Comp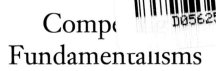
Fundamentalisms

Competing Fundamentalisms

Violent Extremism in Christianity, Islam, and Hinduism

Sathianathan Clarke

WJK WESTMINSTER
JOHN KNOX PRESS
LOUISVILLE • KENTUCKY

First edition
Published by Westminster John Knox Press
Louisville, Kentucky

17 18 19 20 21 22 23 24 25 26—10 9 8 7 6 5 4 3 2 1

Book design by Sharon Adams
Cover design by Mark Abrams
Cover photo: Dika Seva, dikaseva.com

Library of Congress Cataloging-in-Publication Data
Names: Clarke, Sathianathan, author.
Title: Competing fundamentalisms : violent extremism in Christianity, Islam, and Hinduism / Sathianathan Clarke.
Description: First edition. | Louisville, Kentucky : Westminster John Knox Press, [2017] | Includes bibliographical references and index.
Identifiers: LCCN 2016052018 (print) | LCCN 2017006795 (ebook) | ISBN 9780664259884 (pbk. : alk. paper) | ISBN 9781611648102 (ebk.)
Subjects: LCSH: Religious fundamentalism. | Violence—Religious aspects. | Christianity. | Hinduism. | Islam.
Classification: LCC BL238 .C48 2017 (print) | LCC BL238 (ebook) | DDC 200.9/051—dc23
LC record available at https://lccn.loc.gov/2016052018

Most Westminster John Knox Press books are available at special quantity discounts when purchased in bulk by corporations, organizations, and special-interest groups. For more information, please e-mail SpecialSales@wjkbooks.com.

Contents

Acknowledgments

This book took a long time to write, mainly because religious funda- mentalisms were growing more and more fierce, inventive, and vola- tile over the last few years. Every time I described Christian, Muslim, or Hindu extremism, it took on a different incarnation. Thus I had to revise what I thought were completed essays. But the other reason for the delay had to do with taking time to enjoy family and friends, who made life rich and full. My family lives all over the world. My mother (Clara Clarke) moved from India to Australia after my father (Bishop Sundar Clarke) died in 2010. She took on the role of praying that the book would be completed. My late father was my mentor on the Jesus way. He would have been proud of this publication. My parents built a home in Chennai that was open to all, faithfully and joyfully practicing interfaith hospitality without being consumed with theorizing about its challenges and outcomes. Our two sons and their wives (Avinash and Sally Clarke, Ashwin and Laura Clarke) also live in Australia. They, along with our grandson, Roshan, brought much delight, even if it postponed research and shortchanged time in front of my laptop. The larger clan nourished me with affection from different parts of the globe. On my side, there was my sister and brother-in-law (Ramabai and Manoj Chacko) and brothers and sisters-in-law (Amal and Renuka Clarke, Dayalan and Vinodhini Clarke) from Australia and Britain; and on Prema's side, there was my sister-in-law (Shanta Bose) and my brothers- in-law with their wives (Thomas Chandy and Susan Thomas, Mammen Chandy and Anu Mammen) from India. Though many of these loved ones did not know the threads of the book's argument, without them I could not have had as much pleasure in living and writing.

Much of the initial stimulation to think about religious violence and peacemaking came from two good friends. Deenabandhu Manchala invited me to serve on the International Advisers Group for the Decade to Overcome Violence of the World Council of Churches, which stimulated my thinking about religious fundamentalism as a driver of global conflict. Then in 2009 Clare Amos invited me to spend a sabbatical in Sri Lanka and Britain as Thomas Bray Lecturer (jointly endowed by USPG and SPCK) to give several lectures on the competing nature of religious fundamentalisms. Both have remained conversational partners as some of these ideas developed to form a sustained argument. Other friends encouraged and enriched our conversations, even as they cooked and cared for us, while Prema and I transitioned and then thrived in the Washington, DC, area: Bill and Mary Gibb, David and Drema McAllister-Wilson, Beverly Mitchell, David and Corinne Scott, Gerald West, Kiran and Mrinalini Sabastian, Sanjeevi and Shusila Rajasingham, Paul and Annie Namala, Kendall and Allison Soulen, John Chapin and Gabe Kelemen, and Philip Peacock.

Wesley Theological Seminary has been my academic home and intellectual laboratory for the last twelve years. President David McAlister-Wilson has been a probing interlocutor and sojourner in global mission for peace. Dean Emeritus Bruce Birch has been a consistent encourager of my teaching and research from the day I started at Wesley. I am thankful to Bishop Sundo Kim (Seoul, Korea), whose chair I am honored to occupy, for his consistent encouragement. My engaging students, especially those who took my course on "Religion, Violence, and Peace," have pushed me to think through many ideas in new and different ways. I am thankful to the President and the Board of Governors for giving me a semester-long sabbatical in 2012 to research for this project. My colleagues at Wesley have been a supportive and appreciative community for Prema and me. It has become a very special part of our lives.

Robert Ratcliff was a patient, prodding, perceptive, and constructive editor. He was a pleasure to work with through this long process. I could not have wished for a more professional and resourceful editor. I am also thankful to Jennifer Gillyard for help with research assistance and getting copyright permissions.

Prema has been an indulgent spouse, inspiring friend, kindhearted critic, and faithful codisciple on an amazing thirty-six year journey, spanning India and the U.S.A. With her, much has become possible for the sake of peace with justice, through a life of love!

Sathianathan Clarke
December 2016
Washington, D.C.

Introduction

Leaders in public life need to recognize that in a world where people of all religious traditions are migrating and mingling like never before, we ignore the global impact of religion at our peril.

John Kerry, U.S. Secretary of State, September 5, 2015

Peace is unattainable by part performance of conditions, just as a chemical combination is impossible without complete fulfillment of the conditions of attainment thereof. . . . This is clearly impossible without the great powers of the earth renouncing their imperialistic design. . . . It is my conviction that the root of the evil is want of a living faith in a living God.

M. K. Gandhi, Harijan, June 18, 1938

How can you say, "We are wise, and the law of the LORD is with us," when, in fact, the false pen of the scribes has made it into a lie? . . . They have treated the wound of my people carelessly, saying, "Peace, peace," when there is no peace.

Jeremiah 8:8, 11

The twenty-first century has seen religion thunder back onto the stage of history. This is not, in all respects, a good thing. The gods have returned, but it is with a vengeance. Some of their most devout agents are turning fear *of* God into terror *for* the world. While these believers claim to act under divine orders, we cannot indict divinities since we have no way of summoning and interrogating them. Human beings, on the other hand, we do know. Based on our violent past, we can easily imagine how such "divinely sanctioned" violence derives ultimately from human

1

beings misrepresenting divine lords. Violence done in the name of God may not be God's will, but it surrounds us, its human agents and victims, all the same.

No wonder then that U.S. Secretary of State John Kerry wished he had majored in comparative religions. "One of the most interesting challenges we face in global diplomacy today," he notes, "is the need to fully understand and engage the great impact that a wide range of religious traditions have on foreign affairs."[1] He then goes on to admit the following, which should make every religion scholar pleased with the profession they have chosen: "If I headed back to college today, I would major in comparative religions rather than political science. That is because religious actors and institutions are playing an influential role in every region of the world."[2] Religion's resurgence proves to have been ironic; proclaiming "good news," it delivers destruction. Seeking to soothe the soul, it winds up searing the body.

The connection between religion and violence is nothing new to students of history. Yet the magnitude of religious violence is already seriously redefining the overall context of human living in this century. Religious fundamentalisms or extremisms—oftentimes grounded in fiery worldviews, sometimes legitimated by furious gods and goddesses, and always marshaling violent disciples—are taking on new birth and demonstrating effectual growth on our contemporary world stage. They continue to operate dangerously at key global locations and mature into an assortment of violent local expressions. A Pew Report published in 2014 found that a third of the 198 countries and territories studied in 2012 had a high or very high level of social hostilities involving religion, the highest share in the six years of the study. These hostilities—defined in the study as acts of religious hostility by private individuals, organizations, or groups in society—increased in every major region of the world except the Americas. The number of countries with religion-related terrorist violence has doubled over the past six years. In 2012, religion-related terrorist violence took place in a fifth of the countries (20 percent), up from 9 percent in 2007.[3]

Against this backdrop of mushrooming violence, this book probes the theory and practice of violent religious fundamentalism. Fundamentalism is religion stretched to its extremes.[4] Understanding this modern phenomenon by locating its religious features and interpreting them against the currents of present-day globalization is the major objective of this book. Globalism's aggressive competition is the ethos of our twenty-first-century world; it fuels the fundamentalist flame. This book focuses on contemporary violent religious fundamentalism, yet it also reaches into the past to understand the present. In the end I want to challenge and transform this destructive religion—which leads to asking how religious themes might be made to help people rather than harm them.

Why the term "religious fundamentalism"? There are other ways to talk about this phenomenon. We might have started with local examples of violent religion (for example, Christian fundamentalism, Islamic jihadism, militant Hindutva) and then come up with a common tag that would do justice to all three. But this would be impossible because violent extremism within each religion goes by a number of names. To take the Muslim example, we notice Islamic militarism, Islamism, Muslim extremism, Islamic radicalism, Jihadism, Muslim terrorism, Islamic fundamentalism, and Islamofascism.

I am well aware that the term "religious fundamentalism" originated in the United States during the first quarter of the twentieth century. Starting points may explain origins, but they do not constrain further developments. Thus even if the term arises within the development of Christianity in North America, its characteristic features have sprung up in other religions elsewhere in the world. Contesting an identification of fundamentalism with just one religion, Martin E. Marty and R. Scott Appleby spearheaded a more global and multireligious inquiry. Fundamentalism fittingly became spongy as a concept and large-scale as a movement. The Fundamentalism Project investigated a plurality of such movements across diverse global locations.[5] Much more needs to be done in our time. A May 2014 reflective comment, expressed by Marty two decades after this body of research was published, is telling. Taking stock of the global situation of spreading religious fundamentalism, he remarks:

When the American Academy of Arts and Sciences chartered The Fundamentalism Project, with myself and R. Scott Appleby to head it, we promoted local and global studies, which resulted in five fat volumes (University of Chicago Press). Reading up now on the history of Modi's BJP Party, I find that we gave it some attention in all five volumes, but our inquiries remained marginal until the Hindu-Muslim eruptions in 2002. We had pondered why the BJP and RSS (a kind of kin/rival political party in India) were formed in 1925, at about the same time that American Protestant Fundamentalism took name and shape, and just before the Muslim Brotherhood organized in Egypt in 1928. Around the world, pan-religiously, something was

happening in the varied encounters with modernities that led many
to find refuge in 'hardline religion.'[6]

This book, following Marty's cue, strives for a more globally inclusive
understanding of religious fundamentalisms. It focuses on this religious
phenomenon with an eye toward generating solutions to the problem
of fundamentalist "strong religion." It extends and grounds this inves-
tigative process by tapping into recent studies on the concrete expressions and expansions of Christian fundamentalism in the United States,
Muslim radicalism in Egypt, and Hindu nationalism in India. Yet it also
correlates such local manifestations of religious fundamentalism with the
overall pervading and penetrating competitive backdrop of globalization.

Why have I selected these three particular religious fundamentalisms?
First, because they arose around the same point in the first third of the
twentieth century, albeit in separate places: the United States, Egypt,
and India. Second, because they have all enjoyed a resurgence in the
early twenty-first century. Third, because too much attention in Western academic circles has zeroed in on Islam as the "mother of all fundamentalisms." This shift has made one religion endure all the attention
on religious fundamentalism. By the same token, it has shielded other
religions (notably Christianity and Hinduism) from scrupulous and sustained interrogation concerning their role in fashioning and augmenting
this phenomenon. Fourth, because much of the discussion on religious
fundamentalism consciously or unconsciously takes place within the
framework of "the people of the Book." While the common religious
foundations of Christianity and Islam reveal some things about fundamentalism, they obscure other features. Including Hinduism in this
discussion broadens the scope and deepens our insight into what fundamentalism means. Fifth, because my previous research into the threat
that Hindu fundamentalism presents to non-Hindu religions has helped
me discover how this spirit of unhealthy competition informs Christian
and Islamic fundamentalism as well.[7] Finally, because I bring to this work
a non-Arab Indian acquaintance with Islam. Even if I focus on Egypt,
one must be constantly reminded that Islam is much more than what one
sees in the Western media and academy, which project Middle Eastern
Islam as the representative face of the *worldwide ummah* (community of
Muslims).

Let me offer a brief roadmap to how I hope to achieve these ends. In
chapter 1, I examine various popular theories that try to ground religious
violence in primarily nonreligious factors. I argue that no explanation

of violent religion that ignores religious ideas and motivations can adequately account for this phenomenon. I lift out certain fragments of religion that have been unobserved by social scientists in their description of the cultural, social, political, economic, and psychological origins of fundamentalism. Then I turn to a detailed analysis of religious fundamentalism as it manifests itself in three religious traditions. In doing so I ask the following questions: What are the historical backgrounds of religious fundamentalism? What have been its distinctive characteristics in the last century and the current one? What religious themes does it draw upon in each of these traditions?

Chapter 2 is a study of Christian fundamentalism in the United States of America. It uncovers the strong religious beliefs often hidden beneath the political logic and operation of one of the most powerful nation-states in the world. Chapter 3 analyzes Muslim fundamentalism as it emerges from Egypt and spreads around the globe. Chapter 4 looks at Hindu fundamentalism as it arises and spreads in India. Although exhibiting some differences from its monotheistic counterparts, a careful probe finds similar religious themes funding the Hindu branch of this "strong religion." All three expressions of religious extremism are scrutinized, with care to study both the particular historical factors and religious ideas that undergird them.

Chapter 5 frames key features of these violent movements. It highlights and interprets three theological themes: (1) unwavering confidence in and complete submission to *the Word-vision* (the will of God as revealed in sacred scriptures), (2) fixed and straightforward *world-ways* (mandated individual and group behavior), and (3) an imperial *global-order* (the mission to proselytize and dominate the rest of the world). Such religious motifs, I argue, both reflect and draw sustenance from globalism's spirit of fierce competition. These competing fundamentalisms, I suggest, form a surrogate religion. Religious resources are bolstered by extrareligious ends and fused with the forces of globalization to forge a violent movement harmful to religion and hurtful to the whole world. Such a phenomenon thus is a modern and composite invention, which must be separated from any one religion.

Embracing my vocation as a theologian, in the final chapter (6) I propose constructive and peaceful ways to construe my own Christian tradition, with the hope that doing so might serve as a model for those of other religions. I mine two areas through which to contain, counter, and cure twenty-first-century violent religious fundamentalism. First, taking seriously the Word-visions that feed fundamentalism in Christianity,

Islam, and Hinduism, I delve into what we might responsibly do in Christianity to disarm the Bible (especially its "toxic texts") and redeploy its resources to serve the well-being of the whole family of God. Fundamentalists use this key religious resource to aid destruction; I ask how we might deploy it to create harmony and peace. Second, I ask how we might form violence-renouncing and peace-loving Christian disciples to counter violent religious extremism. Christian mission can reflect the aggression and competitiveness of globalization, but it can also be a vehicle for peacemaking in a world of interreligious conflict.

The book in your hands is dedicated not just to comprehending but also to curing the violent competing religious fundamentalisms of our day. I invite anyone interested in a more peaceful world to join me as I seek to understand and answer contemporary violent religion with the hope that swords of destruction leading to death will be transformed into plowshares of restoration leading to life.

Religious Fundamentalism in the Twenty-First Century

A Beast with Many Heads

The twenty-first century is beginning as an age of religion.
Samuel P. Huntington, *Who Are We? The
Challenges to America's National Identity*

Violence can be as essential an element in religion as love, charity,
or any other aspect of the human condition.
Reza Aslan, *Beyond Fundamentalism: Confronting
Extremism in the Age of Globalization*

Introduction

A cademics see and describe the world through the lenses of their own disciplines. From their limited point of view they create explanations for how the entire world works. Thus, for example, some economists see in religion an attempt to compensate those of little or no material resources in this life with an abundance of them in an imagined future heaven. Other economists consider religion to be a belief system whose purpose is to legitimize the excessive accumulation of capital by some at the expense of others. The same thing happens in other fields as well. Politics, culture, psychology, biology, and sociology all have their own panoptic view of human life.

Amid this disciplinary grandstanding, I seek an alternate mode of interpretation that is less parochial and more dialogical. It is also, I believe, more realistic and less portentous. In this chapter I shall not try to construct an argument presuming that because religion is the substance of everything good and valuable in the world, all truth, beauty, and justice in

7

the world must trace its origin and progression within the eternal spring of this blessed source. Nor do I intend to overlook other facets that make up the rich complexity of human life and dump all the responsibility for destruction, despoilment, and death in the world on religion. Instead, I see religion as quite a complex phenomenon, not only sharing in all the good and evil of human life but also operating through and alongside other dimensions of the world. In line with such an organic view of religion, my central purpose in this chapter is to demonstrate that fundamentalism is both a complex phenomenon, involving a number of factors that make up human living, and an irreducibly religious phenomenon at the same time.

Even if not identified with religion, violent forms of fundamentalism are well and alive in our twenty-first century. They are ubiquitous in our contracting globe. They are local, national, regional, and global in network and operation, and their meddlesome reach does not seem easily containable. The origins of such violence are complex even as their effects appear everywhere. But religion cannot be discounted as both a contributor and promoter of such violence. Anthony Parel effectively captures this angle of fundamentalism for our age: "Religious fundamentalism is a very powerful force in world affairs today. It occupies a position not dissimilar to that occupied by Marxism in the twentieth century. Like Marxism, it is not only a belief system but also a plan of action to transform humanity. In addition, the plan in question sometimes involves the use of extreme violence, exercised not only within but also across state boundaries."[1]

As I see it, the most worrisome features of religious fundamentalism in our time are twofold: its reach into the imagination and daily life of the world; and its propensity to generate violence, both on a local and a global scale. Some of this global diffusion has been observed, catalogued, and analyzed by Martin Marty's Fundamentalism Project (five volumes published by the University of Chicago Press in 1991–95). Surprisingly, though, this large corpus of published material does not refer to the term "terrorism" and hardly mentions "violence."[2] In contrast, since the events of 9/11, scholarship on religious fundamentalism has focused almost exclusively on the link between violence and terrorism on the one hand, and "strong religion" on the other.[3] The aggressive movement of religious fundamentalism into various facets of human life in the twenty-first century has ruptured unity and punctured trust. This violence needs to be uncovered and disassembled. To do that we have to understand it, and to understand it we must grasp religion's role in it. But first let's look at other explanations for religious violence, noticing how they sometimes downplay or dismiss the role of religious conviction.

This chapter investigates the phenomenon of violent religious fundamentalism in the twenty-first century by taking stock of existing theories from committed disciplinary standpoints. While describing such models, I seek to pry open analytical space for religion. In critically assessing these schools of interpretation, rather than pressing on toward the illusory goal of capturing a "Theory of Everything," I aim for middle ground between religious self-exoneration and religious self-indictment. I mediate between placing the overall blame for such colossal violence on culture, politics, economics, or psychology on the one hand, and forcing religion to take on all the culpability for widespread violence in the world on the other. After decades of studying world religions sympathetically, Raimon Panikkar can be trusted when he recognizes the mixed makeup of religion: "Religion includes what is best in human beings. It is from religious inspiration that many of the greatest geniuses and works of arts . . . have emerged. Heroic acts have been performed in its name. But religion has also produced what is worst, what is most wicked. Religion has not only been an opiate but a poison as well, and it has served as an excuse for committing the greatest crimes and causing the worst aberrations."[4] My own commitment as a teacher of theology, a scholar of religion, and an adherent of Christianity equips me to keep a fixed analytical gaze on religion, even as I contend that it is one of the central contributors to this multidisciplinary phenomenon of fundamentalism.

Four Theories that Underestimate the Role of Religion

The volatile global situation, with violent local ramifications and pathological social repercussions, has produced numerous explanatory theories. While some of these excuse religion, others subtly maintain the link between religion and other factors in fueling violence. Let me summarize the main assertions of a few of these theories, with a view toward both understanding their points of view and sifting these interpretations for traces of religion, as I seek to appreciate the various factors that support religious fundamentalism.

Clashing Civilizations

The clash-of-civilization thesis conjures up a convenient and convincing way to talk about economics, politics, and religion within the more acceptable and less passionate language of culture or civilization. Thus, for example, particular aspects of religion, economics, and politics are made to fit into a cultural or civilizational template that could broadly account for the predominantly conflictive interrelationship among various groups across the entire globe. Additionally, such a metatheory seemingly offers social scientists an option of highlighting conflictual global encounters while at the same time moving away from their infatuation with dualistic ways of thinking about the world. The habit of thinking along binary lines became entrenched in modern Western political theory through the taken-for-granted oriental-occidental, Islam-Christian, and communist-capitalist categories. When the civilizational interpretive model arose during the twilight of the twentieth century, it created space for more diversity and complexity to be integrated into making sense of the workings of the globalized world.

Samuel Huntington's *The Clash of Civilizations and the Remaking of World Order* (1996) opened up such a general framework for analyzing various contentious aspects of geopolitical currents. Culture, for Huntington, was taken to be discrete elements of human beings that could be assembled into discernable civilizations across different regions in the world, often unified by some form of religion. He describes the manner in which cultures gather themselves into civilizations: "A civilization is thus the highest cultural grouping of people and the broadest level of cultural identity people have short of that which distinguishes humans from other species. It is defined both by common objective elements, such as language, history, religion, customs, institutions, and by the subjective self-identification of people."[5] Using this way of viewing cultures transforming into civilizations, the book skillfully moves away from the cold war bipolar model for explaining global conflict and presses into service a more multicentric one. Huntington identifies multiple civilizational or cultural blocks in such a reconfiguration of the modern world. He theorizes that eight conspicuously formed culture blocks (Chinese, Japanese, Indian, Islamic, Western, Orthodox, Latin American, and African)[6] would be locked in global clashes in the ever-expanding world of competing markets that also aggressively promote cultural patterns. Clearly, Huntington does not see these cultural patterns working together in the globalized world. Instead, he interprets these blocks as more prone to colliding and clashing. His model magnifies the differences. Thus Huntington predicts that such entrenched differences, rather than producing dialogue and adaptation, will propel global clashes. Huntington offers a synopsis of this global trend: "In sum, the post–cold war world is a world of seven or eight major civilizations. Cultural commonalities and differences shape the interests, antagonisms, and associations of states. The most important countries in the world come overwhelmingly from different civilizations. The local conflicts most likely to escalate into broader wars are those between groups and states from different civilizations. . . . Global politics is becoming multipolar and multicivilizational."[7]

A whole range of appreciation and criticism has been directed toward the clash-of-cultures paradigm. For our purpose of analyzing contemporary religious fundamentalism, let me confine this discussion to two issues. First, Huntington does make a connection between cultural patterns and religions but tends to prioritize the lens of culture. Culture appears to achieve the status of metacategory in Huntington's work, often at the expense of other dimensions of human life. He sees culture as a heuristic catchall within which a bundle of substantial elements inclusive of economics, politics, and religion can be collected and studied. There is little doubt that in Huntington's work, culture trumps religion, economics, and politics as he plots anew the role of cultural systems. Thus, in his imaginative thesis, culture is set out to be the basic canopy under which a multitude of religious persuasions, economic orders, political approaches, and social arrangements can be covered.

The breadth of Huntington's cultural analysis, however, does not mean that religion escapes deliberation or eludes accountability. In many ways, cultural phenomena may have enduring life and universal power in Huntington's thought because they are rooted in the mythological world grounded in religion. There is already a role for religion as a frame for cultural meaning and signification in the *Clash of Civilizations* book. Thus, for example, Huntington talks at length about the Islamic or the Orthodox civilization block, patently allowing religion to appropriate the depth and breadth of culture in certain parts of the world. In a 1998 critical symposium on Huntington's work, Freeman alludes to this unambiguous correlation between culture and religion in the clash-of-civilizations thesis: "The sole point on which I agree with Huntington's analysis on contemporary geopolitics is that the major fault lines follow religious divisions. Two important components of religious contentions [that are reflected in his civilizational analysis] are demonizing—making a devil—of the Other and competing cultural mythologies."[8]

The existence of such a tenacious and persistent bond between religion and culture comes through much more freely and explicitly in Huntington's later writings, especially his 2004 work on America. There he baldly asserts that American culture is founded on Protestant religion coming out of England. Religion, Huntington declares, provides the rudimentary scaffolding and core substance of American culture. His own words capture this best:

> Protestant beliefs, values, and assumptions, however, had been the core element, along with the English language, of America's settler culture, and that culture continued to pervade and shape American life, society and thought as the proportion of Protestants declined. Because they are central to American culture, Protestant values deeply influenced Catholicism and other religions in America. They have shaped American attitudes toward public and private morality, economic activity, government and public policy. Most importantly they are the primary source of the American Creed, the ostensibly secular political principles that supplement Anglo-Protestant culture as the critical defining element of what it means to be American.[9]

Huntington, as the master of metanarratives, is clearly not content with only addressing the connection between religion and culture in the United States. He iterates that this spread of religion as a cultural system affects most of the world. Thus he is cognizant of the increased global role of religion as an organized and manifest figuration of culture. Religion thus makes substantial inroads into what was predicted to be a culture of secularity in the twenty-first century. The following comment made by Huntington in the twenty-first century conflates cultural expansion with religious extension and construes politics as the driving force of religion as a cultural system: "In the last quarter of the twentieth century, however, the march toward secularism was reversed. An almost global resurgence of religion got underway, manifest in almost every part of the world—except western Europe. Elsewhere in countries all over the world, religious political movements gained supporters."[10]

A second issue that comes through clearly in Huntington's proposal stems from his lopsided emphasis on the inherent conflict between cultures. Much of the same negativity is transferred to religion as well. He exaggerates the conflict between these cultural blocks while at the same time underplaying the dialogical exchange that accompanies civilizational encounters. Numerous critical voices from across the world have put forth convincing arguments from a multitude of disciplines to debunk Huntington's tunnel-vision approach to the colliding aspects of global geopolitics. Many other reflective voices have tried to complement such a biased model by lifting up the dialogue and interchange that operate between various cultural blocks in the world. Almost as a counter to what was feared to be a self-fulfilling prophecy toward global discord and clashes, "dialogue among civilizations" as a possible trajectory for global currents was formulated by the Iranian ex-president Mohammad Khatami (president in 1997–2005). This Islamic philosopher and political leader made a formal proposal in September 1998 at the 53rd UN General Assembly that 2001 be designated as "the year of dialogue among civilizations." In a Khatami-inspired pathway that was paved with cultural collaboration and cooperation, religious resources were also reassessed and reemployed. The harmonious aspects of culture and religion were located and disseminated to destabilize and subsume the destructive ones. At least such a reminder of another side of cultural encounters allowed for the reassertion of global interreligious voices seeking to promote "dialogue as the vastly superior alternative to conflict among civilizations."[11]

Aware of the similarities and differences, confluences and confrontations, in our paradoxically always-expanding and ever-contracting globe, we must continue to look harder for the interconnection between cultures and religions. This will help to uncover the positive and negative role of religion in the interaction between cultural blocks. How do we lift up the important bond between religion and culture rather than focusing on culture while ignoring religion? We must help cultures of peace to escape the dictates of destructive religion, even as we protect the healing elements of religion from colliding cultures. Both the freedom of culture and the liberation of religion depend on our success.

One contemporary phenomenon might help defang the clash of cultures or religions. Around the world the rigid boundaries between civilizations and religions are blurring. When the lines between one religious or cultural system and the other are rigid and fixed, confrontation between the two is easier. When those boundaries become more porous and flexible, the possibilities for conversation and mutual understanding increase. Global traffic and commerce has led to a loosening of cultural and religious boundaries. As a result human communities have consciously and unconsciously welcomed and assimilated various alien artifacts, ideas, rituals, and aspirations. Communities in the twenty-first century thus are becoming multicultural and multiply religious. While hybridity is not a new phenomenon in human history, it has become more evident in our contemporary global context.

Yet it may be too early to celebrate this postmodern age. A conundrum still remains even if we admit to the twenty-first-century phenomenon of religious and cultural amalgamation. On the one hand, hybridity stands as a testimony to the collapse of well-defined and uniquely patentable cultural and religious models. Multicultural worlds inhabit monoculture-touting communities. On the other hand, this vulnerability to hybrid-ization itself revives religious fundamentalism, which is antagonistic to dangerous mixing of the substance of religion or culture and which is horrified by eroding borders that are necessary to distinguish one reli-gion or culture from the other.

Resistance to Empire

Logically related to the clash-of-civilizations theory is the view that religion as a social and political system is especially adept at assembling resistive and confrontational forces directed toward destabilizing and dis-mantling the expansionist maneuvers of empire(s). Geopolitics, accord-ing to this line of thinking, cannot be understood to be mere cultural clashes that are multipolar. Instead, various movements of resistance and restoration have more in common with the synergistic power of infiltrat-ing and controlling empire(s). Forces of neocolonialism threatening to take control of the whole world are believed to be a continued problem of the twenty-first century. Parag Khanna's work is a good example of such an interpretation, which perceives the global context through the lens of empire. He seems to make Huntington's models diminutive when he announces, "Big is back. It is inter-imperial relations—not international or inter-civilizational—that shape the world. Empires—not civiliza-tions—give geography their meaning. Indeed, empires span across civi-lizations; as they spread their norms and customs, they can change who people are—irrespective of their civilization."[12] In this analysis, empire(s) infiltrate a territory in order to transform its people's beliefs and cultural habits into those of the agents of empire.

Historically, religion and culture have mattered to empire(s). Bodies of knowledge, philosophically systematized into schools of thought, were constructed from the social, culture, and religious beliefs and practices of the Other. The cultures and religions of those outside the empire(s) have long been a special target for inquiry, cataloging, and interpreta-tion. Edward Said[13] and Michel Foucault[14] have inaugurated flourishing schools of postcolonial and postmodern thinkers, respectively, and have worked out the complex and intimate nexus between regimes of power and the bodies of knowledge that they generate, formalize, and institu-tionalize. Labeling this enterprise as "Orientalism" (Said), and associ-ating such manufactured "regimes of truths" with "power/Knowledge"

(Foucault), many groups of intellectuals have tracked and unveiled the vested nature of this dominant and considerable body of Western scholarship. What was notable is that knowledge about the cultures and religions of the "Orient" produced and amassed by the "Occident" reinforced the binary between the West and East. Western scholars described Eastern cultures and religions in such power-imbued categories as rational/emotional, agential/passive, male/female, white/black, and mechanical/spiritual. The empire(s) thus interpreted themselves and the communities that they colonized with an eye toward legitimating, sustaining, and intensifying their own power. Fundamentalism has sought to push back against this colonized knowledge, reclaiming hard and stable templates of religion as a means of resistance to the hegemony of Western worldviews.

Religious fundamentalism, according to these resistance-to-empire(s) theorists, is akin to a cultural and political Trojan horse. Religion offers useful, promising, forceful, confounding, and conventional tools by which those who find themselves subjugated by regimes of imperial power have a reasonable chance to dismantle their unjust world and reconstruct a more acceptable one. In this interpretive tack, religions are varied and clever masks of the weak that serve to resist and overcome the schemes of the strong. Religious fundamentalism is thus primarily a social and political movement set in motion by the resisting masses. Reza Aslan's work has analyzed the relationship between Islam and the United States over the last decade. He is categorical in pushing a line of argument that renders religious fundamentalism as primarily a social resistance movement:

> Despite its fixation on jihad, Global jihad is less a religious movement than it is a social movement, one that employs religious symbols to forge collective identity across borders and boundaries. Social movements arise when relatively powerless people band together under the banner of a collective identity in order to challenge the existing social order. Such movements are, almost by definition, utopian in character, in that they are feverishly engaged in reimagining society. This is particularly true of so-called transformative social movements, such as Global jihadism, which seek a complete upending of the old social order through violent revolution, often in anticipation of cataclysmic global change.[15]

From quite another global context, which has also seen the steady rise of Hindu fundamentalism, Ashis Nandy highlights the political nature of such resistance movements. He submits that, even though fundamentalism proclaims itself to be founded in faith and funded by religion, it is much more about politics: the politics of resistance and politics of representation. Nandy does not mince any words: "Many forms of religious fundamentalism, being themselves progenies of the modern secular world, have a greater appeal to sections of citizens who suffer from doubts about their cultural and religious roots. Though they often elicit passionate allegiance, these forms of faith and piety are only a short step away from being political ideologies trying to pass off as faiths."[16] In another well-argued and widely read essay, which uses M. K. Gandhi (1869–1948) as an example, Nandy points to "critical traditionalism" as a mode by which Hindu Nationalists painstakingly drew upon, creatively reassembled, and resourcefully redeployed Hindu religious thought and cultural practices to gather Indians together to resist and overthrow British colonial rule.[17] Hindu fundamentalists still selectively use Gandhi's selection of Hindu ideas such as *sanatana dharma* (eternal set of moral or religious law governing Hindu practice),[18] *varna dharma* (moral and religious law based on one's caste status), and *ramarajya* (kingdom of Rama, the divine ruler)[19] to bolster their own version of strong religious nationalism. According to this perspective, then, both Muslim and Hindu fundamentalists are principally political ideologues masquerading as militant religionists. Christian fundamentalism in this resistance-to-empire form of thinking, as I see it, finds itself on the other side of the struggle. Historically, from the sixteenth century onward, the spread of Christianity into many parts of the world was associated with the colonial expansion of the West into the rest of the world. More recently, and especially in the twenty-first century, the success of mission is attributed to the Christian West's strategic accompaniment with the forces of aggressive globalization that is calculatingly infiltrating the whole world.

Theorizing mainly from his work on Islam in the Middle East, Baber constructs a popular framework that sees religious conflict as originating from multiple cultural communities determined to fight the pervasive forces of global neocolonialism. Religion is unmistakably employed as a crucial part of this complex pushback. Such religious and political fundamentalist movements violently resist takeovers by colonizing cultural and economic forces. Barber couches all of this in religious terminology:

> I use the term [Jihad] in its militant construction to suggest dogmatic and violent particularism of a kind known to Christians no less than Muslims, to Germans and Hindus as well as to Arabs. The phenomena to which I apply the phrase have innocent enough beginnings:

identity politics and multicultural diversity can represent strategies of a free society trying to give expression to its diversity. What ends up in Jihad may begin as a simple search for a local identity, some set of common personal attributes to hold out against the numbing and neutering uniformities of industrial modernization and colonizing culture of McWorld.[20]

Congruent with the religious fundamentalism as defiance of expanding forms of cultural and political expansionism, Barber is quite willing to posit religious frames to capture the motivation and modality of those who violently subvert the devices of the West. Enigmatically, when talking about neocolonialism's intrusion into the rest of the world, Barber prefers areligious categories. For example, when analyzing the calculating expansion of the United States of America into the globalized world, he uses concepts such as "commercial secularism" (thus his notion of "McWorld" in his 1995 book that incorporates this term in its title) or "imperial democracy" (thus his idea of "CivWorld," the title of a chapter in his 2004 book). Barber's two influential books exemplify these dialectics that steer empire. On the one hand, in *Jihad vs. McWorld*, written in the mid-1990s, Barber "warned that the American world of commercial secularism [was] advanced with such aggressive self-certainty [that it] was on a collision course with fundamentalist Islam and other antimodern movements around the world."[21] On the other hand, in *Fear's Empire*, published almost a decade later, he urges the United States to reverse its ideology of "preventive war" and embrace the goal of "preventive democracy" instead. With grandiose optimism, Barber posits the export of democracy as the empire's contribution to CivWorld. "Preventive democracy . . . work[s] to turn the swamp where terrorism breeds into productive soil, by seeding it with all that it lacks—learning, liberty, self-government, opportunity and security. It saps terrorism of its capacity to build on the alleged hypocrisy and hubris of its Western enemies. Because it empowers the powerless, genuine democracy offers precisely what those drawn by terrorism's self-destructive tactics lack: the capacity to control their own destinies."[22] The underlying polarity between empire advancers, who are fueled by secular frames, and empire resistors, who have embraced religious categories, is markedly preserved.

While on the theme of politics and culture contracting with religion for defiant confrontation of colonial powers, I must also mention political theorists who conflate religious fundamentalism with hypernationalism.[23] The nation-state ignites the imagination of secular and religious nationalists alike. Generally these two movements have been thought of as dreaming up and working toward two opposing visions of the state. The subtitle of Mark Juergensmeyer's book *The New Cold War* sums up this thesis well: *Religious Nationalism Confronts the Secular State*.[24] The argument that is appealing, perhaps because of its simple appeal to a mode of common sense informed by symmetry through mediated duality, becomes the foundation stone for such an either/or framework. The assumption, often uncritically embraced and passionately believed, is that secular nationalism is a materialistic, rational, and nonreligious phenomenon while religious nationalism is its sectarian, irrational and antisecular counterpart.[25] In tandem with such a theoretical framework, secular nationalists accuse religious nationalists of utilizing indigenous religions as conventional and convenient symbol systems to unify citizens for reaching the goal of liberation from former colonial powers. Such a religious vision that stokes mass imagination and steers mass resistance creatively invokes a sense of sacred geography for their homeland and an idea of a strong nation for the state they are constructing. By focusing on the long history of colonial practices over the centuries, political theories of religious nationalism combine the desire to express one's particularism as an organic collective with the traction that can be gained to resist old imperial powers disguised as forces of neocolonialism. A relationship is forged between the yearnings of communities for a free and just nation-state and the communal ideals their religion partially offers them on earth, as is promised in heaven. Such an appeal to religious nationalism is especially persuasive due to the failure of secular nationalism, which was taken to be a Western model that over several decades produced materialism, corruption, and deculturation.[26]

Tariq Ali, the Pakistan-born and Oxford-trained "New Left" secular intellectual, provides another discourse on religious fundamentalism from which we can benefit. Although in agreement that religious fundamentalism represents a distinct form of resistance against global neocolonialism, he insists that scholars retain the label "fundamentalism" when addressing the empire as well. Thus, while Ali employs "religious fundamentalism" as an umbrella term to capture the diverse synchronizations of global resistance to the empire's rule over the whole world, he uses "imperial fundamentalism" as the overarching term that names the neocolonial mechanisms of the United States that threaten to envelop the entire globe in order to subjugate its diverse communities. The conflict for Ali is between two forms of fundamentalism: Resistive fundamentalism of resurgent religions and expansive fundamentalism of the imperial empire. Ali states this categorically:

> My argument that the most dangerous "fundamentalism" today—the "mother of all fundamentalisms" is American fundamentalism—has been amply vindicated. . . . Politically, the United States decided early on to use the tragedy as moral lever to re-map the world. Militarily, its bases now cover every continent. There is a US military presence in 120 of the 189 member states of the United Nations. Domestically, the Bush administration covered up the deteriorating situation of the US economy with the so-called security threat. . . . In the clash between a religious fundamentalism—itself a product of modernity—and an imperial fundamentalism determined to "discipline the world," it is necessary to oppose both and create a space in the world of Islam and the West in which freedom of thought and imagination can be defended without fear of persecution or death.[27]

These various versions advocating that religious fundamentalism is primarily a political, social, and cultural adaptation of religion to resist prior and contemporary Western-led expansion have much to tell us about the global distribution of power. However, one must question the dualistic framework of this political interpretation. "West versus rest," secular versus sacred, or even imperial versus indigenous explanations of religious fundamentalism fail to adequately account for its complexity or dynamism. To begin with, one wonders whether the unipolar geopolitical framework, which either narrowly invests the United States or broadly confers the West with possessing all the keys to the empire, still has many defenders. There are other alternatives to Huntington's multipolar civilizational proposal, if one wants to break away from the lure of dialectic bipolar mappings of how twenty-first-century globalization works. Thus, for example, in Khanna's analysis, China, the European Union, and the United States "are the world's natural Empires." He suggests that this "tripolar world should be thought of as a stool: With two legs it cannot stand; with three it can be stable."[28] The prevailing focus on the BRIC countries (Brazil, Russia, India, and China) as dominant emerging economic and political global power players surely muddies the conceptual waters of any clear-cut notion of the West in opposition to the rest, or the United States versus everyone else in the twenty-first century world. Also, the idea of secular versus religious forms of organizing social and political institutions, especially the nation-state, is riddled with inconsistencies when one analyzes the actual functioning of so-called religious and so-called secular movements. In a convincing study of Egypt, India, and the United States, the three countries on which my own work focuses, Scott Hibbard offers an "integrative approach" that brings together the essentialist and materialist interpretation of religious politics.[29] Relevant to this discussion is the manner in which he ascertains "the promotion of illiberal religion by state actors"[30] and detects the motivation of worldly benefits for the religious fundamentalists, who were "greatly abetted by the modern state and secular elites."[31]

A second objection prompts a reconsideration of the theory that religious fundamentalism is merely a tool for resistance to colonial forces; it comes from an awareness of the universal missionizing dimension of religions themselves. Religions have a primordial world vision rooted in a revelation in Word from the Divine. Thus one must be careful not to underplay the a priori, proactive, primordial claims made by religion to pervade the whole earth with the reigning of God. Ironically, the fundamentals of culture and religion that modernists and Orientalists challenged, deconstructed, and discredited a hundred years ago have in recent years become the principal foundation for banding together and stirring up united resistance against the empire. The stones that were destructively cracked open and dismissively cast out were gathered together, polished, and reassembled to erect monuments of collective self-expression. Thus religious resources—thought to be disgraced, desacralized, and decimated by the intrusive and expansive dynamic of the empire(s)—became historically unearthed treasures and psychologically inspired assemblages for reasserting and refashioning formerly disappearing subjugated self-representations. It is important to restate that in many of the faith traditions, these religious visions have a political and social dimension to them. Thus the pie that may be perched in the sky must also offer a foretaste of its flavor and nourishment "on earth as it is in heaven."

"It's the Economy, Stupid!"

The materialist turn toward explanations for violent forms of fundamentalism may have already been noticed in various renditions of the previous approach that embraced empire as a central analytical concept in interpreting the functioning of imperialistic structures in our contemporary globalized world. There are scholars, however, who will not let economics be undersold as only one component in a multidisciplinary approach for understanding religious fundamentalism. These voices join in the song, sung far and wide throughout history (or at least since Marx), that economics is the fundamental substance of human reality. The class-grievance theory tends to dismiss religion as a by-product and thus constituent of a secondary, often elusive, realm of reality. It promotes the claim that the economic side of human life is obviously the real thing and that those who don't perceive this apparent fact are indeed searching for reality in a house of illusions.

Although Larry Witham's book *Marketplace of the Gods: How Economics Explains Religion* is not about religious fundamentalism, it is a good example of an economic approach that devalues religion. Focusing on six cases from various dimensions of societal life (i.e., new religions of Japan, blue laws, Latin American bishops, church giving, Islamic banking, and religious attire) in different global contexts, Witham makes an argument based on the claim that economics logically and rationally could explain religion better than religion itself. Witham associates the economic approach to all of life as both obviously commonsensical and unquestionably historical. "In many ways," he opines, "the economic approach to life can seem like common sense. It is more than that, however, for it has arisen out of centuries of thinking about human behavior."[32] Witham extols the merits of the economic method for interpreting the goings-on in the world today in contrast to three other approaches that he ascertains to be "black boxes." The first is psychology, "which looks inside the human mind." A second is sociology, which investigates the complex structure and functioning of human society and culture. The third is theology, which he likens to the mother of all black boxes. His terminology is worth retaining in assessing the usefulness of religious thought in comprehending aspects of human life: "One more black box to avoid is theology: the claim to having revealed knowledge about invisible and supernatural things. These claims will be more difficult to adjudicate than even neurons or culture."[33] Interestingly, Witham promotes the economic approach as a "middle path" between these "extremes" to analyze and explain all that is really happening in the world.[34]

Not only does economics best serve as a mode for explaining human activity, inclusive of religion, but also for Witham only an economic model of dealing with religions can be relied upon to influence the relationship between violent and moderate forms of human living in the world. In an essay written in 2011 he speculates on how the economics of religions rather than their theologies can engender either the consensual or conflictual prospects of Islam. Taking into consideration the over-throw of the Mubarak regime in Egypt, he comments:

> For modern-day economists of religion, a perfect test case now faces us: Egypt after the demise of the thirty-year rule of Hosni Mubarak. Since Egypt is a country with strong Muslim and Christian "factions," the question is whether the government should regulate them or allow as much free-market religion as possible? . . . The free market in Egypt could bring Muslim radicals to power. In Egypt, it is still unclear whether the Muslim Brotherhood, if in power, would play host to Al Qaeda, Hamas (even Hezbollah), and other jihadist groups. On the other hand, if jihadist elements competed with moderate Muslims, Coptic Christians, and secular Egyptians, perhaps they would be blunted and become moderate forms of Islam. The outcome will be very significant for the future of Egypt, the future of religion, and for the Economics of Religion.[35]

Of course, because of the benefit of hindsight, we now know that the elected government of the Muslim Brotherhood did not last long enough to experiment with such market-like decisions on managing the free or regulated play of religions. But such confidence in economic models for interpreting and transforming religions has not been quelled as the Arab Spring seems to have been in Egypt.

Paul Collier, another noted economist, continues to promulgate his long-held view that "conflicts are far more likely to be caused by economic opportunities, the chance to get rich, rather than by grievance or religious division."[36] In his compelling book titled *The Bottom Billion*, he cogently explicates four traps that the poorest countries find themselves in: the conflict trap, the natural resource trap, the trap of being landlocked beside bad neighbors, and the bad governance trap. What is remarkable is that even while he spends a chapter discussing the trap of violent conflict in these poorest countries, he makes no reference to religion. In his view, the conflict trap is the handiwork of economic deprivation. Religion appears to play no part in the large scale of violent conflict in the poorest countries of Asia and Africa. If development experts and political leaders can address economic problems and work out economic solutions, such conflict will gradually wane. Thus economic growth is the main way forward to overcome violent civil wars and coups.[37] In a more recent 2015 interview, Collier is willing to concede that there are also "dysfunctional beliefs" that partly contribute to global conflict. Yet, even after all the violence taking place over the last few years that has consistently invoked religious justification, Collier promotes the notion that economic "objective circumstances" principally both fuel conflict and promise peace. While the condition of being "very, very poor" makes communities "prone to conflict" the process of meaningful "economic development gradually makes them safer." The "robust things we know about improving security," he concludes, is that "economic development is a major force of peace."[38]

One problem with using economics as the sole or primary explanation for religious fundamentalism lies in the reductionist assumptions of this approach. Many of these economic approaches are steeped in a hierarchical binary mode of thinking. Thus the materialist base is established as the sure and unshakable foundation, on which are erected all other social edifices. These scholars too easily and uncritically buy into the presupposition that economics makes up the primary stuff of reality. Culture and religion, from this reductionist viewpoint, are derived from the economic activity of a given society. This mode of thinking was founded on an unrealistic interpretation of Marxist orthodoxy, which tried to make a rigid distinction between the "superstructure" and the "base." Accordingly, religion and culture—parts of the superstructure—were secondary by-products of the more fundamental economic base. Jeffrey C. Alexander makes this point clear: "Cultural phenomena, from legal codes to religious rituals to arts and intellectual ideas, are assigned to the superstructure and conceived of as determined by the base. To explain cultural phenomena, one should not investigate their internal structure of meaning but must examine the material elements that they reflect. Because culture was determined by forces outside of itself, it does not have autonomy in a causal sense."[39] In line with this mind-set, scholars of religion and theologians are incapable of offering a true understanding of human society and thus have little to contribute to substantial transformation among human communities.

Populist versions of such economics-alone or materialism-always approaches promulgate that all the violence we see in today's world, even if claimed to be religiously motivated and even though undertaken in the name of God, is nothing other than a working out of economic grievances. To put this sardonically, the phenomena may look like religion, smell like religion, taste like religion, and feel like religion, but it is actually economics! Religious conflict is only a mask that conceals the real economic motives and objectives of violent clashes both locally and globally. In a certain sense this is a continuation of the rationalism of enlightened materialism, which Marx and Engels transformed into a scientific system. Yet this form of economic determinism also manifests a deviation from certain Marxist theories of religion. Thus, no longer are the poor perceived to be manipulated by the false consciousness of religion, akin to opiate for the naive masses. Rather, varieties of religious fundamentalism galvanize economically underprivileged groups to creatively adapt theological beliefs, religious symbols, and ritual practices and thereby subvert the ideological tapestry of the economic elite. The fundamentalist forms of religion, along with their justification of divinely desired and directed violence, become powerful tools for the poor to subvert the economic stranglehold of the powerful and prosperous class. In an ironic way, what appeals to the economics-only approach also proves attractive to the religion-alone explication: a simplistic analytical framework that allows for every action in the world to be reduced to one essential cause. What can be attributed to God, the primordial uncreated Creator, can also be true of Mammon, the primary driver of all human activity. No wonder even Jesus has them being competing and conflicting fundamental realities or principalities: "No one can serve two masters; for a slave will either hate the one and love the other, or be devoted to the one and despise the other. You cannot serve God and wealth [KJV: mammon]" (Matt. 6:24).

Another limitation with the theory that economic grievance of the poor is the driver of religious fundamentalism stems from the fact that such violence does not diminish in economically successful societies. In a well-documented article that elucidates the economic dimensions of religious extremism, Laurence R. Iannaccone and Eli Berma are cognizant that it is not possible to establish a causal link between economic deprivation and religious terrorism. Assessing the situation in numerous contexts, they came up with the following conclusion:

> As scholars have discovered, most radical Islamic terrorists are relatively well off; they are by no means poor and ignorant people with little to lose. We must distinguish between the overall religious organization, which does indeed gain strength and membership by providing material services to the poor, and the composition and motives of the leadership and most active members. Within these organizations, as in all organizations, responsibility and difficult assignments end up in the hands of talented people, most of whom have very good secular alternatives. The pattern has recurred in Palestine, Yemen, Afghanistan, Iraq, and Lebanon during the civil war period. And is it any surprise that when Al Qaeda needed recruits to

attend flight schools in Florida, they tapped a small group of disaffected expatriate Muslims in Europe [who were] students rather than draw from the thousands of illiterate mercenaries they were training in Afghanistan?[40]

Yet oddly the interpretation that religious fundamentalism is stirred by economic deprivation is not made when such violence surfaces in economically successful countries. Thus, when religious fundamentalism strikes out with violence in Europe, Japan, and the United States of America, there is a rush to find psychological, social, and religious triggers that can explain such phenomena. The economic dimensions are not what come to the fore in assessing the reasons behind the acts of violence, even though it is quite well established that there are problems of economic inequity in many of these countries.

One wonders whether there is a certain class bias in understanding the authenticity of religious expressions in the world. It is quite possible that a version of Abraham Maslow's "Hierarchy of Needs" functions tacitly in such divergent interpretations between the less economically developed and more economically developed contexts. According to such a worldview, human beings are assumed to express particular needs based on their specific overall condition. In Maslow's five-stage model, human beings move from (1) basic biological and physiological needs, through (2) safety needs, to (3) belongingness and love needs, onward to (4) esteem needs, and all this toward (5) the highest need of self-actualization. One may notice the logic of how this model instructs the analysis of religious fundamentalism in different contexts of the world. On the one hand, in developing regions religious fundamentalism cannot afford to be rooted in religion since people are still struggling with basic economic needs. In a play on words, according to this form of thinking, we might say that for these stupid folks, it is the economy that matters. On the other hand, in developed countries religious fundamentalism can only be social, psychological, or religious because they have transcended economic deprivation. Implicitly, then, true religion can be cultivated only after persons attain an acceptable level of economic success. Talking about religion as a motivation makes sense only for those who are no longer striving to acquire basic biological, physiological, and security needs.

Let me be clear. I am not suggesting that economic issues play no role in the growth of religious fundamentalism, either in the developing or developed regions of the world. I am saying, however, that religion must play a central role both in understanding religious fundamentalism and in mitigating its expansion. Safiya Afta urges a more complex, multidimensional approach that I find helpful: "There is thus little evidence to support the contention that poverty, in and of itself, fuels extremism. Studies on the socioeconomic profiles of militants would suggest, however, that poverty is a contributing factor pushing people towards militancy, provided an enabling environment already exists. The lack of employment opportunities for the educated, as well as deficiencies in the public school system, also appears amongst the factors that drive militancy."[41] Apart from the "enabling environment" that is listed above, I also identify poverty as an embedded condition that impels the activity of such religious militants. Jessica Stern is able to acknowledge the influence of economic factors and yet highlight the multidimensional role that religion plays to stoke conflict and terrorism. "Poverty's role as a risk factor is controversial, but the frequently cited fact that the September 11 bombers were mostly drawn from Saudi Arabia's elite does not prove that poverty and terrorism are uncorrelated. Several studies have shown that states most susceptible to ethno-religious conflicts are those that are poorer, unstable, and have a history of violent conflict."[42] To put it differently, I am steering away from needing to choose between the options claiming that either economics *or* religious motivations and factors are sufficient *in themselves* to explain the rise of religious fundamentalism. In a full-bodied analysis of fundamentalism, moreover, religion and economics must also be complemented by other dimensions of human life, including the cultural, social, political, and psychological.

Psychological Theories

Thus far I have critically examined interpretations of religious fundamentalism that adopt cultural, political, and economic theories as foundational, often discounting the influence of religion itself. Another cadre of analysts who cannot be ignored focus on the psychological dimensions that fuel religious fundamentalism. Here too the psychological aspects are overplayed at the expense of the religious. This band is sophisticated enough not to project religious fundamentalism as a branch of abnormal psychology. James W. Jones's verdict on this is categorical and instructive: "All psychological studies agree that terrorists are not abnormal psychologically or diagnostically psychopathological."[43] Yet many of these scholars confine themselves to identifying and theorizing upon "certain psycho-religious themes" when investigating religious fundamentalism.[44] Often the former category, "psycho," operates as the predominant, if not overriding, one in this hyphenated idiom, at the expense of the "religious." Without doubt such psychological approaches are dynamic even as they represent a mind-set. In this sense, they fit well into Ruth Stein's model of "psychodynamic approaches." A psychodynamic approach, then, even if dynamic is still limited to the psyche: it "addresses inner psychic constellations of conflicts and affects, internalized relations among representations of self and others, and other dimensions we call psychic reality."[45] From this perspective, religious fundamentalism, even while underplaying religious motivations and factors, is interpreted as a dynamic matrix of maladjusted and discontent minds bonded together by the need to aggressively re-form contemporary global body politics.

In this section, I want to explore the predominantly psychological interpretations of religious fundamentalism. One way to understand this school of interpretation is through the following equation: $RF = A1 + A2 \times H$. The formula asserts that religious fundamentalism (RF) is a collective permutation of unresolved anger (A1) plus acute alienation (A2) multiplied by destructive hate (H) directed toward specific individuals and communities constructed as dangerous others.

Let me unpack this formula. Religious fundamentalism is first a conceptual meeting space and catalyzing launching place for an outflow of unresolved anger (A1) arising from alienation (A2). It is often an anger that arises from forms of rejection that come from being associated with certain religiopolitical beliefs and practices or particular sociocultural ways of life. Thus, because this anger involves the beliefs and practices themselves rather than personal attributes, such rejection is regarded as being undeserved and leads to alienation. Anger within this context is an emotion that is acutely experienced by individuals and groups, who gradually find similar victims with whom to huddle under a religious system. It is in this coming together of victims of alienation from rejection that anger becomes a social force, which then becomes directed against the "principalities and powers" that crush the legitimate yearnings of these religious persons, ideological groups, or ethnic communities. The ingredient that conjoins with alienation to stoke anger is degradation. Psychological explications of fundamentalism posit that it is such anger, which results from being consistently rejected and systematically demeaned, that occasions and stimulates local and global violence.

Numerous labels are given to the principalities and powers that have concertedly alienated and doggedly disgraced religious fundamentalists over the last few decades. Modernity and secularization are often the prime suspects. Many prominent psychosocial analysts and commentators emphasize the psychological effects that modernization and secularization have on global and local communities. Sudhir Kakar, a psychotherapist who analyzes collective violence in India, is one such scholar. Basing his study on Hindu and Muslim communities in India, Kakar highlights modernity's contribution to a sense of humiliation and rejection of self: "Whereas loss and helplessness constitute one stream of feelings accompanying the modernization process, another stream consists of feelings of humiliation and radically lowered self-worth."[46] He then goes on to inquire into why those negatively affected by modernity and secularization find a refuge as well as an armory in religion. Kakar's study of religious violence unearths the deep religious psyches that are ingrained into Hindus and Muslims from childhood. On the one hand, such psychosocial schooling inculcates a psyche of assurance and affection when it comes to one's own religion. Thus religion becomes a familiar abode for safe retreat when under attack by the forces of modernity and secularization. On the other hand, such early socialization also instills a psyche's sense of the Other's religion that is rooted in anxiety and animosity. Modernity and secularization are much more complex and amorphous phenomena. The anger arising from rejection and humiliation is more easily directed against the religious Other. This, Kakar suggests, is the psychological reason why Hindu and Muslim violence becomes morally acceptable and religiously sanctioned when anger needs to be expressed communally.[47]

If such anger generated by humiliation in the context of modernization with secularization leads to violence between Hindus and Muslims, the rising influence of modernization with westernization may be said to fuel forms of violent Islamic fundamentalism. In a 2010 essay on religious fundamentalism in Islam, Farhad Khosrokhavar highlights the generative force of humiliation in the violent turn of jihadism in the world: "Global jihadism is a reaction against humiliation. It is based on a vision of the self as humiliated by the dominant West, and the reaction is to humiliate the humiliator."[48] The anger that initially seeks a fortress in religious fundamentalism gradually acquires a cohort of people and a template of beliefs. These in turn enable one to conjure up radical and concrete remedies for relieving one's sense of degradation through a divinely underwritten plan. In an ironic way anger galvanizes the assembled humiliated ones to relieve God of the responsibility both of avenging them and restoring the divine plan for the world. Instead, the religiously insulted undertake the onus of furiously moving forward God's purposeful and powerful agenda. Thus religious fundamentalism brings together people who are willing to do something about their unresolved anger. They are committed to do something about the source and object of this rage. George Marsden, reflecting on Christian fundamentalism in the United States of America, makes an interesting observation that accentuates this psychological trait. "A fundamentalist is an evangelical who is angry about something. . . . Fundamentalists are a subtype of evangelicals, and militancy is crucial to their outlook. Fundamentalists are not just religious conservatives; they are conservatives who are willing to take a stand and fight."[49] In quite a different historical context, and writing after the Americans claimed to be in a war with "the axis of evil," Barber admits to the pervasive, inscrutable, and confounding element of anger that united those threatening the imperial West. His diagnosis comes from decades of having his hand on the pulse of the Middle East: "The axis of evil can be overcome by prudent intelligence and brute force. The axis of anger—far more encompassing—is difficult to fathom and still harder to address."[50]

Also, those who find refuge in fundamentalism experience a high level of alienation (A2) from the world, which has been overtaken by secularization and modernization. It is deep-felt alienation from the expanding world of strange people, changing life patterns, and shifting religious/ cultural systems. As Martin Marty says, "Psychologists regularly point out that alienated individuals or groups are more likely to work out their insecurities on other groups than are those who have already dealt with their self-estrangement and consequently improved their mental health."[51] This explains the need to construct a collective target that can bear the reproach and thus the punitive onus for this unjustified rejection that has culminated in burdensome alienation. The most commonplace and somewhat handy targets are the usual suspects: secularization, modernization, and other religions competing for power with the religious fundamentalists. Rather than leading to the state of personal melancholy frequently highlighted by Western psychotherapy, alienation also makes individuals seek merger into strong enclaves that promise collective shelter from hurt and alienation. When alienation results from humiliation for religious beliefs and practices, it does not draw the lonely sufferers into unproductive retreat into the self. Rather, they seek afflicted coreligionists who resolve to do something together—often something violent—about relieving their burden of hurt, resentment, and rage. But all this talk of Western interpretations does not exempt theorists from offering mainly psychological motifs for violence that takes place among Christian majority United States of America. There is not a Western versus Eastern way of thinking when it comes to explicating violence emanating from religious fundamentalism. Jessica Stern takes Kerry

Noble—the leader of a Christian cult in rural Arkansas called the Covenant, the Sword, and the Arm of the Lord (CSA)—as her main example in her chapter on alienation. She makes this point: "Learning about Noble's evolution from a mild-mannered pastor to a 'soldier' taught me how cult leaders can harness alienation and anomie to construct group identity, eventually creating killers out of lost souls."[52]

When anger (A1) coupled with alienation (A2) is stoked by hate (H), religious fundamentalism emerges as a potent force. Hate transforms unresolved anger and acute alienation into a concrete project; it motivates individuals to do something about those whom the alienated consider responsible for generating the anger and causing the alienation that Sudhir Kakar describes so aptly: "In defining the other as a competitor with a deadly intent toward one's own group, fundamentalism provided a focus for undue anger and unresolved hate."[53] In this regard, fundamentalism is a psychological program as much as it is a religious project. But of course, one cannot produce wholeness from anger and emancipation from alienation by the directives of hate. For starters, hate further hardens the rift between alienated communities, which in turn churns out more of the anger that should have been resolved through negotiation in the first place. Rather than mitigate their psychological state, such a fundamentalist religious matrix and the actions emanating from it actually exacerbate the wrathful and estranged condition. It is more important and quite unfortunate that fundamentalists are much more likely to become the victims of their own violent designs and deliveries of hate. Acts of violence cooked up in anger seem to offer a way out of alienation, but they usually wind up damaging the alienated far more than their supposed adversaries. Firdous Syed, a retired Kashmiri Militant, makes this point brilliantly: "The first generation of fundamentalists . . . was focused on Dawa—education. We focused on freedom. This generation is much more rigid, stricter, than my generation. They are focused on hate. It is a painful journey. Bitter and sour, like eating a lemon. To hate is venom. When you hate you poison yourself. This is the typical mentality of the fundamentalist movements today. Hate begets hate. You cannot create freedom out of hatred."[54]

I am convinced that simply bundling a collection of negative psychological elements with coherence and persuasion cannot explain the devotion and discipline that religious fundamentalists bring to their vision and mission. Raw and overflowing anger (A1), acute and anxious alienation (A2), and combustible and other-directed hate (H) work in concert through the elements available in religion to craft fundamentalism. The structures and resources of religion thus are of great service for the making of this modern concoction. Religion becomes a metanarrative tapestry that allows one to make sense of A1 and A2 in which H is directed as righteous enmity against those who foil the designs of God and thus insult and marginalize God's true agents in the world. Religion becomes the answer to this problem. It is able to function as both a protective fortress to guard against and an offensive frontline to destroy the regimes of modernity and secularization, which generate anger through enacting rejection and serving out humiliation.

Religion cannot be left out in psychological interpretations of violent religious fundamentalism. Two points may be emphasized to put religion back into the psychological analysis that I just elucidated. First, religion provides overall interpretative scaffolding for psychologically displaced and socially disempowered individuals and communities. The anger, alienation, and hate that are experienced are in a collective search for somewhat ready-made and yet reworkable templates that might explain the psychological and social state to those experiencing A1, A2, and H. There is a real need to make conceptual sense of these feelings that arise in the individual and among communities. Religion becomes an accessible candidate to spell out why certain people are targeted by secular or modern society for rejection and humiliation. In fact, religion offers such conceptual meaning by resorting to interpreting the mundane through the sacred.

Second, religion offers the possibility of gathering an alternate community. It provides a legitimate forum in which the brokenhearted may convene and a subversive arena in which those crushed in spirit might assemble. Aslan's comment is worth noticing: "Religion provides a social movement with a reservoir of ready-made symbols that can be used to create solidarity among members across ethnic, cultural, linguistic, and national boundaries."[55] In religion there is a long tradition of building solidarity among a set-apart (holy) people. Individuals who are set aside or rent asunder by the powers of this world are chosen or elected by the will of the Divine. Religion thus offers more than just conceptual space for the psychologically wounded and socially displaced individuals and communities. It also provides these groups with purposive meeting spaces. In this space solidarity is reinforced, even as rage is baptized into righteous anger; alienation is interpreted to be purification from the taint of the worldly; and hate is sacralized as the force that consumes the power of evil. In this communal assemblage, religion ritually binds those who experience A1, A2, and H. Hence a "covenanted" resolve unites such communities among themselves and with God as they seek meaningful and concrete action against the children of this world who bring humiliation and alienation upon the children of God. What unites religious fundamentalists is a strong belief that within the assurance of religion and through the urging of divine power, they are commissioned to do something about this anger, alienation, and hate that has been churning within them.

The stronger and more inflexible the religious scaffolding, the more security and safety are assured, which is why religious fundamentalism needs to harden the heart of religion. But these shelters of religious retreats do not always merely take restless and raging emotional states and transfer them on to a shock-absorbing god or goddess. Religions also provide strategic locations for regrouping to mount divinely sponsored offense against those who subvert God's rulership over the world. Religious fundamentalism provides legitimate avenues that let believers sublimate such turbulent emotions into the life of the world. This way, something is done in the name of the Divine to push back against the agents of alienation, creating a safe space for others like them in this god-forsaken world. One may say that twenty-first-century fundamentalism is the result of righteous rage seeking and finding alienated partners under muscular religion.[56] It safeguards true believers and offensively subverts those regimes and regiments that stand against its divine agenda.

Fundamentalism as a Religious Phenomenon

Having analyzed cultural, political, economic, and psychological theories as a basis for interpreting religious fundamentalism, I submit that it is irresponsible, especially for nonfundamentalist religious practitioners, to blame the violent manifestations of religious fundamentalism exclusively or primarily on nonreligious spheres and forces. We must be honest with ourselves: religion is part of the problem. We can no longer disregard the fact that a substantial part of the world's violence comes from religion and that religious motivations and convictions must bear the brunt of explaining violent religious fundamentalism. Mark Juergensmeyer puts it well: "Religion is crucial for these acts [of violence and violation in our world], since it gives moral justification for killing and provides images of cosmic war that allows activists to believe that they are waging spiritual scenarios. This does not mean that religion causes violence, not does it mean that religious violence cannot, in some cases, be justified by other means. But it does mean that religion often provides the framework, mores and symbols that make possible bloodshed—even catastrophic acts of terrorism."[57] One must also not gloss over the fact the twenty-first century has put out absurd combinations of militant religious agents. After all, we do not have to look hard to find contemporary cadres of violent religious adherents. There are "crusading disciples" in Christianity, "mullah militants" in Islam, "kshatriya sanyasis" in Hinduism, "Jewish terrorists"[58] in Judaism, and "cowboy monks"[59] in Buddhism. They may all have mixed motives and multiple goals, but the fact that they are situated in the arena of religion is mostly self-confessed and often communally professed.

To conclude: I do not claim that religion can be distilled from and extracted out of the rest of reality. If the previous discussion makes one thing clear, it is that religion cannot help but be expressed though the cultural, social, political, economic, and psychological dimensions of our twenty-first-century world. Yet neither can religion be fully emptied into these other facets of human life. Like them, it makes its own particular contribution. To understand the violence that springs from fundamentalism, we must grasp religion's distinctive role in it. The next chapters will turn much more deliberately to the particularities of religion as it manifests itself in three specific religious fundamentalist movements: one in the United States of America, one in Egypt, and one in India. The histories, contextual triggers, and community manifestations of Christian, Muslim, and Hindu fundamentalism are certainly different from other expressions of religious fundamentalism elsewhere in the world. However, it is important to study how historical situations in these regions have worked with religious sources from these three religions to produce versions of violent religious fundamentalism in our twenty-first century.

Chapter Two

Christian Fundamentalism

How is it . . . that Christianity, allegedly born from the gospel of love, has fallen into the violence of the crusades and inquisitions, and the vengeful threats of apocalypse and hell?

Mark Johnston, *Saving God: Religion after Idolatry*

They only heard it said, "The one who formerly was [violently] persecuting us is now proclaiming the faith he once tried to destroy." And they glorified God.

Galatians 1:23–24[1]

Introduction

As we have seen, fundamentalism is all about religion. Recognizing that other influences contributed to its development does not change this fact. In the next three chapters, I take on the challenge of explaining fundamentalism as a thoroughly religious phenomenon. I do so by moving away from analyzing religion in general to examining religions in their specificity. To understand violent religious extremism, we look at its Christian, Muslim, and Hindu expressions. So as not to dehistoricize these religions in the ocean conveniently dubbed "global," I ground these movements of religious fundamentalism in representative geographical contexts.

This chapter, which focuses on Christian fundamentalism, unfolds in four sections. First, I examine the historical context that gave rise to Christian fundamentalism in early twentieth-century America. Second, I describe aspects of the last quarter of the twentieth century, which

35

become the backdrop for understanding contemporary Christian fundamentalism. Third, taking into consideration the watershed events of September 11, 2001, I sketch the renewed vigor and scope for Christian fundamentalism in our century. Fourth, I identify and explicate key religious characteristics of this Western movement in the twenty-first-century United States. Three of these themes are explicated in detail: cultivated biblical literalism, combative communal dispositions formed by a dualistic worldview, and globally committed (albeit self-serving) political theology. These strong religious beliefs knit together by nationalist ambitions to "keep America great"[2] or "make America great again"[3] violently affect the world. By way of concluding reflection, I observe that more than instigating direct and spectacular violence, Christian fundamentalism operates stealthily through covert forms built into the power of a robust nation-state that also has global reach and influence.

The Origins of Christian Fundamentalism

Throughout its two-thousand-year history and across its astonishing geographical expansion, Christianity has manifested itself in a multitude of ways, becoming the largest religion in our twenty-first-century world. A 2012 Pew Research Study put the Christian population at 2.2 billion, representing 32% of the world's population.[4] Christian fundamentalism's origins lie buried within the mountain of information that is Christian history; fully accounting for those origins represents searching for the proverbial needle in a two-millennia-old haystack of historical data strewn across an assortment of geographical locations.

Nonetheless, we can know much about Christian fundamentalism by attending to certain noteworthy details regarding how it came to be. The first is surprising: while violence has been part of Christianity at other times and places, Christian fundamentalism is a modern movement arising out of the United States of America. Harvey Cox puts this matter across adeptly: "Fundamentalism has roots everywhere, but it was born in America"[5] Less than one hundred years ago, Christian fundamentalism emerged in the modern West, "on the soil of American Protestantism." Martin Marty reminds us that this term, "which cannot be found in dictionaries before the 1920s," has now appeared in "various translations—not all of them welcome in all cultures—[and] has traveled internationally."[6] Commenting on the contextual nature of this term, he underscores the fact that "the effective invention of the word, and its rapid spread in usage, occurred because a new phenomenon was present."[7]

Second, when this term "fundamentalism" arose during the early decades of the twentieth century, it did not have the pejorative meaning that accompanies it today. In fact, at the time, Christian fundamentalism was an identity marker chosen and propagated by its members. Two events support this claim. One is the publication and distribution between 1910 and 1920 of three million copies of a series of twelve pamphlets with the title *The Fundamentals*.[8] Another is a column written by Cutis Lee Laws, a Northern Baptist newspaper editor, on July 1, 1920, suggesting "that those who still cling to the great fundamentals shall be called 'fundamentalists'"; hence originally this label represented a "compliment" rather than a "disparagement."[9] It was a distinct identity beneath which convicted Christians, feeling threatened by the sea change of sweeping modernity in the United States, would stand up for their beliefs as compiled into uncompromising core statements of religious faith.[10]

A third point to keep in mind has to do with the political impulses of early twentieth-century fundamentalism. It was an age in which modern science, rational philosophy, and spreading secularism rattled the secure religious foundations of the United States of America. Christian fundamentalism was a spirited counterattack in a perceived war for the worldview of the Bible. This God-given, tried, and tested worldview had made the nation of evangelical Protestantism stable and prosperous; modernity imperiled that stability and prosperity. Fundamentalism, in this sense, was a "rebellion against the hegemony of the secular."[11] It brought together a militant movement fearing that rationality rather than revelation, science rather than the Bible, and pluralism rather than Protestant Christianity would be the building blocks for the twentieth-century United States of America. Two representative foundational theories were singled out: the theory of evolution, which undermined the biblical account of creation; and historical-critical theories in theology, which destabilized the literal interpretation of the Bible. What is interesting is that this fear of "the hegemony of the secular" was fueled by the fundamentalists' own "sense of entitlement to exercise hegemony in American life."[12] These evangelical Protestants of the first two decades of the twentieth century were convinced that they had the "right to claim that historically their expression of Christianity was the majority view in America."[13]

The fundamentalists' passionate battle for right doctrine as a means of reclaiming the land for God, however, did not ignite the imagination of the nation. Instead, fundamentalism found itself losing steam after the first quarter of the twentieth century. For one thing, Christian fundamentalists were unable to capture leadership within the various churches in the United States.[14] Ironically, another reason for the lack of growth of fundamentalism can be attributed to its aggressive fighting spirit. Such a disposition, useful in fighting enemies outside their camps, spilled over into instigating clashes within the fold. In the words of Cox, "Fighting fundamentalists fought other fighting fundamentalists over how the fight against the enemy should be waged."[15] But more important, even the fundamentalists' victories against their secular enemies wound up looking like defeats: thus after the 1925 Scopes "Monkey Trial" in which John Scopes was fined $100 by the Judge Raulston for teaching the theory of evolution in Dayton, Tennessee, the tide of public opinion turned against them.[16] Beside the fact that the Tennessee Supreme Court reversed the decision based on a technicality just over a year later, the attention of the nation as a whole turned to less religious and more pressing matters.[17] After an initial effervescence in the public mind, fundamentalism's fizz went flat over the next several decades. Other events, notably the Great Depression and World War II, displaced fundamentalism's concerns from public attention.

Christian Fundamentalism's Resurgence

After waning for fifty or so years, the Christian fundamentalists resurged in the United States during the last quarter of the twentieth century. Three factors may have contributed to this reemergence. The first was the 1970s wave of new immigrants coming from traditions that were not Christian. This was a threat to the hegemony of Christianity in a religiously changing nation. Although "not the immediate catalyst," this wave of immigrants from "other religious traditions largely alien to most Americans" did form "a backdrop to that revival" of fundamentalism.[18] I have edited a 1999 U.S. census data report to show the gradual decrease in the number of immigrants from Europe (traditionally from Western and Christian backgrounds) in reverse proportion to a steep increase in the number of immigrants from Asia (traditionally from non-Western and non-Christian backgrounds).[19] Thus, while there were 7,256,311 immigrants from Europe in 1960, this figure fell to 4,350,403 in 1990. In contrast, while there were only 490,996 immigrants from Asia in 1960, this figure rose exponentially to 4,979,037 in 1990.

Region and Country or Area of Birth
of the Foreign-Born Population: 1960 to 1990

Region/country	1990*	1980*	1970*	1960*
Total	**19,767,316**	**14,079,906**	**9,619,302**	**9,738,091**
Reported by region/country	18,959,158	13,192,563	9,303,570	9,678,201
Europe	4,350,403	5,149,572	5,740,891	7,256,311
Asia	4,979,037	2,539,777	824,887	490,996
China	529,837	286,120	172,132	99,735
Japan	290,128	221,794	120,235	109,175
India	450,406	206,087	51,000	12,296
Iran	210,941	121,505	(NA)	(NA)
Pakistan	91,889	30,774	6,182	1,708

Source: U.S. Bureau of the Census, March 9, 1999[20]   * Indicates sample data.

Apart from the overall change in the numbers from Europe and Asia, this selectively presented table encapsulates the increase in numbers from China, India, Japan, and Iran-Pakistan to indicate the likely proportional jump in the inflow of Confucian, Hindu, Buddhist, and Muslim immigrants entering the United States from the 1960s to the end of the twentieth century.

Second, from the 1970s onward, evangelicals and fundamentalists seized upon new technologies to beam their message into the homes and hearts of U.S. Christians, thus consolidating an activist religious constituency. Coming to be known as the New Christian Right (NCR), fundamentalists led their radio and television audiences to embrace "totalism" (fusing economic, social, cultural, and religious realms) and political "activism."[21] Ironically, the forces most resistant to the ideas of modernity made best use of modern technology to further their orthodox worldview. The gradual dominance of the evangelicals and fundamentalists over religious broadcasting stations during this period is astounding: "Station managers dropped programs airing free religious time and sold time to evangelicals and fundamentalists. By 1970 there were thirty-eight independent evangelical programs; by 1977, 92 percent of all religious programming was commercial; by 1990, 75 percent of all religious broadcasting on radio and television was evangelical or fundamentalist."[22] The fundamentalist agenda went viral in remarkable ways throughout this period, creating a wider and more diverse base in the United States.

Third, a class of charismatic yet militantly fundamentalist leaders—such as Jerry Falwell (1933–2007), Pat Robertson (b. 1930), James Dobson (b. 1936), and Bob Jones III (b. 1939)[23]—systematically labored to animate and shape the hope that the United States would be a Christian nation. One camp among the fundamentalists adopted a separatist strategy. Thus, for example, the Joneses (Bob Jones Sr., Bob Jones Jr., and Bob Jones III) established Bob Jones University, where students could be kept safe from what they perceived as a godless, secular society. For them, theological purity implied "separation from the mainstream, whether it was from the secular world or even among their own fundamentalists rank."[24] The purpose of these separatist institutions was to exert a leavening influence on the rest of society through the example of their fundamentalist convictions.

Another camp among these fundamentalists was avowedly political. For example, Jerry Falwell launched his Moral Majority organization in 1979 to influence national politics, and Pat Robertson unsuccessfully sought the Republican presidential nomination in 1988, aspiring to bring an overtly Christian perspective into U.S. politics. The bid by fundamentalists to control the United States both as a nation-state and as the leader for the entire world might explain the covert manner in which Christianity could carry out massive violence through the state while still personally professing to be committed to living the (nonviolent?) way of Jesus. Of course, this was not a new strategy in the history of Christianity. Constantine the Great (272–337 CE; emperor 306–37) was successful in an experiment of amalgamating the violence of empire with the gospel of peace, which Christianity was known to proclaim. Gregory A. Boyd presents Falwell and Robertson as the representatives of such a Constantinian shift in the United States. In this political turn of robust religion, the nation-state becomes a cover for righteous violence to be exercised in the world in the name of the Lord and for the sake of God's purposes. As he puts it,

> While the violent expression of Constantinian mind-set has been largely outlawed, the mind-set itself is very much alive today . . . within the borders of America. When Jerry Farwell, reflecting a widespread sentiment among the conservative Christians, says America should hunt terrorists down and "blow them all away in the name of the Lord," he is expressing the Constantinian mind-set.

When Pat Robertson declares that the United States should assassinate President Chavez of Venezuela, he also is expressing the Constantinian mind-set.[25]

Christian fundamentalism was against the spirit of Enlightenment-influenced modernity, which gradually took away the right of the church to discipline and punish by shifting these powers to the nation-state funded by reason. However, it now tried to regain political control so that Christians could continue to chasten and reprimand religious and irreligious others not aligned with their beliefs and practices.

As history approached the threshold of the new millennium, this openly political brand of fundamentalism expanded its reach. The extreme among the separatists were announcing preparations for the end of the world. But many more fundamentalists were both "present[ing] themselves as movements against social modernization" and situating themselves within "the long U.S. tradition of projects to create in America a new Jerusalem, a Christian community separate from both the corruption of Europe and the savagery of the 'uncivilized' world."[26] The political role for Christianity in the United States also had consequences for violating the religious and ideological rights of others within the nation and across the whole world. Pat Robertson quite categorically declared that in the Christian-led country he hoped to lead in 1988, "those who believe in the Judeo-Christian values are better qualified to govern America than Hindus and Muslims."[27] He then envisioned the role of such a Christian-led nation as ushering in "The New Global Order" and asserted a bold claim to put Christians in charge of bringing peace to the world: "There will never be world peace until God's house and God's people are given their rightful place of leadership at the top of the world. How can there be peace when drunkards, drug dealers, communists, atheists, New Age worshipers of Satan, secular humanists, oppressive dictators, greedy moneychangers, revolutionary assassins, adulterers, and homosexuals are on top?"[28]

Before I get to the twenty-first century, let me make two observations that may help us understand Christian fundamentalism in the United States better as it entered the new millennium. First, the reinforcing of violence through concerted aggression is also on display among other religious fundamentalist movements across the world. The militant spirit and violent activity of fundamentalism became magnified among other religious movements throughout the world during the last quarter of the twentieth century. Competing fundamentalisms fueled particular religious mobilizations in a more connected global community. I will look closely at the escalation and spread of fundamentalism in Egypt and India in subsequent chapters. At this point it is sufficient to simply state how the Muslim Brotherhood and the forces of Hindutva were poised in these countries during the time. Even though the Muslim Brotherhood was founded in Egypt in 1928, it was during the last quarter of the twentieth century that its violence became more intense and widespread. The impressive encyclopedia on world terrorism sums this up well: "From the assassination of [President Anwar] Sadat in 1981 to the mid-1990s, Islamic terrorism in Egypt continued to escalate."[29] Similarly, the idea of India as a Hindu nation not only grew in influence among the masses but also began to consolidate as political power, prepared to govern the country. As the noted historian K. N. Panikkar stated in 1999, "A [Hindu] communal agenda is now before the nation, initially conceived by the ideologues of the Hindutva and later elaborated by its politics. The main thrust of the agenda is the construction of a sociopolitical order that would privilege the culture and the religion of the Hindus."[30] After the Hindu Nationalists came to power in 1998, such a Hindu order, Panikkar argues, singled out Muslims and Christians for "marginalization" and brutalization."[31]

Fundamentalism, as an identifier of strong and militant religious expression, percolated into the world as the twentieth century came to an end. As I see it, one result of this intensification and expansion of Muslim and Hindu fundamentalism in the Middle East and South Asia was that Christian fundamentalism gained newfangled meaning and global relevance into the twenty-first century. To begin with, the inter-religious characteristics of violence and violation, which may not have been explicit in the early expressions of Christian fundamentalism, came to define its engagement in the world. Violent means of furthering one's own religious beliefs and practices not only in the United States but also in the shrinking world, which often resulted in violation of the rights of other religious worldviews, gave religious fundamentalism an added trait. It is this connection with violence against other religious worldviews and legitimizing of violation of the right to be religiously different that characterizes twenty-first-century Christian fundamentalism in the United States. In chapter 5 I shall explore this competing dimension among Christianity, Islam, and Hinduism in much more detail.

Second, another hallmark of Christian fundamentalism as it entered the twenty-first century was the convenient alliances between politically active fundamentalists and theologically conservative evangelicals. The coalition of Bible-based and secular-wary Christians known as the New Christian Right often showed signs of strain between its fundamentalist and evangelical components through some of the twentieth century. While the lines between the two were often blurred, they were nonetheless evident. Yet one can see a gradual coming together of these two strands of Christian fundamentalism toward the end of that century. After 9/11 a more closely aligned body of theologically conservative and politically activist believers emerged.[32] The serious difference between these two camps could now be consistently interpreted more in terms of attitude than belief. In a short 2012 book titled *Militant Christianity*, George Marsden, a renowned scholar of Christian fundamentalism, stressed that a militant "attitude" came to be an important marker for both fundamentalists and evangelicals. "Our broad definition of fundamentalism," he opined, "involves both an attitude (militancy) and a set of beliefs (evangelical)."[33] While fundamentalists and evangelicals "parted company mainly over manners and demeanor,"[34] they found commonality beyond shared doctrine. There were dire threats against them from both within and without the United States. Both came to see a newly militant Christianity as the great need of the new millennium.

Violent Rebirth in the Twenty-First Century

After September 11, 2001, Christian fundamentalism upped its game beyond strong beliefs and strident manners. On one hand, the nationally catastrophic and diabolically spectacular attack on the United States emboldened the forces of fundamentalism to reclaim the Christian character for the nation and, on the other hand, stimulated the imagination of fundamentalists to extend their worldly reach into governance of the whole world. The first idea was in continuity with the fundamentalist objective of the preceding century. Its aim was to reassert the Christian worldview and culture as foundational to the nation and reintegrate future generations into this way of thinking and living. The internal threat within the nation came from the colluding worldviews of secularism and modernity. Steve Bruce's words are perceptive: "American fundamentalism is essentially a voluntary association of self-selecting individuals, competing to define the culture of a stable nation-state."[35]

Yet for the first time, after 9/11, Christian fundamentalism in the United States began to overflow its national boundaries. The terrorist attacks kindled in the fundamentalist movement a new kind of global imagination. Here we should recognize that for centuries American mission agencies have worked toward the goal of converting the whole world to Christ. We should likewise recognize how U.S. transnational corporations have infiltrated the global markets over the last several decades. It is not as though no globally ambitious Christian mission or capitalist enterprise emanated from the United States before September 11, 2001. Yet the 9/11 attacks ignited and fueled a religious vision of a larger role for the American nation-state in the world. This fertile event loaded Christian fundamentalism's national ambitions with weighty responsibilities on the global stage. Previously it was a national movement in the United States, wrestling with the secularization in its own country; now Christian fundamentalism found itself poised to assume a role in the drama of all of humanity.

In framing its response to the events of 9/11, the United States might have chosen simply the language of neoconservatism, speaking of military responses to outside attacks.[36] Instead, the country's leadership played into the religious agenda set into motion by the bombers and their sponsors. This religious script was outlined, not only by the much-publicized rhetoric of Osama Bin Laden (the symbolic voice of the Islamic jihad), but also by the preparation and the execution of the events of September 11, 2001, themselves. The letter found in the luggage of Mohamed Atta, one of the hijackers who flew a plane into the World Trade Center, is laced with Qur'anic quotations and littered with invocations of the will of Almighty God. George W. Bush's address, less than a week after the attacks, mirrored, to a lesser extent, some of this religious language. Even if unintentional, his public statement symbolically put in place a global theater, quite familiar to Christian fundamentalists, within which one might extract meaning for these clashing forces. As a historical-mythical clothesline on which Christian fundamentalists might hang their individual garments of belief, let me point to three such references in his speech given on September 16, 2001, from the South Lawn at the White House in Washington, D.C.[37]

First, Bush couches his address to the American people on what is claimed to be a day of "prayer," "the Lord's Day," and a "day of faith." Using the Christian idea of Sunday as a prayerful day that commemorates the resurrection of Jesus Christ over death and the forces of evil, Bush, at the very beginning of his address, reminded the people of the United States that although "today, millions of Americans mourned and prayed, . . . tomorrow we go back to work." Toward the end, just in case they had forgotten the auspiciousness of the time of his address, the president reminds them that "on this day of faith," he has "never had more faith in America" than "right now." Second, the language of "crusade" against terrorism that he invoked stimulated the Christian imagination. The term "crusade" clearly was a careless shift away from Bush's official script since it was used in answer to a reporter's question. Yet it categorically and sensationally projected a global clash between the "holy war" against infidels (Osama Bin Laden) and the "war on terrorism" (George W. Bush). Third, the connection between prayer and "job" to be done took on religious imagery akin to a battle between good and evil. The work that Bush was referring to involved the specific "job" of the U.S. military to "rid the world of evildoers."[38] The war between good and evil may not have been painted explicitly as a war of religions between Christianity and Islam. Yet Bush's global prognostications of the macroplot and universal script were peppered with so much imagery and symbolism that they evoked a clash of these two religious traditions.

Undoubtedly, President Bush did much to prevent making his War on Terror (so named by Bush on September 20, 2001) an assault on Islam. Yet, apart from setting up a "prototypical fundamentalist" Christian paradigm, which shared "far more in common with the [Muslim fundamentalist] enemies he fought," George W. Bush also brought the reach of religious fundamentalism onto the theater of the whole world.[39] The alliance between neoconservative political ideology and religious fundamentalism swept the country, which believed it was under massive and violent threat, both from secular and liberal "pagans" within and religious and anti-Christian "terrorists" abroad. More important, this politically muscular Christianity found an even more secure foothold in the Congress after the mid-term election of 2002 and in the White House after the reelection of the Bush-Cheney ticket in 2004. The strong collaboration between communities of Christian fundamentalists and collectives of clash-of-civilization ideologues united by a national and global political "will to power" had violent consequences for the world. It became much harder to tell the differences between the War on Terror, the battle of religions, and U.S. ascendency as the global superpower. Most of the first decade of the twenty-first century witnessed a convergence of conflict-prone foreign policies of the neoconservatives, who directed a New World [dis]Order and a theology of "violent retribution, paranoia, and revenge"[40] propagated by Christian fundamentalists.

The Beliefs that Move Christian Fundamentalism

Thus far we have been looking at the history and ethos of Christian fundamentalism. In the rest of this chapter, I want to focus and comment upon the religious ideas that frame and fuel the fundamentalist movement in the United States. The theological aspects that I identify below have emerged throughout the historical development of Christian fundamentalism (from the 1920s to the 2000s), even if they have not always been equally acknowledged. In what follows I zero in on three foundational convictions on which Christian fundamentalism depends to construct a worldview and nourish a way of being religious individuals and communities in the world.[41]

Biblical Absoultism

Religious fundamentalism flourishes within an absolutist world where all truth that justifies belief is authorized by God and given through an objectively trustworthy narrative. Even in our so-called postmodern age, it espouses the worldview of modernity. Douglas Pratt accurately portrays this aspect of religious fundamentalism as a "modernist project writ large." On the one hand, there is an unequivocal insistence on "only one truth; one authority; one authentic narrative that accounts for all; one right way to be." On the other hand, there is another self-exalting claim: "That way is my way."[42]

Christian fundamentalists invoke the Bible, *the* divine Word to human beings, as the sole authority that directs them toward the overall objective of being wholly faithful to God and fully fruitful in the world. Setting the Bible on a pedestal this way, claiming that it reveals God's plan concretely, historically, and literally, has been a feature of Christian fundamentalism from the 1920s to the present day. This belief in the absolute truth of the Bible is intended to protect the movement from the radical historical shifts, with their competing forms of authority, that have characterized the last century. Allegiance to such an absolute authority of the whole Bible is termed "scripturalism" or "biblicism." While acknowledging that literalism and inerrancy are key features of such a commitment to the absolute authority of the Bible, Richard Antoun rightly points to the emotional and inspirational relationship between Christian fundamentalism and the Bible. Through unqualified and unchangeable belief in the complete authority of the Bible, religious persons and communities are "transformed, inspired, and comforted"[43] as they find in this sacred divine communication "certainty in an ever changing world."[44]

The absolute authority of the Bible as the historical-literal vision of God for all of humanity offers Christian fundamentalists in the twenty-first century a bulwark against two competing foundational frameworks: (1) the persuasive legitimizations of secular reason and (2) the formidable assertions of other sacred scriptures. The first has a long history of wooing the West. Secularism's project of advancing the progress of reason as a sure way to undercut the hold of biblical truth on Western civilization goes back to the age of Enlightenment, beginning in Europe in the late seventeenth century. The fear that this spirit of secular reason would move from the East and West coasts to seep into the broad center and Deep South of the United States of America has been very real for fundamentalism from the early twentieth century. It continues to function as a threat to fundamentalists' notion of a "Christian America." Much of the struggle pits the authority of the Bible over against the weight of reason and the lure of modern scholarship. Christian fundamentalists pursue a form of reasoning that insulates the Bible from the attack of both secular reason from outside of religion and liberal reason employed by modern scholarship from within Christianity. Thus, in concluding her study on distinguishing between evangelicalism and fundamentalism, Harriet Harris unearths a form of circular reasoning utilized by Christian fundamentalists to ward off the threat of modern foundations of scholarship. Fundamentalism is, in her judgment,

> a commitment to a priori reasoning that scripture cannot contain any error because it is inspired by God; an almost contrary commitment to demonstrating empirically that scripture is indeed inspired because it contains no error; a feeling that by moving away from either commitment one is making concessions to modern scholarship; and a hesitancy to make such concessions lest they detract from the authority of the Bible and so threaten the very foundations of the Christian faith.[45]

This circular reasoning also might explain why the conflict about whether the Bible contains the literal word revealed by God or symbolic divine truths communicated through human beings is so intense. Through its alliance with secular reason, modern scholarship threatens the stability of absolute, biblical truth. The stakes are thus high for the fundamentalists. Robert P. Jones invokes metaphorical language of war to describe this contestation: "The main reason the battles over how to read the Bible have been so brutal is that they were at their heart about how to find a stable source of truth and guidance for life in the rapidly changing modern world."[46] The Christian fundamentalists are fighting a two-front war with the forces of reason-driven modernity: they battle the secular camps outside of their religious community while at the same time defending against the schools of biblical realism that have arisen within Christianity itself.

The second threat to the absolute authority of the Bible is more recent. Christian fundamentalists stridently uphold and disseminate firm belief in the absolute truth of the Bible within a globalized world where similarly confident claims are made by other religious communities. In the United States, this has taken on a public and aggressive posture of demonizing the Qur'an. The days after September 11, 2001, saw a series of diatribes against Islam from fundamentalist leaders such as Franklin Graham, Jerry Falwell, and Pat Robertson. President Bush made it a point to distance himself from these blanket criticisms of Islam. He also tried to humanize the prophet Mohammed and suggest resemblances between the Bible and the Qur'an. Chuck Baldwin, a popular radio broadcaster, syndicated columnist, and Christian fundamentalist leader, who served in 2004 and 2008 as the U.S. vice-presidential and presidential candidate, respectively, of the Constitution Party, took on Bush for assuming common ground between these religious traditions. On December 13, 2002, Baldwin's caustic attack on President Bush challenged his understanding of the Bible. In extolling a Christian belief that the Bible is the only revelation of God, Baldwin deplored Bush's suggestion that the Qur'an could also be a revelation of God. President Bush, he said, "has repeatedly demonstrated colossal ignorance of Biblical truth" by remarking that "Ramadan commemorates the revelation of God's word in the Holy Koran to the prophet Mohammed." Baldwin reiterates his own fundamentalist Christian view in contrast to Bush by means of a rhetorical question: "Does Mr. Bush not realize that the Holy Bible, not the Koran, is the one and only written revelation of God to man? Is he that ignorant of Christian teaching? Or, was he deliberately denying Christian doctrine in order to curry favor with his Muslim hosts?"[47]

The most sinister, public, and violent attack against the Qur'an, however, came many years later. Terry Jones, a fundamentalist pastor of Dove World Outreach Center, caught the attention of the world when he announced in January 2011 that he was going to "put the Koran on trial." Claiming that he "didn't hear a single complaint," which he took to be American Christians' endorsement of his plan, "Jones dressed in a judicial robe, . . . ordered a copy of the Koran to be torched [on March 20, 2011] in a portable fire pit." Reflecting on the planning of such a desecration of Islam's Holy Scripture, "the pastor said the church also debated whether to shred the book, shoot it or dunk it in water instead of burning it."[48] The defacing of the Qur'an must be viewed in light of the pastor's fundamentalist belief in the absolute authority of the Bible. This conviction can be found on the website of the church: "We are a New Testament, Charismatic, Non-Denominational Church that believes in the whole Bible and that we are to act in response to the Word of God in order to change the times we are living in. Those times have gotten further and futher [sic] away from God; full of deception."[49] Jones seemed unconcerned that his act of symbolic violence against the Qur'an could lead to real bloody violence from Muslim fundamentalists in many parts of the world. His point was to publicly demonstrate a violent denunciation of the symbol of Muslim authority while holding true to the conviction that Christians are bound together by espousing the authority of "the whole Bible."

Christian fundamentalism in the United States is thus a movement against both the secular reason of modernity and the sacred narratives of other religions. Modernity threatens to let assured reason and liberal reasoning shake the secure foundation of the Bible as absolute authority in the life of the community of believers as they seek to bring about the divine purposes for world history. The other sacred narratives jeopardize the fundamentalist myth that as a "Christian nation" the United States must be grounded upon and guided by God's Word as revealed concretely, historically, and literally only in the Bible. There is, one might notice, much re-creating in this process about "what is imagined to be a past social formation based on sacred texts."[50]

But of much more concern is how such an absolute allegiance to the authority of the Bible fosters and feeds violence in the present and into the future. It is dangerous that Christian fundamentalists find their own purpose organically and missionally connected to the nature of God's powerful and even violent work in the Bible. Philip Jenkins is honest when he admits: "If Christians . . . needed biblical texts to justify terrorism or ethnic slaughter, their main problem will be an embarrassment of riches."[51] Behind the veil of redemptive purpose, there are parts of this divine narrative that authorize God's faithful to deal violently with those who undercut the divine vision so completely revealed in this authoritative

Word. "Religious convictions that become locked into absolute truths can easily lead people to see themselves as God's agents, . . . capable of violent and destructive behavior in the name of religion."[52] It is not just the matter of believing but also the injunction to act against the belief of others that justifies violence and warrants violations.[53]

Jenkins helpfully classifies violent scriptures found in both the Bible and the Qur'an into three categories (arranged from lesser to greater): disturbing, alarming, and extreme. Where Jenkins takes this is astounding, especially since the author is himself a distinguished Christian scholar. Although he admits that the Bible and Qur'an share in a sinister array of alarming and disturbing violent texts, Jenkins is able to state "with confidence" that it is the Bible that "abounds" with "extreme texts," "while the Qur'an has nothing strictly comparable."[54] He goes on to add, "Through all of the centuries of controversy between Islam and its enemies, Christian and Jewish critics have devoted intense effort to finding Qur'anic texts that expose the brutal nature of that faith, and they find many to parade. None, however, damns whole races, inflicts hereditary curses, or issues a command to exterminate. . . . No Qur'anic passage teaches that enemies in warfare should be annihilated or exterminated."[55]

Cosmic Struggle between Good and Evil

Dualism is more than just a logical way of seeing the world as constituted by light and darkness, right and left, male and female, north and south, east and west, yin and yang. It suggests a template of reality that puts the twofold division of all existence, both physical and metaphysical, into active conflict between the powers of good and evil. In an insightful introduction to *The Fundamentalist Mindset*, Charles B. Strozier and Katherine Boyd suggest that "fundamentalism often treat[s] dualistic thinking as a primary characteristic of the mindset."[56] Thus, a clash of contrasting pairs trumps the complementarity of halves within the whole of reality. By placing this cosmic warfare at the heart of reality, religions can then claim that any limited, temporal conflict is an expression of the fundamental, eternal battle. This mind-set assures us that sacred power accompanies us in every struggle, legitimizing whatever means we use to achieve a victory already promised to us by God. By drawing on conceptions of this warfare between good and evil, often presided over by God versus Satan, religions inject such cosmic clashes with moral legitimation and divine assurance that sacred power accompanies such a duel to ultimate victory.

Let's look at three dimensions of this complex web of dualistic world-views within Christian fundamentalism. First is the violent language with which dualism saturates the minds of Christian fundamentalists. Whether one is reflecting upon personal spiritual striving as a Christian disciple or faithful engagement in the world as a Christian community, fundamentalists espouse and disseminate imagery that bespeaks the clash between the powers of good and evil. Thus battle symbolism permeates the individual Christian's thought while confronting the "wiles of the devil" and "all the spiritual forces of evil." Such Christians take on the battle-like instruction in Ephesians to "take up the whole armor of God," which includes belt, breastplate, shield, helmet, and sword (Ephesians 6:10–17). Preachers dole out such language lavishly. Although meta-phorical in nature, since they mainly refer to combat within the spiritual rather than the material realm, the opposing agents are envisioned within a binary oppositional worldview. Thus these enemies of the good more generally, or of God more specifically, are othered at a minimum and demonized at a maximum. Harriet Crabtree's study many decades ago is still true in the contemporary world of fundamentalism: "Preachers everywhere have encouraged the flock to wage war against the forces of evil, and their homilies are followed by hymns about 'Christian soldiers,' fighting 'the good fight,' and struggling 'manfully forward.'"[57] Since the language and symbolism of warfare permeate Scripture, the overzeal-ous Christian disciple and militant Christian community will find there a wealth of resources with which to equip their struggle with the forces of darkness. The Old Testament acclamation that "with God we shall do valiantly; it is he who will tread down our foes" (Psalm 108:13) is woven into the New Testament affirmation that Christ's reign is characterized by "put[ting] all his enemies under his feet" (1 Cor. 15:25). From this conjoining emerges the central thread around which a dualistic religious narrative is woven, which then persuades disciples and communities to join in an ongoing struggle between God and Satan.

The second dimension of this dualistic worldview marks the overflow of such conflicting language and symbolism from the mind of individuals and communities into real life. Because dualistic worldviews are an orien-tation to the *whole* of reality, they also become an invitation to translate religious belief into everyday living within a world demanding that one take sides between competing forces of good and evil, God and Satan. Raimon Panikkar is suspicious of all forms of metaphysical *dvaita*, or twoness, especially as manifested in Western Christianity. He anticipates that they will have disastrous consequences for the real world. "Once an ontological separation is accepted between two ultimate realms of reality," he contends, "there is going to be a fight to the bitter end. The war cannot be waged on logical grounds because logical coherence does not need to be metaphysically binding. It will have to be fought in the field of praxis, with the will to power being its theoretical ally."[58] Radical ways of thinking may not always result in radical behavior, but the latter always starts with the former.

In the United States, the movement from a dualistic mind-set to violent behavior is influenced by a combination of suspicion and antipathy toward those who are conventionally othered and thus easily demonized. Christian fundamentalism's suspicion and antipathy toward Muslims were either the source of, or drew its inspiration from, the larger society's rejection of Islam. Perhaps a bit of both contributes to the truth.[59] Whatever the case may be, the national search for evil has, in the predominantly Christian United States, meant a turning of the collective eye toward Muslims. In a 2014 survey commissioned by the Arab American Institute, "Zogby Analytics found that 42 percent of Americans believe law enforcement is justified in using profiling tactics against Muslim-Americans and Arab-Americans."[60] The survey also shows American attitudes toward Muslim-Americans deteriorating between 2010 and 2014. Thus, favorable impressions of Muslim-Americans on the part of their fellow citizens dropped from 36 to 27 percent in that four-year period.[61] Also in 2014, another study by the Pew Research Center gathered atheists along with Muslims as those most negatively viewed by the American public. When asked to rate religious groups on a "feeling thermometer" ranging from 0 to 100—where 0 reflects the coldest, most negative possible rating and 100 the warmest, most positive rating—Jews, Roman Catholics, and evangelical Christians all receive a rating above 60. By contrast, the poll scored atheists at 41 and Muslims at 40.[62] A mind-set of "friend-enemy thinking"[63] always seems to seek and find religious friends of God alongside whom to combat religious enemies.

The third element of this dualism is the religious conviction that this conflict between good and evil will end in a cosmic showdown in which God will completely crush and conquer Satan and all the forces of evil. The belief that history is moving toward an apocalyptic end that involves the whole cosmos makes this dualistic drama pregnant with meaning for fundamentalists. "One of the most widespread beliefs of violent religious movements is their apocalyptic vision of the cosmic struggle of the forces of the all-good against the forces of the all-evil."[64] For fundamentalists, this conflict is the grounds for hope rather than fear, since they know that in the end God will be victorious over the powers of evil. Religious warriors are emboldened and strengthened in the sure hope that God's "mighty arm" and "strong hand" (Psalm 89:13) will prevail in the end. This sure belief in the ultimate victory of the forces of God over the forces of evil is a concertedly reinforced and collectively rehearsed faith affirmation, which is why it prevails even if all the facts attest to God's faithful losing ground in the conflict with their evil opponents.

Contemporary Christian fundamentalism within the United States has demonstrated a fascination with the imminence of the final battle between God and Satan at Armageddon. Based on a dramatic interpretation of Revelation, "Armageddon" is represented as the site of this violent historical battle between the forces of God and the forces of Satan (16:16 NIV; NRSV: "Harmagedon"). The scenario envisioned by this divinely revealed end-times master plot in the book of Revelation has seeped into the imagination of American fundamentalists (and indeed much of the rest of American culture) through the amazingly successful Left Behind series of sixteen books published in 1995–2007 by Tim LaHaye and Jerry B. Jenkins. The books in this series had already sold over 65 million copies by 2009 and have launched four full-length movies, as well as video games.[65] The biblical road map from the book of Revelation animated the imagination of these authors, who have influenced many twenty-first-century adherents to embrace this dualistic end-time showdown. Armageddon is reconfigured to represent a culminating world war, which Christian fundamentalists anticipate by faith and participate in with hope. It is here that "the kings of the whole world" assembled by "demonic spirits." (Revelation 16:14) will be violently defeated by "the rider" on the "white horse," accompanied by "the armies of the heaven" (Revelation 19:11–15). Jürgen Moltmann suggests that it is from such a dualistic cosmic vision of the end times that "American fundamentalists have developed a modern, fantastic scenario about the final struggle."[66]

Christian fundamentalism, as I have sketched it in this section, possesses a collective dualistic mind-set that calls its followers to take concerted action in the world against the forces of evil, energized by hope in the victorious final battle of God that will vanquish Satan once and for all. Christian fundamentalism embodies a hope manifest in faithful practice rooted in a binary and oppositional worldview: hope for God's ultimate triumph through dualistic struggle. Conflictual politics flows from a metaphysics that pits good against evil both spiritually and materially. Capturing the nation-state to implement the Master's metanarrative within the country and across the whole world, as human history marches toward the end times, becomes an important goal for Christians in the United States. As I mentioned earlier, the nation-state's exercise of hard power to carry out retributive and redemptive violence is what makes a robust United States attractive to Christian fundamentalists. Acts of well-intentioned and providence-attributed violence against religious and ideological others are not executed by the church, which continuously lifts up the soft power of the Christian gospel. Instead, such aggressive practices are the responsibility of the nation-state committed to the politics of God's battle within and without its borders, which the United States intends to serve boldly and faithfully. Michael Ignatieff's words, although from another context of terrorism, are relevant to this analysis. Christian fundamentalism, as I argue, taps into "a desire to give ultimate meaning to time and history through ever-escalating acts of violence which culminate in a final battle between good and evil."[67]

"Chosenness" and God's Rule over the Whole World

Religious fundamentalisms are comprehensive in their theology: souls need bodies, the chosen ones need a nation, and God needs an earthly kingdom. Such a this-worldly, immanent focus within religious movements centered on a transcendent Other may sound contradictory, but it is no anomaly. Throughout history this correlation has been remarkably consistent within the religions that are the focus of our study. It forms the third source of religious fundamentalism, expanding the reach and invigorating the mission of these religiously sectarian groups, causing them to morph into large-scale aggressive movements. No wonder, then, that the goal of religious fundamentalists is to shift their focus outward, moving from cultivating small groups of like-minded followers to altering the beliefs and practices of the larger community. Religious fundamentalists paddle in the backwaters of religion now, but they aim to make their way into the ocean of human life in all its comprehensiveness.

Christian fundamentalism in the twenty-first century fuses a universal God with a chosen people sent to infiltrate the world for the sake of the kingdom inaugurated by Jesus Christ. This grand narrative has captured the imagination of the United States of America. It involves a universal God, his chosen people, the divine promise to make this nation "the light of the world [as] a city built on a hill" (Matthew 5:14), and the role that this chosen people through their nation will play in establishing the kingdom of God on earth. We have already looked at the religious authority that undergirds this vision of history: on the one hand, absolutist belief in the Bible; and on the other, a dualistic worldview that prepares one for battle in the struggle between good and evil. America as the "city on the hill" thus becomes neither simply a religious nor a political reality, but rather a "package deal" comprised of the two.[68]

Let me try to unpack the reality of this package deal. What elements go into this committed political theology? At the most basic level, Christian fundamentalism is founded on the idea of an absolute divine sovereignty. God creates and governs the whole world. Represented as "the LORD," he "is a great God, and a great King above all gods." (Psalm 95:3). Three characteristics of this absolutely sovereign God contribute to Christian fundamentalism's character as a committed political theology.

Christianity shares the first of these qualities with other monotheistic religions. The absoluteness of God in theology is referred to as monotheism, and for Christian fundamentalists the sure knowledge of this God is revealed through the inerrant word of Scripture. But the power conferred by this absolute God must be appropriated and employed by faithful disciples to affect the relative world. This is how theology is translated into theopolitics. Lloyd Steffen makes a convincing argument that the "demonic turn" in religions occurs when absolutism of monotheistic belief operates in tandem with ultimacy of divinely sanctioned singular action. This amalgam of ultimacy with absolutism overflows into destructive power in Christian fundamentalism. The monotheistic God as a "self-contained and exceptionless" personification of "The Absolute" grows in "totalizing power" to "encompass everything."[69] Such an absolute God with the "tremendous power" co-opted by Christian fundamentalists has at times led to "disastrous results,"[70]especially when violence is read into God and enacted on earth for the sake of heaven. Monotheistic affirmations of the absoluteness of God create conceptual extrapolations that such a sovereignty has sole governance rights of the all-knowing and all-powerful creator over God's entire world.

The other side of absolute monotheism is its preoccupation with all the other religious loyalties that undermine its sole authority over all creation. God's absolute status ironically is threatened when it does not translate into ultimate power over all things in heaven and on earth (specifically, when we humans do not grant God that ultimate power). This leads to a strangely anthropomorphic feature of the control-wielding Divine One. The scriptural term that best captures this character of God is "jealousy." The Bible makes "Jealous" an actual name for God: "The LORD, whose name is Jealous, is a jealous God" (Exodus 34:14). God can be named Jealous because this is part of God's essential and consistent nature. In spite of the logical contradiction of positing jealousy to an absolute, sole, and supreme being, since there can be no other comparable to the ultimate One, such an affirmation casts a suspicious eye on all other religious loyalties. Moltmann is cognizant of the more violent converse side of such an absolutist monotheistic credo: "The one God permits no other gods beside him. For that reason religious societies which are termed monotheistic are usually intolerant towards the gods of other religions."[71]

When the absolute God "whose name is Jealous" acts against those perceived as a threat to this God's ultimacy in the world, we humans see ourselves as authorized to commit violence. Again, the name of this God converts this feeling of jealousy into the action of securing ultimacy through a concrete, aggressive image of one doing battle: "The LORD is a warrior; the LORD is his name" (Exodus 15:3). Jerry Falwell insisted that U.S. Christians embrace the idea that "God is pro-war." During the lead-up to the Iraq War (2003–10), this message could not have been more timely. Conservative political hawks within the George W. Bush administration were seeking the support of evangelical and fundamentalist Christians to endorse the Iraq War, which began in March 2003.[72] In typical fundamentalist terminology, Falwell appealed to the authority of the Bible, invoked the history of "God-ordained wars," dehistoricized Jesus, and offered violent scriptural metaphors to charge up his base. Consider Falwell's declaration:

> However, if one depends on the Bible as a guidepost for living, it is readily apparent that war is sometimes a necessary option. In fact, just as there are numerous references to peace in the Bible, there are frequent references to God-ordained war. . . . Many present-day pacifists hold Jesus as their example for unvarying peace. But they ignore the full revelation concerning Jesus pictured in the book of Revelation 19, where He is depicted bearing a "sharp sword" and smiting nations, ruling them with "a rod of iron."[73]

One must not fail to notice Falwell's reference to the apocalyptic Christ, who comes to accomplish God's victory in a final battle with the powers of evil. The war against the regime of Saddam Hussein in the Muslim-majority regions of the Middle East (in concert with the bold urging of Israel's Conservative Prime Minister Netanyahu as early as in 2002)[74] was cleverly linked to the cosmic battle of the second coming of Christ to "smite nations" with a "sharp sword' in order to rule them with "a rod of iron."

A second element in the political theology of U.S. Christian fundamentalism is that the United States has been chosen by God. The idea of being a "chosen people" of God goes all the way back to the Puritans, who came to America from England in the seventeenth century. This aspect of fundamentalist belief exists in tension between their reverence for the Bible and their sense of divine favor on America. In one sense, the fundamentalists' language of being a chosen people derives from and mirrors Yahweh's original choosing of the Israelites in Deuteronomy 7:6: "For you are a people holy to the LORD your God; the LORD your God has chosen you out of all the peoples on earth to be his people, his treasured possession." However, in another sense it usurps this "chosen" status of God's original elect by representing America (the new community fleeing the oppression of England's crown and church) as the "new Israel." As Moltmann says, "Just as God has liberated Israel from Egyptian slavery, so the migrants from slavery in feudalist, absolutist Europe, with its state churches ('Pharaoh's Britain' was a catchword) felt liberated for a free life in the New World: 'A new nation conceived in liberty.'"[75] In this imaginative construction of providential history, which became a stepping-stone for America's ideology of manifest destiny,[76] "Europe is Egypt [and] America the promised land."[77]

The fundamentalists' theology of chosenness has distinct political implications. Let me point to at least two of these, which I label "the politics of self-elevation" and "the politics of anxious aggression," to prove divine favor in the world of mundane power.[78] The politics of self-elevation claims that God chooses a nation for reasons that might be obscure to us yet are clear to God. This fact in itself elevates that nation above its peers.[79] Yet according to the politics of anxious aggression, this chosen status "can be 'removed' if the individual in question does not maintain high standards of conduct and faith."[80] This means that the nation must engage in beliefs and actions that demonstrate its fidelity to God, justifying its status as chosen. Some of this ambivalence of embracing the political theology of collective divine favor can be read into the manner in which Christian fundamentalism engages the world well before September 11, 2001. The chosenness thus that the fundamentalists claim for the United States is ambiguous, in that God chooses the nation but can just as quickly withhold that status, if the chosen nation is not faithful to its given mission. The politics of self-elevation over all other nation-states, when entwined with the politics of anxious aggression to display divine favor, needs a global stage to lay out theatrical victory over the forces of evil.[81] From this description of Christian fundamentalism's vision and mission that I have laid out, the way the United States should demonstrate its fidelity to God is through violent relations with other nations who do not evince the "Christian" values of the United States. Although the focus of such aggression in the twentieth century was much more secular ideologies, such as Socialism and political Islam, after 9/11 the main target of this violence has been Islam itself.

This connects to a third component of a committed political theology, which is the self-perception of Christian fundamentalists that the United States must embrace its calling to be "the Redeemer nation" within the world. The obligation that comes with being the chosen nation in this divine dispensation compels the United States to establish God's kingdom "on earth as it is in heaven," thus carving out a global stage for fundamentalist Christianity. When the *status* of being a chosen nation becomes the *imperative* to become a redeemer nation, the result is a religionizing of politics, both within the United States and beyond, in those countries to which its global reach extends. David Domke and Kevin Coe have tracked the high rate and overt manner in which the four presidents who occupied the White House from 1981 to 2009 exploited religious imagination and language to appeal to their citizens. They note that "Presidential invocation of faith were 57% higher among the four presidents beginning with Reagan"[82] than those before them. They further go on to expose the manner in which such national leaders acted as "political priests by speaking the language of the faithful" in their strategy of "fusing God and country, by linking America with divine will."[83] Political theology has local, national, and global implication when the collective will of a supposed "Christian nation" conforms to the divine will for the world. It is important to reiterate that "Protestant Christianity has informed [such] a more exclusive and aggressive religious nationalism."[84] As Scott W. Hibbard puts it, "This variant of the American idea provides an explicit Christian narrative to American history and links national purpose with the execution of God's will on earth."[85]

This marriage of the passionate religion of a chosen nation and the robust politics of a redeemer nation affects the collective future of the United States and the whole world. It might not be the case that all the violent intrusions, brutal expeditions, and aggressive invasions of the United States around the world derive from Christian fundamentalism. There are other political, economic, and cultural reasons that also drive expansive and antagonistic U.S. foreign policy. Nonetheless, just as Christian fundamentalists kept a watchful eye on Muslims and secular others within the United States, they manifested global enthusiasm for violently disciplining and punishing similar enemies around the world. In this regard notice the United States' overt and covert violence toward nations whose hopes for expansion upon the world stage derive in any way from Islamic identity. Recognize as well its antipathy to the growth of nations like Cuba and China (or the former Soviet Union), whose secularism has a strong antireligious component. When the United States acts within the world as a redeemer nation, its triumphs are evidence of having been blessed and chosen by God. Boasting of its possession of the most sophisticated weapons of war and most efficient military establishment in the world, what is in fact a violent nation-state sees itself instead as a divinely blessed Christian nation, humbly claiming that it only seeks to bring honor to God's purpose to rule the world. Yet such a fundamentalist boast of divine power seriously glosses over the loss that its exercise of violence has brought to the rest of humanity. In his bluntly titled book *America's Battle for God*, Geiko Müller-Fahrenholz puts it this way: "Again, one cannot deny that the United States has experienced great triumph. The point is that, when a nation sees its great victories in the image of a divinely ordained triumph, it prevents itself from perceiving the impact of these victories on others. . . . It also helps us understand why its citizens have so casually accepted the new mission that has been officially designated as the 'global war on terrorism.'"[86]

As I come to the end of this section on the religious themes that frame and direct Christian fundamentalism in the United States, let me rework Martin Marty's observations. Commenting on the early development of fundamentalists, he says, "First, they believed that they must, as one of them put it, 'do battle for the Lord.' Second, the arms they would use to fight off the moderates were appeal[s] to doctrines that they regarded as fundamental."[87] If we want to complete this picture of Christian fundamentalists, we might add a third element. This movement of militant activism, rooted in a rigid worldview and strident posture, was united in the overall business of building a God-pleasing Christian nation that can expand to God's whole world. "It was a way of bringing God back into the political realm, . . . to re-create a lost wholeness."[88] In its origins, early growth, and present manifestation, Christian fundamentalism thus nicely weaves together theology with militancy in the service of communal polity for the welfare of the world.

Stealthy Roots and Violent Fruits

Most Christian fundamentalists are not *direct* participants in the violent destruction we see in our communities, our country, and our world. Some do engage in acts of individual violence, of course; the United States is particularly fertile soil for the "lone wolf." There have been sporadic expressions of this type of violence within the United States both against Sikhs, ignorantly mistaken to be Muslims, and liberal representatives seen to be furthering antifundamentalist Christian practices. For example, on August 5, 2012, white supremacist Wade Michael Page used a semiautomatic weapon to murder six people at a Sikh temple in Oak Creek, Wisconsin. Although he was not a self-proclaimed Christian, I agree with Mark Juergensmeyer that "it is fair to call Page a Christian terrorist since the evidence indicates that he thought he was defending the purity of white Christian society against the evils of multiculturalism."[89] Similarly, Scott Roeder, a fundamentalist Christian, shot and killed Dr. George Tiller on May 31, 2009, for providing abortion services to women. Carrying out "an assignment from Almighty God," Mr. Roeder came to Reformation Lutheran Church, Wichita, Kansas, where Dr. Tiller was worshiping, to take him down execution style.[90] In spite of these and other examples, one can say that the public acts of violence by individual Christian fundamentalists have gradually become less spectacular and less widespread.

This does not mean, however, that Christian fundamentalism has changed course and disengaged from violence. Much of the long history of Christian missionary expansion has been intertwined with violent Western colonial conquest, so much so that it is hard to say where one set of motivations and methods ends and the other begins. The twenty-first century has seen merely the adaptation of this partnership, not its end. Christian fundamentalists in the United States have allied themselves with (supposedly) secular military and political leaders, not only to evangelize the lost, but also to do battle with God's enemies. This makes the violence of Christian fundamentalists harder to detect, yet far more potent and pervasive.

Look, for example, at the way the United States carries out warfare. This nation has proved itself capable of inflicting massive loss of life, even as it hides that destruction with a sophisticated machinery that kills efficiently without obviously connecting the agents of death to the communities being killed. By legitimizing and valorizing this kind of violent conflict instead of gruesome targeted beheadings or grotesque mass executions, Christian fundamentalists consider themselves peaceful and nonviolent. Yet when Christian fundamentalism speaks of "Islam as Antichrist" while legitimating and sanctifying a global military regime, it makes itself complicit in that regime's violence. Daniel Hill makes a useful "distinction between a hot-blooded and a cold-blooded violence." Because Christian fundamentalism in the United States has been so adept at supporting cold-blooded violence, it has convinced itself that hot-blooded violence is the only variety that exists. While this builds up the idea that only other religions are violent and hurtful, it hides the violence perpetuated with stunning success by the collusion of Christian fundamentalists and the expanding U.S. empire.[91]

Christian fundamentalism, as I have reported, started out with a thorough rejection of the Enlightenment. The separation of religion from political and social life, the ascendency of reason over revelation, and the right of individuals and groups to freely think and live out their own convictions were threats to the dominance of Christianity as the worldview that united and directed the United States as a nation. Some such thinking describes the path down which Christian fundamentalists still continue to tread. Reverting back to Judeo-Christian values to revive the greatness of America continues to gain traction as the U.S. moves toward the 2016 election. Yet I think Christian fundamentalists' relationship to the age of modernity that was influenced by Enlightenment is a bit more complex than that when it comes to the question of justifying and executing religious violence. One of the principal accomplishments of the Enlightenment was to delegitimize violence committed in the name of God. This doesn't mean, of course, that Western society became less violent. Rather, the justification for violence and responsibility for war was effectively transferred by Enlightenment modernity from the church to the nation-state. So how did fundamentalists deal with the situation? They became thoroughly modern and creatively political. As Susan F. Harding put it, "American fundamentalists once described themselves, and were widely described, as being opposed to modernity. . . . However, fundamentalists were in fact always fully inside modernity."[92] On the one hand, Christian fundamentalists became much more vested in gaining control of the nation-state. I have highlighted the way in which the Bible, flag, and God were entwined by fundamentalism to forge an imagined "deification of the nation."[93] On the other hand, Christian fundamentalists could utilize the state to carry out violence against those who were demonized by religious and political leaders of the chosen nation. This fact has bearing on my argument in that most Christian fundamentalists would be far more likely to couch their calls for violence against Muslims in terms of national security rather than in religious terms. They reject Islam as a false religion, a creation of the devil, yet they are sufficiently children of the Enlightenment to refrain from using that as the justification for violence against Muslims.

In concluding this discussion, I must acknowledge that fundamentalist Christianity is only one brand of Christian faith within the array of choices in the United States. Yet it has exercised an outsized role on the country's engagement with the world. Fortified by a deep-seated, "biblical" belief that the United States is a chosen people called to serve a jealous God, in a dualistic battle between good and evil on a global stage, fundamentalists see the United States as a "redeemer nation," created to serve God's cosmic purposes. Such mythical appeal to the privileged status of "redeemer nation" is fused at the hip with engaging the myth of "redemptive violence." This idea that the status of redeemer nation is tied to a divinely commissioned redemptive mission is said to be as old as the republic itself. Tuveson has skillfully argued that such a high calling for the United States is taken by fundamentalists to be a literal interpretation of biblical prophecies leading all the way to the millenarian ideal of God's blessed ends. He also points to the way in which Christian fundamentalism has impelled U.S. foreign policy to be aligned to such a religious worldview.[94] I am aware that Walter Wink calls the myth of redemptive violence "the simplest, laziest, most exciting, uncomplicated, irrational, and primitive depiction of evil the world has ever known."[95] However, we have also witnessed how the marriage of these myths has successfully inspired political action steeped in violence that has the sanction of religiously committed Christians devoted to furthering God's will on earth. In this case the nation-state becomes the instrument of sacralized violence, which is sanctioned by the Bible's absolute, historical divine vision to take the dualistic cosmic struggle between good and evil into the whole world, so that God will be Lord of all creation.[96] No wonder then that the United States pursues, in Jack Nelson-Pallmeyer's words, "a foreign policy presenting itself as 'Mother Teresa with a gun' . . . backed by a 'Rambo Jesus.'"[97] In this configuration of "strong religion," an all-encompassing worldview, founded on an absolutely truthful divine revelation contained in Scripture, captivates a passionately committed community to "set the world right" by undertaking the calling to serve as "religious soldiers," to fight for God "against the forces of evil."[98]

Chapter Three

Muslim Fundamentalism

Gunmen were heard shouting "Allahu Akbar" [God is Greater], but I did the same tonight, in my room, praying for those killed and their families.

Ayisha Malik's tweet after ISIS terrorists shot 129 persons dead on November 13, 2015, in Paris[1]

Islam has retained its imperialistic ambitions to this day.

Efraim Karsh, *Islamic Imperialism*

Introduction

Any discussion originating in the United States about Muslim fundamentalism must begin with a couple of honest reflective comments. At the outset, it must be acknowledged that Islam is the most negatively viewed religion in the United States. A 2009 Gallup Report surveying the opinion of Americans states, "More than 4 in 10 Americans (43%) admit to feeling at least 'a little' prejudice toward Muslims—more than twice the number who say the same about Christians (18%), Jews (15%), and Buddhists (14%)."[2] Not surprisingly, this jaundiced stance conforms to perceptions in other Western countries. A more recent Gallup Study focusing on the United States, United Kingdom, France, Switzerland, and Germany from 2008 to 2011 reports that "within key Western societies, there are genuine negative perceptions, prejudices, and discriminations targeted against Muslims." It suggests that "seeing Muslims as not loyal, voicing prejudice against Muslims, and avoiding Muslims as neighbors are all symptoms of Islamophobia that exist in the West."[3]

One does not have to buy into the current idea that any rejection of liberal Western causes and commitments constitutes a "phobia." However, we cannot ignore the multiple ways in which mind-sets of prejudice contribute to discrimination against Muslims. Gottschalk and Greenberg's understanding of Islamophobia, which stems from a multimedia study of the depiction of Muslims in the United States, may convince us that this term could still be a useful descriptor. "Islamophobia," they suggest, "accurately reflects a *social* anxiety toward Islam and Muslim cultures [and communities] that is largely unexamined by, yet deeply ingrained in, Americans."[4] The stress on the social nature of this mentality is important to note: Instead of "arising from traumatic personal experiences," such communal anxiety of Muslims results from "distant social experiences that mainstream American Culture has perpetuated in popular memory."[5]

Apart from this general shared negativity and social anxiety, which have contributed to Western societies' religious outcasting of this faith community, Muslims have also been branded more specifically as terrorists. At present an unexamined mentality—pervasive in the United States, other Western countries, and Hindu-majority India—equates Islam with violence. N. C. Asthana and Anjali Nirmal have observed the role "the media" and "security establishments" have played in spreading terms like "Islamic," "Islamist," and "Jihadist terrorism" across the world over the last decade. They strongly believe that such a conflation of Islam and terrorism produces a default social mentality that equates violence in the world with one specific religion. In their view, "it has created an impression in the minds of a large number of people that terrorists who happen to be Muslims are to be found in the world because their religion inexorably drives them to terrorism and that an approval of terrorism is integral to Islam."[6] In the United States, Muslims are represented as a community that embodies the converse of American beliefs and practices and thus as more likely to violently endanger its Eurocentric and Judeo-Christian worldview and way of life. John Esposito puts it well: "The taint of 'foreignness' and terrorism continues to brushstroke Muslims as 'the other.'"[7] The problem with this seamless identification of Islam with terrorism is that it equates eliminating terrorism with eradicating Muslims just as it easily likens taming violence in the world with controlling the adherents and curbing the growth of Islam.

This chapter on Muslim fundamentalism tries to move away from populist caricatures and negative misrepresentations of Islam while also keeping a close watch on the movements of violence that have surfaced from segments within the religion over the last century. It unfolds in five sections. The first section goes back to the historical origins of Islam, to locate the context within which it arose. It uncovers a religious vision and mission that integrated politics, economics, and culture. The second section scans the history of Muslim fundamentalism in Egypt before the twentieth century. I take Egypt to be the site from which Muslim fundamentalism emerges as a modern movement. Here I examine the need of an evolving nation-state to carve out a stable and secure Muslim identity in Egypt's interaction with the Ottoman, French, and British Empires. The third section focuses on the origin and development of modern Muslim fundamentalism as it surfaced in Egypt during the 1920s, through the formation and agency of the Muslim Brotherhood. Strikingly, this was around the same time that Christian fundamentalism became a phenomenon in the United States and Hindu fundamentalism emerged in India. The fourth section takes stock of where this movement is poised today. It observes the more recent trends and quite dramatic prospects of Muslim fundamentalism in this century. While I do keep one eye on Egypt in this segment, I also focus upon the violent expansion of Muslim fundamentalism in the rest of the world. Even if we grant that taking over the world for Allah is "mission impossible," the effect of violent destruction is a growing threat in many regions across the globe. The fifth section identifies and comments on the religious motifs that fire up and add fuel to Muslim fundamentalism. Three of these features of strong religion (i.e., preserving radical monotheism, flourishing of the faithful [*ummah*] through an absolutist belief in the Qur'an, and protection and promotion of global religious civilization) are discussed in some detail.

Islam's Beginnings

The Pew Research Center's Forum on Religion & Public Life (December 2012) reports that Islam is the world's second largest religion. The demographic study, which is based on analysis of more than 2,500 censuses, surveys, and population registers, estimates that the world has 1.6 billion Muslims (23% of the world's population), behind Christianity, which has 2.2 billion Christians (32% of the world's population).[8] The report provides further evidence that while the heart of Islam might beat in the Middle East, its numbers "are concentrated in the Asia-Pacific region, where six-in-ten (62%) of all Muslims reside."[9] Yet much knowledge of Islam in the West, as I have reported, marries fear with ignorance compounded by imagination. "Most Europeans and North Americans have never met a Muslim," concedes Prothero, "so for them Islam begins in the imagination, specifically in the corner of the imagination colonized by fear."[10] The growth of Hindu fundamentalism in India has led to a similar situation there. Muslims in India, who number around 170 million, are the second largest Muslim population in the world, behind Indonesia. Yet they too have been the butt of an inventive narrative based in fear and ignorance among the 80 percent Hindu majority. In the next chapter I will deal with this vested and imaginative caricature of Muslims in detail. At this juncture, it suffices to merely register this point by quoting a recent article from *Foreign Policy*. "Indian Muslims, like African-Americans in the United States," states James Traub, "are marginalized members of a culture they have done so much to shape. The Sachar Committee, which studied the condition of Muslims nationwide, reported in 2006 that 'Muslims complained that they are constantly looked upon with a great degree of suspicion not only by certain sections of society but also by public institutions and governance structures.'"[11]

The birth and rapid expansion of Islam during the seventh century of the Common Era is recognized as a momentous event in world history. Not only was a new religion born on the vast and arid desert sands of Mecca, but a new political and economic system as well, one that eventually affected the whole Arabian peninsula and the entire region. The integrative character of Islam, which reached out to claim and shape the totality of the life both of the community of faithful and the inhabitants of the world, was at the center of its vision and mission. "From its roots in seventh-century [Arabia], . . . Islam has always been connected with politics."[12] This explains how Islam expanded by overpowering the Byzantine Empire (the Eastern and Christian part of the Roman Empire, with its center in Constantinople), leading to the eventual conquest of Syria, Egypt, and Byzantium's North African territories. The religiopolitical movement known as early Islam also caused the collapse of the Sassanian Empire (the Persian dynasty, with its capital in Ctesiphon), which had for almost four centuries ruled Iran and Iraq. The distinguished historian Hugh Kennedy draws our attention to the rapid and radical political change that took hold during, yet especially after, the time of Muhammad (570–632 CE): "In the year 632, Islam was confined to Arabic-speaking tribesmen living in Arabia and the desert margins of Syria and Iraq."[13] Few of the populations in Syria and Iraq, and none of the populations in Iran, Egypt, Afghanistan, and North Africa, were Muslim at the time. But this was soon to change. "The scale and speed of the transformation are astonishing; within a century of the prophet's death, all these lands, including Spain, Portugal, Uzbekistan, Turkmenistan, and Southern Pakistan (Sind) were ruled by an Arabic-speaking Muslim elite, and in all of them the local population was beginning to convert to the new religion."[14]

It was not politics alone that changed dramatically through the birth and rise of Islam. Wealth also traded hands as a result of this multifaceted religious vision. Economically, the wealth moved from the rulers into the new hands of the subjects. Till this point Arabs lived in the vast stretch of deserts in the Arabian Peninsula. The great An Nafud wilderness in the north and the Empty Quarter in the south were two of the most parched sand terrains in the world. Their people were mainly skilled traders living at the crossroads of the empires that surrounded them. The prophet Muhammad himself was a successful merchant in the city of Mecca. Economics was surely on his mind. After the prophet's lifetime, the Arabs gradually changed places with their imperial neighbors and promoted themselves as the rulers who controlled economic production, financial legislation, and taxation. The Arab Muslims brought to this role a concern for the economic commitment for redistribution of wealth and for the care of orphans and widows. These concerns stemmed from the Qur'an and the teaching of the prophet. Yet raiding the possessions of one's competitors was a long tradition among the nomadic Arab tribes who first joined Muhammad's cause, and after his death this tradition morphed into an economic motivation for conquest.[15] Thus did ambitions for economic justice, political power, and financial gain intertwine among Muhammad's followers as they spread his integrative religious vision around the world.

The culture and the religion of Islam provided the skin and sinew for this political and economic movement on its journey outward. The Arab community would likely never have courageously ventured beyond the Arabian Peninsula without the endowment of the wondrously revealed religion of Islam, claiming one of their own as the prophet called by God to recite a universal message applicable to all of humanity. The self-confidence born of being chosen as bearers of this new religion is an important foundation for the self-assuredness required to recommend Arabic language, culture, and religion to other peoples and nations. "The early Muslims brought with them a great cultural self-confidence. God had spoken to them through His Prophet, in Arabic, and they were bearers of true religion and God's own language."[16] The architecture of governance, the ambivalent economic interests of desert peoples, the sacred worth imparted upon the Arabic language and culture, and the missionary thrust of Islam—all these resources intermingled in a highly successful combination. No wonder then that in Islam's early expansion "this cultural self-confidence meant that . . . anyone who wished to participate fully in government or intellectual activity had to be literate in Arabic and preferably a Muslim."[17]

The self-confident character of Islam, identified with one culture and language and integrally connected with politics and economics, must be seen against the backdrop of a world of confusing plurality and confounding polytheism. Islam arose as the "straight path" and the "pure truth," firmly rooted in a formidable and vibrant monotheism, within the context of a perplexing mix of utilitarian polytheism. "Arabia was in ferment" during this time, Ira M. Lapidu reminds us; it was "a society touched by imperial influences but without a central government; marked by the monotheistic religions but with competing polytheistic and henotheistic beliefs; a prospering society caught between social and moral conflicts."[18] It was in such a befuddling historical situation that "Muhammad was born, was entrusted with the Quran, and here he became the Prophet of Islam."[19] The radical nature of Islamic monotheism arose in the historical context where many other divinities were vying for attention and honor. Partly due to the gods and goddesses that were brought in by the traveling merchants from various parts of the region and partly because of idol worship imported from Syria, the Arabian Peninsula was teeming with a variety of deities. Allah, as "the lord of the Kabah [Ka'ba, Kaaba]" was "the most important God" for the Quraysh tribe, of whom Muhammad was a member.[20] Yet Allah was dependent on the whims and fancies of utilitarian bands of people who moved from god to goddess, pleading for them to grant their wishes and fulfill their demands. Muhammad's divine encounters, which reveal the oneness of God (Allah), unseated all the other divine pretenders. The widely recorded symbolic act of Muhammad's triumphant journey into Mecca to cleanse the Kaaba[21] epitomizes the forceful and even violent nature of monotheism's triumph over utilitarian polytheism. There were said to be 360 idols housed in and around the Kaaba, representing every god and goddess recognized in the Arab peninsula, when Muhammad rode into Mecca in 630 to cleanse the sacred shrine by smashing all the idols housed inside.[22]

In its origins and through its early development, Islam also had to nurture its self-assured monotheistic revelation in variance from the claims of Judaism and Christianity. There can be little doubt that both before and during the time of Muhammad, Judaism and Christianity "had an influential presence in the Arabian Peninsula."[23] I am not convinced by the popular though quite controversial theory that Islam arose from an intramonotheistic combustion involving elements of Judaism and Christianity. This proposal, put forth forcefully by Tom Holland,[24] makes Muhammad a creative storyteller and disestablishes the narrative of faithful Muslims, including all their scholars. Yet neither can I accept the fanciful alternate theory that all Islamic revelation was uninformed by the Arabs' long history of knowing the Jewish and Christian sacred narratives. After all, as Karen Armstrong points out, "Jews had probably lived in Arabia for over a millennium," and "some of the Arabs had become Christians" long before the birth of Islam.[25] It is noteworthy that the relationship between these monotheistic traditions and polytheistic Arab communities was peaceable. For one, "at the time, Arabs did not see Judaism or Christianity as exclusive traditions fundamentally different from their own. Indeed, the term 'Jew' or 'Christian' usually referred to tribal affiliation rather than religious orientation."[26] But more importantly, "because no imperial power was seeking to impose any form of religious orthodoxy, Arabs felt free to adapt what they understood about these traditions to their own needs."[27]

Was there cross-fertilization of religious ideas between Islam and the other two Peoples of the Book (Judaism and Christianity)? Much contact certainly took place between the three faiths, and concepts of peace and justice surely flourished in all three (however imperfectly they were put into practice). Relations between the three were multilayered and organic, helping explain why the idea of justice and peace was so important in Islam's origins, even against the backdrop of persistent warfare. Thus, while Islam arose as a religious, political, economic, and social movement, its heart was richly stocked with concepts of justice and peace that it shared with other Peoples of the Book. "As a religion that emphasized equilibrium and justice in all aspects of human life, Islam [like Judaism and Christianity] also accentuates the outward and public aspects of religion to complement the inward and private ones."[28]

Muslim Fundamentalism in Egypt before the Twentieth Century

Being cognizant of the historical origins of Islam prevents us from falling into the trap of simplistically asserting that Islam is essentially a fundamentalist religion that legitimizes violence against other human beings and engenders violence in the world. It lets us see the various factors that gave rise to this all-encompassing monotheistic faith (integrating politics, economics, culture, and religion) as it strove to bring individual adherents and political entities into submission to God. Holding together the obligations of justice with the objectives of peace, which exhibit the heritage of Judaism and Christianity, Islam worked out a pragmatic theology for life in a conflict-packed seventh-century world. In the birth of Islam, then, is a struggle to mediate between the "straight path" of Allah and the good life on earth, justice and mercy, pursuit of peace and command to fight, and brutality and compassion. Fundamentalism, as we have seen in Christianity and we will see in Hinduism, is a modern ideology and movement. It cannot be facilely read back into early Islam. Yet even in this brief description of the genesis of Islam, we cannot deny that there are violent and exclusive strands of theology and practice that cannot be covered over or explained away. In the ensuing discussion, I focus on the Muslim Brotherhood, a radical Islamic project in Egypt, to inquire into how such religious capital has been employed by Muslim fundamentalism throughout the last hundred years. And in order to understand that, we first must spend a moment getting to know Sunnis and Shiites.

There are two main branches of Islam: the Sunnis and the Shias. In 2010 the number of Sunni Muslims was between 1.41 billion and 1.46 billion, while the number of Shia Muslims was between 162 million and 211 million.[29] This would make the Sunnis the overwhelming majority of the global Muslim community. Comprising between 85 and 87 percent of all Muslims, the largest Sunni-majority populations are in Egypt (99%), Indonesia (99%), Bangladesh (99%), and Pakistan (87%). The Shiites are a minority that constitute between 13 to 15 percent of the global Muslim population. The largest Shia-majority populations live in Iran (93%), Azerbaijan (70%), Bahrain (70%), and Iraq (67%).[30] While some have posited Sufis as a third branch, I defer to the consensus among Islamic scholars, such as Nasr and Esposito, that this grouping refers to those who ground themselves within their respective Sunni or Shia traditions while pursuing "the inner or esoteric" (mystic) path to God by "meditation" and "cultivation of spiritualized virtues."[31] What is pertinent to this discussion is to note the effort of both these branches of Islam to consolidate and expand their religious communities through most of the history of Islam; and yet it is also important to be mindful of the fundamentalist vision and mission of Sunnis and Shiites that has developed over the last century on the modern global stage. Contemporary geopolitics serves almost as well as recent history to illustrate the point. Egypt, Pakistan, and Saudi Arabia are firmly rooted in a Sunni vision of an extremist, politically expansive Islam. At the same time, Iran leads the world in embodying and nurturing fundamentalist political Shiism. In the background of such competition appears Islamic State (IS, also known as ISIL, the Islamic State of Iraq and Levant, and ISIS, the Islamic State of Iraq and Syria), aspiring to reconstitute a Sunni-based state in the form of the IS Caliphate.[32] The most salient political fact in the Muslim world today is the emergence of a strong Shiite state in Iran and the weakening of Sunni political power in Iraq, Syria, and Egypt (a list to which some would add Saudi Arabia). As one of the most highly visible expressions of Muslim fundamentalism, IS is itself an outgrowth of the rivalry between the Sunnis and the Shiites. As the power of Egypt and other Sunni states wanes, IS wants to reconstitute a violent fundamentalist Sunni-based state in the contemporary world.

For centuries Egypt has persistently been the focus of a Sunni hope for a nation-state that would embody the beliefs and practices of Islam. Islam arrived in Egypt as early as 639 CE. It came when Amr Ibn al-As, a contemporary of the prophet Muhammad, invaded Egypt from Hijaz in 639 and established control over the whole country by 642. Islam thus gradually took over the well-established Christian territory, which since its arrival in the first century had gradually displaced Egyptian religion with a Coptic (a language descended from ancient Egyptian) form of Christianity. It was only by the ninth century, however, that most Egyptians had converted to Islam. From that time onward, Egypt has remained a Muslim country. There was a takeover of Egypt by the Shia Fatimid Caliphate between 969 and 1171, which was not without many internal revolts. However, apart from these 202 years, Egypt was a Sunni region ruled by a sense of what it means to live collectively as a Muslim ummah. Estimates of 2014 suggest that 90 percent of Egypt is Muslim, with close to 99 percent of this number being Sunni. Of the rest, 9 percent in Egypt are Coptic Christians.[33]

In spite of this broad and deep Sunni Muslim heritage and aspiration, from the early sixteenth century onward Egypt was entangled with three imperial powers that compromised both its Egyptian identity and its Islamic character. In 1517 Egypt was annexed into the Ottoman Empire, which maintained political control and cultural sway over its peoples until 1867. Selim I, who even took on the title caliph, gained a foothold for the Ottoman's expansion by defeating Egypt's Mamluk sultanate. The Ottoman Empire spread under the banner of a modernizing Islam, which was a far cry from what the Sunni Muslims wanted for a state. The second modern imperial influence on Egypt came from the French, whose rule over Egypt was brief (1798–1801) yet whose values lingered long after their defeat and departure. That defeat came at the hands of Muhammad

Ali, who restored Ottoman rule in Egypt and became, in 1805, the Sultan's viceroy. From1805 to 1848, Ali went about systematically purging Egypt of the influence of traditional Mamluk leaders, with the objective of restructuring Egyptian society and rebuilding it along modern lines.

The concrete symbol of the passage into modernity, carved out hand in hand by the Egyptians and the French, was the Suez Canal. With much enthusiasm from Ishmael Pasha, grandson of Muhammad Ali and viceroy from 1863 to 1879, the French designed and managed this 101-mile long colossal project to connect sea trade between the East and the West. European capital conjoined with Egyptian labor to bridge seas, peoples, and ideas. By creating a water-level sea route connecting the Mediterranean Sea to the Red Sea (and from there to the Indian Ocean), the Suez Canal ushered in speedy, easy, and free flow of goods, peoples, and services between East and West without having to go around the continent of Africa. Ishmael Pasha celebrated the canal as "the dazzling symbol of new Egypt, not just a cut through the isthmus but a link between continents."[34] Under the backdrop of the Ottoman Empire's protection, Egypt was recasting political Islam by freeing it from Africa and marrying it with Europe. Pakenham encapsulates this sentiment in the boast of Ishmael: "'We are not now a country of Africa,'" he proudly said, 'but a country of Europe.'"[35]

This ambitious project, by which Egyptian and French cooperation brought political Islam into the modern world, attracted another colonial actor. Along with other infrastructural projects in Egypt, the building of the Suez Canal forced Ishmael Pasha to borrow heavily, primarily from the British. When the Egyptian government couldn't pay its debts, the British used the resultant bankruptcy to make substantial inroads into the economic and political life of Egypt in the latter part of the nineteenth century. Initial cynicism about the canal project gave way to opportunism: British investors took control of Egyptian shares of the Suez Canal in 1875, with the result that Britain became yet more economically and politically vested in Egyptian life. Finally, to suppress a revolt in the Egyptian Army in 1882, the British invaded Egypt, ultimately making it a British protectorate in 1914. While becoming nominally independent under King Fuad I in 1922, Egypt remained under British influence into the 1950s.

Muslim Fundamentalism in Modern Egypt

Egyptian religious identities were assimilated into modernity through the infiltration of the Ottoman, French, and the British Empires, creating the necessary background for understanding the rise of Islamic fundamentalism in the twentieth century. While one reform-minded option open to Egyptian society involved stretching and straining Islam to fit into "the will to power" characterized by its political rulers, another option involved confronting and destabilizing the empires to help the faithful conform to "the will of Allah." As Egypt entered the twentieth century, the reformist pathway was symbolized by Muhammad Abduh (1849–1905), who served as mufti of Egypt (the Muslim legal expert who gives rulings on religious matters) and adviser to Al-Azhar University (the chief center of Islamic learning in the world). Abduh carved out a way forward for religion and academy to work in concert to reshape Islam and reconfigure modernity. The assessment offered by Ahmad N. Amir, Abdi O. Shuriye, and Ahmad F. Ismail is compelling: "[Abduh's] work and struggle has brought unprecedented change in [the] legal, social, and political structure of Egypt, and help to revitalize modern Islamic aspiration. The modern worldview he projected had significant impact in engineering the force of rational spirit and reviving modern and liberal ideas and contributing to dynamic change in [the] social, cultural, educational, political and religious paradigm of modern Egypt."[36]

Muslim fundamentalism in Egypt grew out of the latter option to undercut and overpower the wily and corrupt worldly rulers by retrieving and advancing the pure and sure way of Islam. Rashid Rida was an influential thinker who advocated such a conservative and illiberal future for Egypt. Although born in Syria in 1865, Rida moved to Egypt in 1897, where he lived till his death in 1935. While influenced greatly by Muhammad Abduh, Rida was much more adamant about reinstating "original Islamic sources—the Qur'an, Sunnah, and ijma (consensus) of Muhammad's companions—as the basis for reform."[37] As the leader of the Salafi Movement[38] in Egypt, he pushed for "a strict interpretation of Islam,"[39] including the restoration of the caliph. The Salifis worked in early twentieth century Egypt toward "an alternative to the secularism of the 1920s and 1930s as well as to Abduh's liberal or 'modernist' Islam."[40] It was out of this theological vision and political dream that the Muslim Brotherhood was founded by Hassan al-Banna (1906–49) in March 1928 to serve as the platform for Muslim fundamentalism, initially in Egypt and gradually across much of the region in this part of the globe.

Many notable books examine various dimensions of this "grassroots reformation of Egyptian society."[41] I shall limit this discussion to briefly sketching the roller-coaster nature of this fundamentalist movement and then lift up key features of "strong religion" evident in the Muslim

Brotherhood, which is said to be the "largest Fundamentalist group in Egypt and the Arab world" with a "history [that] is the longest"[42] of any such Muslim fundamentalist organization. From its origins in 1928 until today, the Muslim Brotherhood has cast a long shadow on religious fundamentalism both in Egypt and the rest of the world. Al-Banna is often regarded as "the founding father of modern Islamic fundamentalism."[43] Jabbour formulates this aptly: "We see the 'trunk of the tree' of Fundamentalism in Egypt in the twentieth century personified in al-Banna."[44]

The initial vision of the Muslim Brotherhood was to transform the historical, social, and cultural imagination of the masses by turning to Islam. In conformity with the early origins and development of Islam, which I discussed in the earlier section, the Muslim Brotherhood looked to religion to ground the aspirations of a people traumatized by Ottoman quasi-secular and Western quasi-Christian Empires. Al-Banna worked from the ground up, focusing on educating children within the family, then youth in the local community, and finally all members of the larger society. He was mostly apolitical when he started the movement even though he recognized the comprehensive demands of Islam. It was just a matter of time, however, before the Muslim Brotherhood came to engage in the affairs of the state, during the years leading up to the ouster of King Farouk in 1952. From the 1940s onward, the king ruled Egypt by precariously balancing three swelling and violent movements: the revolutionary but not Islamic Wafd party, the increasingly political and fundamentalist Muslim Brotherhood, and the traditionalists who supported the waning monarchy. This three-way struggle unfolded against the backdrop of significant ongoing British influence, even in the midst of the Second World War (1939–45). The prime minister of Egypt dissolved the Muslim Brotherhood in December 1948 by an order due to the threat it posed to the ruling power, including advocating violence against the state. But the real blow came with the assassination of al-Banna in June 1949, in retaliation for the gunning down of Prime Minister Mahmud Fahmi al-Nuqrashi by a member of the Muslim Brotherhood. Yet the rising swell of anti-Farouk sentiment made it impossible for the authorities to shut down or even contain the late al-Banna's movement.

It was a time of turbulent transition in Egypt as nationalist pressure mounted to do away with the monarchy. The Muslim Brotherhood joined forces with the Wafd party and the Free Officers movement's military conspiracy against the monarchy. In 1952 revolution brought an end to Farouk, who was known for colossal corruption, blatant anti-Islamic indulgence, and conniving collaboration with the British. After the successful revolution Gamal Abdel Nasser, one of the generals of the Free Officers, took over, with the promise of building a strong nationalist country. Although Nasser initially tolerated the Muslim Brotherhood as he carved out a socialist, state-controlled, secular-leaning Egypt, his patience with them abruptly ended when one of their members tried to assassinate him in 1954. The government banned the Brotherhood and imprisoned its leaders in the thousands, a repression that continued throughout Nasser's rule. In spite of the government's measures to maintain a tight grip over the Brotherhood, Muslim fundamentalism continued to attract attention, partly due to the work of Sayyid Qutb (1906–66), the most influential of the Muslim intellectuals during Nasser's time. Although more of a mystic and saint in his early days, Qutb gradually became radicalized, bringing his absolute faith in God to counter the faithless ways of the leaders of Egypt. While he was popular as a writer and intellectual well before 1953, only then did he join the Muslim Brotherhood. It was mostly in prison that he developed an oppositional and violent activist agenda for the faithful Muslims as they united to unseat the present "usurpers of God's sovereignty."[45] In Qutb's indictment, "Nasserism and Arab Nationalism were generally mere avatars of European discourses that put the 'people' ahead of God." His lucid and passionate analysis, along with his legitimizing of violence against nominal Muslim regimes, led to his imprisonment and execution by Nasser in 1966. Yet even today Qutb is heralded as an iconic intellectual/activist among radical Muslim fundamentalists across the world as they seek to fend off "irreligion, vice and exploitation . . . in the name of God."[46] In his massively circulated *Milestones* (1964), Qutb provided many violent Muslim fundamentalist organizations—including al-Qaeda and Hamas—with the theological and moral rationale they sought for undermining organizations and governments not run on Sharia principles.

Nasser died in September 1970 and was succeeded by Anwar al-Sadat. Sadat gradually relaxed the government's repression of the Muslim Brotherhood even though he did not remove the ban. In fact, Sadat's regime gave back some freedoms to the organization in exchange for its support in fighting off his political rivals. Sadat also moved Egypt away from the secular and socialist direction pursued by Nasser's pan-Arab nationalism and peppered his official communication with Muslim slogans. However, much against the wishes of Muslim radicals, he signed a peace treaty with Israel in 1979. The peace accord, along with his dubious commitment to Sharia, led to his assassination in 1981 by a Muslim fundamentalist and former member of the Brotherhood.

Hosni Mubarak took over the mantle of leadership in 1981 and for three decades ran Egypt with an iron fist made strong by his training as a military leader. Mubarak consistently kept Muslim fundamentalists under check, redefined the Muslim Brotherhood as a religious rather than a political organization, and brokered a serviceable relationship with the United States that would guarantee a formidable military state. But even an organization confined to the religious realm by the state knows how to infiltrate the political sphere. From the 1980s onward, the Muslim Brotherhood methodically and progressively entered into politics. It started by forging alliances with other like-minded Salafi parties; eventually the Muslim Brotherhood fielded its own members as independent candidates. "In 2000, the Brotherhood won 17 parliamentary seats, a figure which leapt to 80 following the 2005 election."[47] Muslim fundamentalists changed tactics publically and in a big way. Instead of undercutting the quasi-Muslim state, they affiliated with the Salafis and worked through the process of democratic elections to capture state power. Yet this shift in tactics should not be seen as a dramatic exchange of bullets for votes or militant violence for democratic elections. After all, as Tarek Masoud reminds us, a commitment to making inroads into democratic elections was part of al-Banna's practice from the early years of the Brotherhood.[48] All the same, we should recognize the sheer magnitude of this collective effort. "The Brotherhood" had decided to hoist the crescent (Islamic flag) "under the dome of the parliament."[49] It did this by floating the "Freedom and Justice Party (FJP)" in April 2011 as the Muslim Brotherhood's political wing. The Muslim Brotherhood's success with the masses in the twenty-first century was in sync with their desire to dismantle a corrupt, inept, repressive, and unpopular political regime, one that had impoverished the state and increased the burdens on Egypt's poor. This massive tide of discontent turned into a people's revolution in 2011, bringing about the free elections that made Mohamed Morsi, a senior leader of the Muslim Brotherhood, President of Egypt in June 2012.

But the historic change that installed Muslim fundamentalism in political power was short lived. Mohamed Morsi only served as President of Egypt for just over a year (June 2012 to July 2013) before being deposed by the army chief General Abdel Fattah el-Sisi, who was later elected president in May 2014. Sisi overthrew Morsi after massive protests in the mid-2013 stalled the Muslim fundamentalist regime's plan to implement a new constitution and rearrange the judiciary. The new constitution had the fingerprints of the Muslim Brotherhood and other fundamentalist allies all over it. Along with being "hurriedly drafted," it was also accused of being "undemocratic and too Islamist," leaving "minority groups [such as Coptic Christians] without proper legal protection."[50] Since 2014 the Muslim Brotherhood has been banned, Morsi was jailed and sentenced to death, and several religious fundamentalist leaders have been rounded up and imprisoned.

The Global Spread of Muslim Fundamentalism

Well before Egypt's recent ban on the Muslim Brotherhood, Salafism as a violent and extreme ideology was spreading in Europe, the Middle East, and North Africa. The Salafi movement, inspired by the Brotherhood, may not have had a massive following through the turn of the millennium. Estimates suggest they were about 1 percent of the Muslim population in 2005.[51] Yet those who joined the movement operated with a passionate commitment to violently attack all pseudo-Muslim, Western-supported, and secular-leaning regimes that veered away from the "straight path" of Islam, even as they worked toward forging a state that mirrored their understanding of the ummah inaugurated by the prophet.

Contemporary Muslim fundamentalists have many of the same goals as their predecessors. Thus Salafism as a "movement of movements" is committed to the following two overarching objectives. The first is practical: the "establishment or reinforcement of Islamic laws and norms as the solution to economic, political, and cultural crises."[52] The aim here is the incorporation and implementation of the Sharia as the basis of individual behavior, social relationships, and statecraft. The second goal is more symbolic. It involves consolidating a Muslim ummah that reflects the community led by the prophet Muhammad and his "pious forefathers." This may explain the banding together of various fundamentalist factions in Syria, Iraq, Afghanistan, and Tunisia under the common vision of carving out a present-day caliphate.

The scope of Muslim fundamentalism in our own time has expanded markedly over the last fifteen or so years. There is a radical shift from being content with nationalist aspirations in the twentieth century to yearning for global outreach in the twenty-first. Thus, for example, through the last century the national objective of Muslim Brotherhood was predominantly focused on inaugurating and consolidating an Islamic state in Egypt. Such a vision and mission was to offer an Islamic model for Egyptians in stark contrast to the Western-imitating, pseudoreligious monarchy on the one hand and the secular-leaning, quasi-modern military state on the other. For sure, the ideology and influence of the movement spilled over into other regions, such as Palestine, Syria, and Libya (Brothers on the Run); Jordon, Kuwait, and Morocco (Brothers under Monarchy); the Sudan (Brothers in Power); and Tunisia (Islamists Sharing Power).[53] Yet the scope of such fundamentalist movements was to liberate their respective nation-states and establish Islamic values and laws within their borders. The passage into the new millennium, however, has seen a shift in focus from thinking nationally to reaching out globally.

In many ways globalization has influenced such a shift from a contained mesoscale vision to a macroscale reach for religion. Of course, globalization was already a process in motion well before the twenty-first century. However, the new millennium initiated a much more interconnected social condition of global connection, which made the flow of goods, services, human bodies, and ideas impervious to borders and boundaries.[54] Accompanying the social condition of globality was also a mounting "consciousness of belonging to a global community."[55] Globalism seeks to weaken national boundaries and strengthen international bonds. With the arrival of the twenty-first century, this globalist vision captured the imagination of Muslim fundamentalists as well.[56] Their vision and mission burst national borders and reached out across the world.

The spectacularly violent attack on New York's Twin Towers (the World Trade Center) by a Sunni fundamentalist organization (Al-Qaeda) on September 11, 2001, and the awesome display of the United States' offensive in retaliation eventuating in the invasion of Iraq in 2003 (often called operations of "shock and awe") galvanized Muslims around the world. Whether we thought of it as West versus East or Islam versus Christianity or imperial terrorizer versus resistant terrorist, the battle was now played out on the world stage. The "global jihad after September 11, 2001" was in part stimulated by "the dramatic character of the 2001 attacks" that was impressive to Muslims keen on fighting westernization and modernization at its source and fundamentalists who had bought into the story line of "a cosmic war between Islam and the West, cast as a struggle between light and darkness, good and evil."[57] Reza Aslan draws attention to such a broadening of aspirations for reach between "religious nationalism" and "religious transnationalism" occurring at the crossroads of the millennium. While there are still many Muslim fundamentalist movements with "a nationalist ideology," most emerging militant ones "want to erase all borders, to eradicate all nationalities, and to return to an idealized past of religious communalism."[58] The words of Nasir Ahmad Al-Bahri, a militant Muslim fundamentalist who was a Yemeni from Saudi Arabia fighting in Bosnia, makes this point straightforwardly: "The issue of nationalism was put out of our minds, and we acquired a wider view than that, namely, the issue of the [global] *ummah*."[59]

The reimaging of a transnational Muslim ummah from merely representing a nation-state has opened a pathway for Muslim fundamentalist movements to return to violence as the means to achieve their ends. The Islamic State (IS/ISIL/ISIS) is the best known and most notorious expression of such a transnational Islamic movement that works within the framework of an authoritarian structure, with the caliph as the supreme leader. The vision to set up an actual territory with Caliph Abu Bakr al-Baghdadi, in the regions of Iraq and Syria, is a military experiment to reestablish the caliphate.[60] National borders are collapsed for a transnational ummah that mirrors a state. However, the imagery of such a state is a fallback to the past rather than an imitation of the modern Western nation-state. For a group that uses modern weaponry to spectacularly violent effect and successfully employs cyber technology in recruitment and propaganda, their religious and political vision is surprisingly medieval. Graham Wood puts it this way: "There is a temptation to rehearse this observation—that jihadists are modern secular people, with modern political concerns, wearing medieval religious disguise—and make it fit the Islamic State. In fact, much of what the group does looks nonsensical except in light of a sincere, carefully considered commitment to returning civilization to a seventh-century legal environment, and ultimately to bringing about the apocalypse."[61] He goes on to conclude, "The reality is that the Islamic State is Islamic. *Very* Islamic. Yes, it has attracted psychopaths and adventure seekers, drawn largely from the disaffected populations of the Middle East and Europe. But the religion preached by its most ardent followers derives from coherent and even learned interpretations of Islam."[62] One must not downplay the role of economic grievance, cultural maladjustment, political disempowerment, and psychological malaise that contributed to the emergence of the Islamic State (IS). Yet Bernard Haykel advises that the Islamic State (IS) cannot be explained by only focusing on "the ideology of Jihadi-Salafism" or "the dire political and economic realities of the Arab world."[63] If we ignore or downplay the religious ideology that drives this Muslim fundamentalist movement, we are blind to the Islamist goal of forming and spreading (by violent means) a transnational universal ummah. "Its goals," according to this Princeton professor, who has spent years studying such Muslim fundamentalist movements, "lie beyond Iraq and Syria, inasmuch as its ideologues boastfully claim that world conquest and the establishment of Islamic rule everywhere is their ultimate aim."[64]

Adding Religious Fuel to the Muslim Fundamentalist Fire

Thus far in this chapter, we have looked at how the seedlings from the origins of Islam, historical intermingling between various peoples and empires in Egypt, cultural aspiration of Egyptians, and religiopolitical self-determination globally have cooperated in intriguing ways to produce Muslim fundamentalism as a modern phenomenon. Although Islam from its inception was a universal worldview with one eye on the totality of life and the other eye on the whole inhabited earth, it has journeyed through multiple historical stages, with complex modalities that attest to reception, hostility, and ambivalence to its comprehensive vision and binding practices. The religious nature of Islam, which emanated from a divine revelation and forged a human civilization, routinized a framework and put together a wellspring of sources by which peoples could be gathered, contained, and united. In this section I endeavor to focus on the religious themes that constitute this alluring and compelling corpus, which fires up and fuels Muslim fundamentalism.

If there is one thing that jumps out when studying Islam, especially when one pays attention to the theological thread that links origins, growth, and contemporary Muslim belief and practice, it is that religion matters before anything else and has consequences that must shape other realms of life. In other words, Islam as a divinely revealed Word about God comes first, after which comes transforming the whole world to fit such a Word-vision. At the end of giving the reader a palpable sense of the violence perpetuated by Muslim fundamentalism in twenty-eight Muslim-majority countries, Karima Bennoune concludes that we need to go beyond cataloging the symptoms of these overt undertakings to inquire into the causes that generate all of this destruction. "But we should focus not only on fundamentalist violence," Bennoune states, "because the problem is also the discriminatory and hateful ideology that underlies it, the yeast that makes the beer."[65] I take seriously her exhortation to delve deeper into the substance of such hate-filled and violence-emitting ideologies adopted by Muslim fundamentalism. What are the religious motifs that power up such an ideology so that fundamentalists will give their lives and take the lives of others to reshape the world? In the rest of this section, I will locate and comment upon the religious convictions that frame the divine vision and shape the sacred mission of Muslim fundamentalists. Some of these have already been mentioned while interpreting the origins and development of Islam and observing its transformation into Muslim fundamentalism in Egypt. Three religious cords intertwine to hold together the religious narrative of the fundamentalists: (1) complete surrender to the one God and conforming to Allah's will made available in the Sharia; (2) absolutist Scripture interpreted by authoritative leaders committed to a divinely scripted view of the world; and (3) promotion of global religious civilization that extends the Muslim way of life in a world of westernization and modernization.

Submission to The One God Alone and Pleasing Allah by Conforming to the Sharia

We must consider first things first when reflecting on religious convictions that matter to Muslim fundamentalists. Such a beginning may be located in the *shahada*, which is universally acknowledged as the first and most important pillar of Islam.[66] It compresses and makes explicit the Muslim credo and is often heard as a call to prayer from the minaret first thing in the morning.[67] Although recited in Arabic, it is translated as "There is no god but God, and Muhammad is his messenger."[68] If there is one universal faith statement that makes a human being into a Muslim, it is this concise credo. The first part of the confession is rooted in the willingness to completely surrender to the God who is solely and unqualifiedly one. The theological affirmation "There is no god but God," though, not only sets Allah as one but also opens up a pathway to undercut all others that may pose a threat to this singularity of the Divine.

It is the radical and unconditional oneness of Allah that inspires unequivocal passion for God and justifies smashing other expressions of the divine in Muslim fundamentalism. I have traced some elements of such a theology of God through Islam's long history. Most of this becomes pathological when it is not correlated with the compassion and expansive mercy of God that is communicated in the Qur'an. Dealing with the trauma of multiple forms of Western colonial and quasi-secular Muslim empires pushed Muslim fundamentalism to focus on God's exclusivity while forgetting God's mercy. This resolute and uncompromising belief that "there is no god but God" has taken on an often-heard mantra on the battlefields of fundamentalists in the exclamation "Allahu Akbar," which translates as "God is great [or greater]." With singular passion and violent assertion, the unequivocal Divine One refuses to countenance other divine pretenders.

Much has already been said about the religious motivations of the 9/11 hijackers,[69] so let's look instead at three other examples of violent fundamentalists acting on behalf of a radically monotheistic God. The first is far away from the fundamentalist ethos in the Middle East that has been the focus of this chapter. On November 5, 2009, a U.S. army psychiatrist preparing to be "deployed to Afghanistan allegedly shouted 'Allahu Akbar,' or 'God is greatest,' as he opened fire at a military base in Texas, killing 13 people and wounding 28."[70] A second example can be seen in two acts of violence directed toward Coptic Christians by Muslim fundamentalists: the bombing of a Coptic church in Alexandria on December 31, 2010, killing 21; and a shooting of Coptic Christians aboard an Egyptian train by an off-duty policeman who shouted "Allahu Akbar" as he pulled the trigger. In these cases Muslim fundamentalists see religious otherness as in itself threatening to the divine oneness and sovereignty.[71] The third is more recent and also involves the invocation of the One God and Muhammad his prophet. On January 7, 2015, gunmen inspired by a version of violent Muslim fundamentalism shot dead 12 people at the Paris office of the French satirical magazine *Charlie Hebdo*. Among those killed were four of the magazine's well-known cartoonists, including its editor, all of whom were thought by the terrorists to have been involved in insulting Islam. It was reported that "witnesses said they heard the gunmen shouting, 'We have avenged the Prophet Muhammad' and 'God is Great' in Arabic (Allahu Akbar)" as they carried out this horrendous act suggestive of a religious execution.[72]

While submission to the One God purifies the adherent, the goal of violent Muslim fundamentalists is to please this awesome God by smashing others whom they see as somehow threatening God's honor and supremacy. In both life and death, Allah is the objective. Let me go back to the example of the Muslim Brotherhood. "The Brotherhood survives and thrives in Egypt," opines Andrew McCarthy, "because [of] its credo: . . . 'Allah is our objective, the Prophet is our leader, the Koran is our law, jihad is our way, and dying in the way of Allah is our highest objective.'"[73] Living for Allah in a world of *jahiliyyah* (sin of ignorance of God's guidance) and *shirk* (sin of idolatry or associating other beings above the One God) also means being willing to die for Allah. Muslim fundamentalists' embrace of suicide bombing is a modern expression of violently promoting the cause of the Great God, who alone must reign over all things. Such dying in the service of this One God thus is equated with martyrdom. The Hamas leader Sheikh Ahmed Yassin (1937–2004) brings together the themes of martyrdom, service of the heart, and pleasing

Allah quite logically: "Love of martyrdom is something deep inside the heart. But these rewards are not in themselves the goal of the martyr. *The only aim is to win Allah's satisfaction.* That can be done in the simplest and speediest manner by dying in the cause of Allah."[74]

Muslim fundamentalists commit themselves uncompromisingly to reinstate through reinvention a form of Islam that alone can be pleasing to Allah. In conformity with their particular understanding of the origins and early development of Islam, which I discussed in the earlier section, the fundamentalists look to religion to ground the political, economic, and cultural aspirations of a people traumatized by the plethora of modern options. The core of this integral vision as pleasing to God was proffered to be the Sharia. In contrast to the Western ideals of human agreements and social contracts, the Sharia, which literally means divine "pathway," returns the faithful to giving themselves up to God as the sole sovereign and "the ultimate legislator."[75] The comprehensive divine law of God holds together an all-embracing religious framework through which convinced individuals and complying communities "surrender their whole will to the Will of God."[76]

Islam, as framed by Sharia, was presented by al-Banna as "a state, a place of belongingness, a nation and a government, . . . the record of creation, of God's power, His mercy and justice."[77] In this instance a fundamentalist vision was developed by reaching backward to reclaim a divine blueprint and offering such a plan as a collective way to fuse a revealed religious worldview demanded by the One God. Such a religiopolitical comprehensive divine pathway (Sharia) unfolds as "the practical way to reach the glory of Islam and to serve the welfare of the Muslims."[78] The welfare of those who submit (Muslims) cannot be achieved by following human legal and political wisdom. It can only be attained by submitting to Allah's legal prescriptions contained in Sharia, which alone can guarantee a righteous and just human society. Ray Takeyh and Nikolas K. Gvosdev capture this idea cogently: "A hallmark of all Islamist movements is the conviction that all modern sociopolitical ideologies, being man-made and elevating the sovereignty of the individual over that of the Divine, cannot succeed in forging a truly just society."[79] Yet all of this talk of submission to God is not without vested worldly interests. At the end of a meticulously researched and convincingly argued book on the Muslim Brotherhood, Hezem Kandil rather comprehensively brings together the spiritual and the material, religious and political, and hope after life and before death, all in the vision of Muslim fundamentalism. "Islamism is, at bottom," he concludes, "an ideology that attributes worldly success to religious devotion." Furthermore, according to Kandil, even while the Sharia claims to mold submission to Allah, it "is not just a set of duties imposed on Muslims in this life in hope of reward in the next, but also a tool for worldly accomplishment."[80]

Absolutist Scripture, Authoritative Leaders

The unflinching authority attributed to the Qur'an is an important element that binds Muslim fundamentalists. However, it is the authoritative interpretation of the content of such an absolute Word from God coupled with the frame of mind cultivated for such a dutiful reception that reveals how fundamentalists utilize religions. In the reflections that follow, I shall focus on the manner in which Muslim understandings of God's pure revelation in the Qur'an is transformed by staunchly assertive leaders into a set of marching orders. These leaders hope to cultivate a group of believers eager to see the unfolding of the divine drama in every mundane reality.

The Qur'an is as scriptural as a scripture can get with regard to religious authority over adherents of the faith. Michael Cook uncovers the immediacy and inflexibility ascribed to this mother of all scriptures: "The Koran is emphatically a scripture rather than classic. Indeed, it could well be described as the paradigmatic scripture, the word of God in the most immediate, uncompromising sense."[81] The idea that the Qur'an is a literal and uncontaminated voicing of God to mediate the absolute (in the sense of both 'final' and 'independent of human conditions') truth to human beings is built into the content that was revealed and the process by which it was transmitted. The word "Qur'an" means "recitation," representing the fact that it is a verbally revealed set of scriptures. The Qur'an is the direct Word of God spoken to the prophet Muhammad through the angel Gabriel in Arabic. Muhammad could not read or write. His illiteracy, rather than being an obstacle, bolsters the claim that he did not contaminate the revelation with his own interpretations. What Muhammad heard from God was recited by him, committed to memory by his followers, and written down verbatim by them during his lifetime under his supervision.

To safeguard the direct and original character of revelation, the Qur'an can only be read and interpreted in classical Arabic. Thus the spoken language of God was Arabic, and the whole community of faith must learn Arabic to know what has been spoken. Refusal to accept translations as scriptural or authoritative bolsters the belief that the Qur'an derives from no human wisdom or reason. Its wording is letter for letter fixed by no one but Allah. This high view of Qur'an as "scripture of scriptures" for interlinking the way, the truth, and the life is expressed cogently by Hans Küng:

> Indeed, for all Muslims, the Qur'an is *the truth*: the original source of the experience of God and piety and the mandatory criterion of right faith; *the way*: the true possibility of coping with the world and the eternally valid standard for correct action (ethic); *the life*: the abiding foundation of Islamic law and the soul of Islamic prayer, already the material for the instruction of Muslim children, the inspiration of Islamic art and the all-permeating spirit of Islamic culture. The Qur'an is at the same time a religious, ethical and legal-social codex which however is only the way, the truth and the life to the degree that it is the word of God.[82]

While such an exalted understanding of scripture is widely ascribed to by most Muslims around the world even to the present time, Muslim fundamentalism uses this belief to lionize the authority of its leaders and valorize the uncritical obedience of its disciples. Fundamentalist movements have revered and powerful ideologues who cannot be opposed because they speak, not on their own authority, but on that of an infallible scripture, thus granting the leaders the scripture's own religious and political authority. They become both commanders of operations and defenders of the faith. But alongside the leaders' unquestionable authority is a related characteristic just as crucial to the fundamentalist movement: the cultivation of fired-up activists rather than complicated thinkers. Hassan al-Banna challenged the Muslim Brotherhood to turn the focus from endless deliberate argumentation on matters of Islam to develop concrete practices that can transform everyday life. Kandil does a remarkable job of lifting up this dimension of members of the Muslim Brotherhood:

> Brothers are expected to be passionate and active believers, but not ones too keen on learning. The principal justification for this is that Islam is practical religion. Life is short, and would be better spent loving and serving God and His creatures. A second, though no less important, justification is that the independent pursuit of knowledge invites arguments, and arguments poison the peace between Brothers. Banna had, in fact, paired the two justifications in his well-rehearsed maxim: 'Be practical not argumentative.'[83]

The need to cultivate a movement of less argumentative and thus less critical disciples for Muslim fundamentalist organizations may explain the proliferation of madrasas (schools for children and youth to learn Arabic and the Qur'an) in regions where they are active and expanding. Accompanying the growth of the madrasas is a concerted effort to dismantle and destroy the systems delivering so-called Western education. The bombing of schools providing un-Islamic education in Afghanistan, Pakistan, and Nigeria represents an offensive against the possibility for critical reflection to enter the minds of children and youth. In this context, it is pertinent to note that the name for one of the most feared, violent Muslim fundamentalist organizations (Boko Haram) operating in Nigeria, Niger, northern Cameroon, and Chad means "Western education is fraud."[84] Uncritical education based on a scripture one little understands because its language is not one's own, combined with no opportunities to learn alternative viewpoints, cultivates not only nonargumentative but also subservient followers for the cause of fundamentalist movements. The Muslim Brotherhood spread the art of inculcating an Islamic worldview and transforming that education into actual practice. Its strategy through the twentieth century was to start with children within the family and youth in local communities, in order to cultivate the Islamic way of life. The hope was that gradually, from the family through the local community, the Muslim Brotherhood would "enlarge the circle of 'committed' Muslims until it eventually encompassed society as a whole."[85]

Abetting their absolutist notion of scripture is Muslim fundamentalists' view of a divinely scripted world. According to this view innate qualities and attributes apply to individuals, human societies, and divine agents irrespective of time, historical change, and laws of science. God rules over all of creation in a direct and perceptible way as revealed within the Qur'an, and for this reason immutable forces will govern individuals, societies, and global history till the end of time. To be knowledgeable about this true nature of reality and consciously commit to the process of its unfolding and concretization is the purpose of a world-transforming fundamentalist faith. Seyyed Hossein Nasr refers to this mind-set, which stems from an absolutist interpretation of the Qur'an as "the Islamic worldview." It connects divine and human agency in a simplistic yet direct manner, often giving religious leaders a role in bringing God's will to bear on human affairs. "Muslims might be fighting over the question of political authority and the types of laws that should govern Islamic society, but very few differ concerning the belief that God is still sitting on His Throne (*al-'arsh*) and is the ruler of the universe."[86] Muslim fundamentalism unites God, God's rule over the universe, and the faithful community as it enacts God's will into one reality. The threads of all three strands weave theology into history where the absolutist saga of God continues to form individuals, societies, and global history through the deliberative beliefs and actions of the ummah led by dogged Muslim leaders.

Their belief in a divinely scripted world, buttressed by an absolutist notion of scripture and constantly reinforced by interpretations of human events as immutable signs of God's will, keeps Muslim fundamentalists hoping for ultimate victory despite all realistic odds being against them. The God who shows forth his mighty arm of triumph in the Qur'an is the same God who inspires and directs his faithful in their struggle for the divine vision. It thus was not surprising that on the eve of the collapse of the legitimately elected Morsi government of the Muslim Brotherhood in 2013, members of this Egyptian fundamentalist movement "were visibly shaken by the absence of divine intervention" as during "Prophet Muhammad's epic battles" and as testified to by "biblical stories, from David and Moses to Armageddon."[87] As the army in Egypt gradually dismantled the Muslim fundamentalists' yearlong reign of power, the daughter of the Brotherhood's effective leader was videotaped confidently proclaiming on television: "God will part the sea for us! Just wait and see!" Commenting on this incident, Kandil throws light on the linkage this expectation has with the unfolding narrative of Scripture. "She was echoing one of the many prophecies circulated during the sit-in: that the soldiers of Pharaoh had trapped the Brothers just as they had the ancient Hebrews, and if the Brothers keep faith with Morsi, as their predecessors did with Moses, a miracle was shortly at hand."[88] The fact that God did not miraculously intervene in their struggle did not change the simplistic religious worldview of the Muslim fundamentalists. In their eyes, they remain compatriots with God in the unfolding of Allah's will, revealed in the Qur'an and sure to materialize on earth for the glory of God and welfare of God's people.

A Global Religious Civilization

In addition to radical monotheism and faith that God intimately and directly guides human history, Muslim fundamentalism insists on the need to cultivate concrete everyday practices in the unfolding global conflict between the forces of God and powers of evil. In service of their vision of a universal Islamic civilization, Muslim fundamentalists have promoted a startlingly divisive us-versus-them mentality toward other people. The "flip side of the godly brotherhood is antipathy to others," a maxim fundamentalists believed came from the Qur'an.[89] Let me hark back to the Muslim Brotherhood. Not only did the dualistic worldview informed by the Qur'an call for an increased zeal of "loyalty" to the Brotherhood; it also implied an intensified fever of "antipathy" toward both non-Muslims, who might lead the faithful into secularization and westernization, and other Muslims, who might do the same in the guise of modernization.[90] These binaries were simplistic and tangible but were also loaded with religious and political implications for taking over the world for Allah. Sayyid Qutb repackaged and reformulated the Islamic heritage to challenge authority, including those who deceptively claimed to be Muslim, by appealing to its oppositional, antithetical, and therefore mutually exclusive character. Drawing on a cosmic duel that needed faithful and courageous Muslims to infiltrate the world for God, he "hardened the lines between *hizb* Allah ('the Party of God') and *hizb al-shaytan* ('the party of Satan')."[91] Thus, the battle for this version of religious fundamentalism involves deadly opposition to specific historical embodiments demanding active and even, at times, violent service.

In an earlier segment in this chapter, I sketched in some detail the deep oppositional worldview that forged communal action during the birth and expansion of Islam. Yet much of the fundamentalist shape and surge of the movement, I have argued, was a modern phenomenon. Arising from the historical experience of fending off the liberal Muslim Ottoman Empire on one side and the Western Christian French and British Empires on the other, the coordinated dualistic mind-set and dueling scheme for action were successfully developed through the religious, social, and political reach of Muslim fundamentalism. Although applicable to the movement well beyond early twentieth-century Egypt, Moaddel lifts out this dualistic dimension of fundamentalism that characterizes the formation and development of the modern ideologues in the Muslim Brotherhood: "A series of binaries defined its identity and distinguished the MB from other movements: Islamic activism versus religious retreatism and apathy, Islamic unity versus the political parties' disunity and factionism, puritanism and modesty versus sexual laxity, gender segregation versus mixing of the sexes, Egypt's Islamic essence versus Pharaonism, Spiritualism versus Western materialism."[92] Over the last century modernity and globalization have gradually transformed Muslim fundamentalism's reach from merely a national or regional phenomenon to a worldwide movement. Local conflicts take on cosmic significance in such a universal political theology.

The global scope for an imagined universal religious civilization that guided a tight-knit ummah fighting for God against the forces of evil has roots in the origins and continued spread of Islam. The combative and passionate acting out of Muslim fundamentalism through the twentieth and into the twenty-first centuries certainly has a crowded registry of complaints against various populist ideologies, cultural challengers, and economic currents. However, one cannot discount the global missionary dreams of expansionist Islam, which, like Christianity, accompanies Muslim theology from its inception. "Contrary to widespread assumptions," states Efrain Karsh, "Arab and Muslim anti-Americanism, have little to do with US international behavior or its Middle Eastern policy. If, today, America is reviled in the Muslim world, it is not because of its specific policies but because, as the preeminent world power, it blocks the final realization of this same age-old dream of regaining the lost glory of the caliphate, . . . a universal Islamic empire (*umma*)."[93] Karsh is no doubt overstating his case, even as he underplays the considerable affects U.S. imperial ambitions have on other cultural and religious worldviews in various parts of the globe. Yet one cannot deny the universal vision that galvanizes Islam and its link to conflictual dynamics on a global scale. A universal hope that Allah will rule over all creation so that justice and peace may be established on earth through embracing the laws of God (Sharia) tends to become pitted against other universal theologies and ideologies. I am highlighting the deliberate attempt of Islamic fundamentalism to revive and restate the relevance of Islam in the modern world by falling back on this universal vision steeped in a cosmic dualistic struggle. While this leads to violent reactions against the modern West, it also leads to violence within the Islamic community itself. Jihad is the catchall term that has given religious justification for this aggressive struggle against the far-off enemy in the abode of the West and the close-at-hand enemy within the household of Islam itself.

Beverly Milton-Edwards's words, even if penned a decade ago, are still true today. Referring to Westerners' perceptions, especially those who assume that the high-profile Muslim extremists represent all Islam, she states, "Jihad not *Salaam* (peace) is the word most commonly associated with Islam."[94] But what does this Arabic term mean, and how is it so central to the vision and mission of Muslim fundamentalism? "Jihad," which literally means "striving," is interpreted as a form of religious flexing to protect and promote purity both within believers and in the world. In order to ensure that Muslim faith and practice is governed by the ideal of peaceful submission to God in an ethical or spiritual and material or socioeconomic-political world, scholars make a distinction between "lesser jihad" and "greater jihad." The distinction goes back to a hadith, which records the sayings of the prophet Muhammad. It is said that when the prophet returned from a violent battle to defend his newly established ummah, he instructed his followers coming home from waging *jihad al-asghar* (the lesser war) to be prepared to wage the *jihad al-akbar* (the greater war) against the baser forces that lie deep within each follower and prevent them from submitting fully to the true human nature that Allah has created in human beings. The point being made by sympathetic advocates is that Islam prioritizes and even privileges inner striving toward bringing all affections, thoughts, and actions within oneself into conformity with the will of Allah.

Greater jihad is a form of holy struggle within, which trains individual Muslims to submit fully to the pattern of God's demands. This is the struggle that all other strivings must be accountable to in Islam, the straight path revealed in the Qur'an. "Piety, knowledge, health, beauty, truth, and justice are not possible without jihad—without sustained and diligent hard work. Therefore, cleansing oneself from vanity and pettiness, pursuing knowledge, curing the ill, feeding the poor, and standing up for truth and justice even at great personal risk are all forms of jihad."[95] Islamic scholars accentuate that it is this "act of striving to serve the purposes of God on this earth"[96] that the Qur'an points to when it uses the term "jihad." Lesser jihad, on the other hand, involves social, economic, and political forms of holy struggles to construct a world that allows for the flourishing of the Islamic way in the world. According to most Islamic scholars, violence is permitted in lesser jihad, through which faithful Muslims struggle against other religiopolitical regimes that threaten the Islamic way of life, even as they work toward extending this straight path for all of humanity. This type of striving, which can even be termed "fighting for God," is sanctioned in "the Quran as legitimate armed struggle."[97] However, "even verses employing that term are typically followed by exhortations to patience in adversity and leniency in strength, the essence of being of gentle disposition."[98]

Muslim fundamentalism exploits the Qur'an's religious justification of armed struggle. It also creatively interprets these scriptural sanctions for lesser jihad by drawing on strands of Islamic theology that testify to Allah's help in protecting the ummah from other religious and political regimes and its expansion into regions controlled by these same powers. What is notable in contemporary Muslim fundamentalism, however, is the manner in which the greater jihad has become a means to the end of the violent expressions of the lesser jihad. Thus the purpose of controlling and purifying the self is not simply to make one a better servant of God but to make one a better warrior in the violent struggle to realize God's sovereignty over all the earth. While the short-term goal of Muslim fundamentalism is regional and confined to Muslims, the long-term goal is global and embraces the whole of the inhabited world. The words of Abu Musab al-Zarqawi (1966–2006), one of the founding ideologues of the Islamic State (IS), is categorical: "We will fight in the cause of God until His shariah prevails. The first step is to expel the enemy and establish the state of Islam. We would then go forth to reconquer the Muslim lands and restore them to the Muslim nation. . . . [At last,] the Muslims would still be required *not* to refrain from jihad but go forth and seek the enemy until only God Almighty's shariah prevailed everywhere in the world."[99] Abdelhamid Abaaoud, the suspected mastermind behind IS's Paris attacks on November 13, 2015, symbolizes the global danger from such chosen-by-God violent Muslim fundamentalists. Although "raised in Europe by not especially religious parents," Abaaoud displayed "an abrupt fixation on fundamentalist Sunni Islam and a turn to terror, bringing about scores of deaths on European soil."[100] His own justification is solidly backed by prayer to Allah that God's enemies be vanquished, for which he is willing to play his part. "All my life I have seen the blood of Muslims flow," he said in a recent video made in Syria; "I pray that God breaks the backs of those who oppose him."[101]

From this discussion of its promotion of a worldwide Islamic civilization, we might conclude that "religious conviction, hatred of secular society, and the demonstration of power through acts of violence" frequently coalesce in Muslim fundamentalism.[102] One focus of Muslim fundamentalist jihad has been the struggle against the westernizing and secularizing West. Partly to blame for this focus is the fact that Western, secular culture has itself been engaged in a "hostile takeover" of Muslim hearts and minds for the last two centuries. Bernard Lewis puts it this way: "In the course of the nineteenth and twentieth centuries, the primacy and therefore the dominance of the West was clear for all to see, invading the Muslim in every aspect of his public and, more painfully, even his private life."[103] This explains the twenty-first-century striving of fundamentalists to destroy the systems that represent expanding westernization. New York, London, and Paris became symbolic targets of violent jihad.

Yet one must not ignore another dimension of Muslim fundamentalism: its struggle against the forces of reform and modernization within the Muslim world. Reza Aslan may be overplaying his argument when he asserts, "What is taking place in the Muslim world is an internal conflict between Muslims, not an external battle between Islam and the West."[104] Yet his desire to lift up the magnitude of violence affecting various Muslim communities rather than fixate on the lesser extent of casualties in the West makes good sense. Aslan helpfully reminds us of the striving taking place right now among the adherents of Islam between fundamentalists and modernists over the future of the faithful: "a rivalry . . . is raging in Islam over who will write the next chapter in its story."[105]

Conclusion

As one peers into the future, one can say that Muslim fundamentalism of the Sunni kind has carved out two trajectories. One is exemplified in the violent conflicts frequently seen in the news. It displays revolting, raw, cruel, and spectacular violence laced with clichés of "Allahu Akbar," intent on forming an Islamic State (IS) in the tradition of the earlier caliphate. Taking advantage of the dismantling of Iraq, Libya, and Syria, the Islamic State (aka Islamic State of the Levant; Islamic State of Syria) has banded together thousands of discontents, including hundreds of Muslims from the West, to set up a state with Sharia as the rule of law and the companion of Muhammad as its leader. The West, along with most of the nation-states belonging to the United Nations, is at war with this fundamentalist movement and its affiliates.

The other is the consolidation of a Quranic-based ummah living under the Sharia within an already existing nation-state. Though a close ally of the United States and Europe, Saudi Arabia is the best example of this type of Muslim fundamentalism, shrouding the systemic violence that it perpetuates within its borders and scheming to spread its political power in the Middle East through the dissemination of its toxic version of Islam.[106] As a repressive government, which curtails the rights of women, foreigners, and its own citizens, this Muslim fundamentalist country continues to be the main proponent of its modern version of Salafism, i.e., Wahhabism. As a major ideology of Sunni fundamentalism, Wahhabism is still propagated and funded by Saudi Arabia in various parts of the world. Even more troubling is the reality that Saudi Arabia has now become the world's largest arms importer. According to IHS Jane 360, "Saudi Arabia has become the world's biggest importer of weapons and defensive systems" among the 65 arms trading countries examined in 2014. Data revealed by examining Global Defence Trade Report, "shows that Saudi Arabia spent over $6.4 billion on defense purchases in 2014, dislodging India from top spot. India's spending stood at $5.57 billion, placing it second."[107]

Both these brands of Muslim fundamentalism claim to be taking Muslims back to the rudiments of the ummah that Muhammad advocated and instituted in Medina from 622 CE. Yet they conveniently cast off some of the core features of the prophet's community. In concluding this chapter, let me list some of these with the hope that they will be instructive to Muslim fundamentalist movements that truly want to live out the straight path as represented by Muhammad and his successors.

Most biographies of Muhammad point to his religious piety, deep compassion for the poor, and zeal for social and economic reform.[108] As the heads of this Islamic state, Muhammad and his ensuing caliphs (successors), were in charge of the civic and religious leadership of the entire Muslim community. These devoutly spiritual yet shrewdly pragmatic leaders were committed to establishing a just society in submission to God. They were united in the conviction that "the message of the Quran was not a new abstruse doctrine . . . but simply a 'reminder' of what constitutes a just society that challenged the structural violence emerging in Mecca: that it was wrong to build a private fortune but good to share your wealth with the poor and vulnerable, who must be treated with equity and respect."[109] "Economic redistribution" and "social egalitarianism" were embraced as principles by which the ummah ought to reorder their community life. Aslan surmises that, for Muhammad, such a just social order included ensuring "the protection of every member of his community;" "reforming the Law of retribution" to both extend to slaves, orphans, and widows and incorporate forgiveness; instituting the compulsory tithe (*zakat*) to aid the poor and the needy; and bestowing "rights and privileges . . . upon the women in his community."[110]

While presiding over the operations of justice within the community of the faithful, the prophet and his successors also had to lead the faithful in violently defending Islam from aggressors even as they kept expanding the ummah into other regions through caravan raids, ambushes on other tribes, and full-fledged battles. Muhammad too led some of these aggressive operations. However, through the course of his life, claiming to use the content of the revelation communicated to him, the prophet provided sketches of a "primitive just war theory."[111] The defensive and offensive use of aggression, interpreted by leaders to be in compliance with the divinely revealed law from God, must be understood in conjunction with another overall goal of Judaism, Christianity, and Islam:

the pursuit of peace. "Quranic verses," states John Esposito, "underscore that peace, not violence and warfare, is the norm: 'if your enemy inclines toward peace, then you too should seek peace and put your trust in God' (8:61)."[112] Much of this invocation of peace in all three of these religions has not been easy to understand considering the conflict that each has initiated. Yet the fact that *shalom* (*šālōm*, Judaism), *eirene* (*eirēnē,* Christianity), and *salaam* (*salām*, Islam) are central ideals that hold together both peace as a gift from God to individuals and peace as a state of becoming for communities under God reminds us to acknowledge peace as a fundamental constituent of Muslim belief and practice. As Sayyed Hossein Nasr suggests, it not enough to counter the accusation that Islam is a "religion of the sword" by naively pointing out that the word "Islam" itself means *salaam*, or peace. Rather, just as Hindus pursue *shanti*, Jews hope for *shalom*, and Christians pray for *pax*, Muslims "need to point out that, since the goal of every authentic religion is to reach God who is Peace and the Source of all peace, Islam also aims to lead its followers to the 'Abode of Peace' and to create peace to the degree possible in a world full of disequilibrium, tension, and affliction."[113]

Chapter Four

Hindu Fundamentalism

The western world after 9/11 was obsessed with extreme Islam. But here in India was evidence that every major religion can be hijacked by the forces of fundamentalism.

Edna Fernandes, *Holy Warriors: A Journey into
the Heart of Indian Fundamentalism*

Introduction

"Hindu fundamentalism" should be an oxymoron. The open-ended and inclusionary kernel of the Hindu religion does not appear to fit into the closed and exclusionary shell of fundamentalism. Yet, as we have seen in Christianity and Islam in the previous chapters, religions brazenly contradict even those beliefs most central to their identity. This chapter argues that Hinduism, with about one billion followers and close to 15 percent of the world's population, has not avoided the fundamentalist turn seen so often in this and the previous century

Hinduism is hailed as one of the most diverse of the world religions. It is a religious jigsaw puzzle of sorts, encompassing a host of images, theologies, and practices. Stephen Prothero captures this diversity eloquently. "Under Hinduism's sacred canopy," he says, "sit a dizzying variety of religious beliefs and behaviors practiced in the wildly complex and contradictory subcontinent of India and its diaspora."[1] This diversity ought to make Hinduism immune from any drift toward fundamentalism. In many ways Hinduism's diversity implies its opposition to rigidity of theological dogma and strictness of religious practice. In its 3500-year history Hinduism has exhibited fluid boundaries, predisposed to incorporating

95

all forms of religiosity. This open, inclusive, and embracing character, however, is only one face of Hinduism. Another face has been growing stronger and spreading: Hindu fundamentalism.

This chapter proceeds in four sections. First I describe the historical context of multiple conquests during the last five hundred years as a backdrop to Hindu fundamentalism's emergence in early twentieth-century colonial India. Second, I examine the last two decades of the twentieth century, which witnessed the resurgence of Hindu fundamentalism and its accession to political power. Third, I describe the momentous influence of Hindu fundamentalism in the twenty-first century, which culminated in a sweeping victory for the Hindu Right, with the Bharatiya Janata Party (BJP) being voted into power in May 2014. Fourth, keeping this historical commentary in mind, I locate three religious characteristics of this resilient and swelling fundamentalist movement in the twenty-first century. Three themes predominate in the analysis of this phenomenon: an idealized scriptural authority cultivated to unify the Hindu community; combative communal dispositions to form a social body that manifests the body of god; and the contradiction of violently *dualistic* religiopolitics based on *monistic* philosophy. These strong religious beliefs knit together by nationalist ambitions violently affect India.

Fundamentalism and Conquest: The Mughals and the British

Hinduism goes back at least three millennia, even though the term itself was not used until the early nineteenth century. This is when Europeans put a label on a family of religious beliefs and practices prevalent in the Indian subcontinent. The need to define itself as a religion in the modern sense of the term was an ongoing challenge, beginning in the sixteenth century. Seen from within, the term "Hinduism" describes a number of Indic streams flowing across the subcontinent, encountering and coalescing with numerous local tributaries. Seen from without, the term represents an attempt by aggressive external forces to delineate Indian beliefs and practices without bothering to consult the communities being defined.

Hindu fundamentalism, I submit, emerged as a self-conscious, widespread, and religiopolitical worldview and national movement in the first quarter of the twentieth century. To understand the circumstances that contributed to its formation, however, one must situate it within the historical currents of Mughal and British rule.

The Mughal occupation (1526–1757) and British colonization (1757–1947) of Hindu India were aggressive in strategy and management, extensive in reach across the subcontinent, and varyingly linked with the aims of Islamic and Christian mission. Although both empires ruled with the alliance of the Hindu majority that formed a significant portion of their armies, they had all the markings of colonial intervention, expansion, and control in the subcontinent. Each of these colonial takeovers of the Indian subcontinent has its own long and complex history. A brief word on each should suffice to shine some light on the impact they had on defacing the self-image and undermining the sense of agency of local Hindu communities, giving rise to twentieth-century Hindu fundamentalism.

The Mughal occupation commenced formally in 1526, when Babur, its first emperor, defeated Ibrahim Lodi at the First Battle of Panipat, a town outside of Delhi. This was the first time that gunpowder was used in India, leading to the Mughal Empire joining the "gunpowder empire" club.[2] As with most empires, gunpowder (brute force) and genteel ideas (ideological co-option) were used by the Mughals to rule over the bodies and minds of native subjects. The long line of Mughal emperors engaged in both violent destruction and respectful acceptance of the culture and religion of native Hindu communities. Babur started by destabilizing the religious self-identity of Hinduism. He began building mosques as a tribute to "Almighty God" for his victorious expansion into the land of the Hindus, "Hindustan." Two mosques in particular flaunted his devotion to Allah in the face of the many temples already built to various Hindu deities. The first mosque was completed in 1527, soon after the historic battle in Panipat (1526), to commemorate "the Moghul conquest of Hindustan."[3] Another mosque was built between 1528 and 1529 in the "highly charged" site of Ayodhya. The contemporary popular assertion that this mosque was built by erasing a Hindu temple, which marked the site of Lord Rama's birth, may not have much historical support. However, Catherine Blanshard Asher documents that "an important Mughal Chronicler, writing about seventy years after the mosque's construction, acknowledges Ayodhya's sanctity as Rama's dwelling, but says nothing of the exact site of Rama's birth."[4] This mosque, called Babri Masjid or Mosque of Babur, is a metasymbol of the conflict between Hindu fundamentalists and Muslims until today.

The ruthless and militantly pro-Muslim and anti-Hindu emperor Aurangzeb (1618–1707) erased much of the harmonious Hindu-Muslim diplomacy that had been characteristic of his grandfather Akbar's reign. One side of his violent rule overtly advantaged Muslims. For Aurangzeb, "the Mughal Empire must become a Muslim state governed by the precepts of the Sharia for the benefits of the Indian Muslims."[5] The other side of his violent rule blatantly harassed and hounded Hindus. In an edict of 1669, Aurangzeb "ordered that all temples built or repaired contrary to the Sharia be torn down."[6] Not content with this destruction of Hindu temples across the empire, "Aurangzeb's ultimate aim was conversion of non-Muslims to Islam. . . . The message was very clear to all concerned. Shared political community must also be shared religious belief."[7]

The Mughal Empire, though, was not without its paragons of pluralistic governance. Akbar the Great (1542–1605) was known to be a tolerant, inclusive, and benevolent emperor. Attested to be the greatest of the Mughal emperors, he extended Mughal rule to most of the subcontinent between 1556 and 1605. Under his leadership "the empire shifted from an Islam-imbued to a more pluralist project."[8] Akbar issued an "edict of universal tolerance, . . . forbade the forcible conversion of prisoners to Islam, . . . ended the *jizya* tax levied only on the non-Muslims, and ordered the translation of the Sanskrit classics into Persian."[9] Yet the fact that the overwhelmingly Hindu majority was ruled by a Muslim dynasty for centuries, which now and again demolished their temples, converted native Indians, and subjugated their culture and religion, meant that the models of Babur and Aurangzeb cast a long shadow over other more tolerant and pluralistic Mughal rulers. In the process, Hindu self-esteem and self-respect, along with confidence in their own agency, took a long and hard battering.

Colonization did not end with the Mughals; the British Empire took over from them almost seamlessly. In this case colonialism followed commerce, as the British East India Company's 1619 establishment of a factory in India led to ever more involvement of the British crown in the affairs of the subcontinent. In the end the company became so profitable that the British government had to protect it by assuming political control over both it and the Indian peoples, whose wealth it was so effectively extracting. William Dalrymple does a remarkable job of showing how the tail of "corporate looting" wagged the dog of British Raj (rule): "At the height of the Victorian period there was a strong sense of embarrassment about the shady mercantile way the British had founded the Raj. . . . They liked to think of the empire as a *mission civilisatrice*: a benign national transfer of knowledge, railways and the arts of civilisation from west to east, and there was a calculated and deliberate amnesia about the corporate looting that opened British rule in India."[10]

A small factory gradually led to a strong corporation, which then led to British rule in India. This company, it must not be overlooked, had built up a regular army with as many as 200,000 men, which facilitated its expansion across the subcontinent. The East India Company's control over India was decidedly established with Robert Clive's victorious battle over the Nawab of Bengal in 1757. As a lead essay in *The Economist* puts it, "Sir Robert Clive won the battle of Plassey and delivered the government of Bengal to the Company."[11] Simply put, India so tempted the expanding British Empire that it could no longer allow the East India Company to control it. By 1784 the British government formed a board to guide the directors, and by 1813 it revoked the rights for "monopoly of trade" with India. The East India Company was banned from trading with India in 1833 before India was officially declared a British colony in 1858.[12]

One cannot whitewash the economic looting and repressive violence that accompanied the exploitation of India by the East India Company and the British Crown. After all, the company sailed into India with authority bestowed in 1600 by Elizabeth I for monopoly of trade over anything east of the Cape of Good Hope. However, the British did not set themselves to ravage and destroy the religion of India. Their attitudes toward Hinduism ranged from systematic devaluation and strategic criticism to systemic enchantment and charmed Orientalism.

An Amalgamated Religion for a Modern Nation

The advent of the twentieth century animated various anticolonial movements around the world. Hindu fundamentalism was one of these movements. "India's fundamentalists," Edna Fernandes states, "were radicalized by anger over the past and fear for the future."[13] They urged the Hindu majority to get back to the fundamentals of a chosen vision, which was indigenously religious and inventively political. Fundamentalists reached inward to reclaim a primordial Hindu essence that evaded capture and reached outward to reconfigure a religiopolitical nation-space that grew out of this autonomous vision. It is from this foundational sense of corporate self, dubbed "Hindu-ness" (Hindutva), that India would live out its future in courageous response to Mughal and British colonialism. The Hindu reaction to Mughal and British colonial rule was paradoxical. On the one hand, it accepted the simplistic myth that colonialism had constructed for India, that India is one unitary and homogeneous entity held together by its essential religiosity. In an ironic way, the early twentieth-century self-understanding that conflated being an Indian with being a Hindu reflected, as if in a mirror, the image constructed by the Sunni Muslim-allied Mughal and the Protestant Christian-laced British

Empires. India was embraced as mysteriously though collectively Hindu. On the other hand, the emerging Hindu self-image rejected the tendency in colonial policy to divide the Indian community into numerous disunions according to the colonialist's own whims and fancies. The divide-and-rule tactic of Mughal and British colonialism almost succeeded in making Indians believe that they were merely a disparate conglomeration of human tribes loosely held together. A unitive principle rooted in a comprehensive vision that was truly Indian and uncorrupted by Islam and Christianity was needed by Hindu fundamentalists, around which their religion, civilization, and nation might be constructed into the postcolonial future.

Hindu fundamentalism is thus not simply a reactionary countervision and oppositional movement. It professes to emanate from a primordial metaphysical and materialistic religious vision, which was revealed through the Ancient of Days to the Hindu seers and testified to by the Hindu scriptures (Vedas). Copiously but selectively drawing from Orientalist scholarship propagating notions that "India was the cradle of all civilization" and "the original homeland of humanity," and that "Hinduism represented humanity's primal philosophy" and "offered redemption for contemporary humanity," Hindu fundamentalists fused together a religiously grounded and politically viable unitary identity for a non-Mughal and non-Christian future.[14] Angana P. Chatterji captures this aptly: "Hindutva has made the unification of Hindus central to its mission. Overlooking wide distinctions in tradition and tongue, sect, grouping, ethos, eros, forms of worship, theology, it steers Hindus into fulfilling their 'manifest destiny,' essentializing Hinduism as a monotheistic, canonical religion, 'natural'/sui generis to, and uniform across, the immense heterogeneity of India."[15] Hindu fundamentalism thus was put into motion as a deliberate process of restoration, consolidation, and construction. It projected Hindu India as one composite and tangible "national soul," which, even if fragmented by colonialism, was in the process of restoring its lofty religiopolitical and sociocultural primordial self. In all of this construction through restoration, religion was utilized to frame, source, and animate a unitary vision.

Around the same time that Christian and Muslim fundamentalism was germinating in the United States and Egypt, Vinayak Damodar Savarkar (1883–1966) was developing the rationale for Hindu fundamentalism in the 1920s. Savarkar carved out a vision counter to that of Mohandas Karamchand Gandhi (1869–1948; aka Mahatma Gandhi) by pushing for a much more militant and much less religiously inclusive India. Both these visionaries, who met in London in 1906 and in Ratnagiri in 1927, combined religion and politics with fertile imagination. But while Gandhi carried over the ethical dimensions of religion to develop an inclusive and nonviolent politics, Savarkar harnessed the narrow and exclusivist elements of religion to foster political militancy in India.[16] Savarkar was not merely "untroubled by the violence" but also his writings "are steeped in a desire for revenge against those who have humiliated Hindus."[17] His aim for his coreligionists is straightforward: "I want all Hindus to get themselves re-animated and re-born into a martial race."[18] Commenting upon the Hindu fundamentalists' mythology spun around Savarkar, who is referred to with the prefix Veer (fearless) by his admirers, Bhatt surmises: "The overarching themes in his hagiographies are undoubtedly those of uncompromising Hindu militancy, violence, masculine strength and daring, both against British colonial rule and against Indian Muslims."[19]

Savarkar's influential form of nationalist thinking strengthened the idea of India as a united region, a common race, and a militant religious civilization. He creatively reworked Hindu fundamentalism in brawny and broad terms. Savarkar moved away from merely representing Hindu ideals and practice as a religious phenomenon confined to rituals, myths, deities, and social norms. He promoted a larger and more expansive understanding, one that encompassed national identity and encouraged people to live by the fundamental essence of being Hindu (Hindutva). Savarkar's ideas have influenced the modern resurgence of Hindu fundamentalism, making him one of its patron saints. His muscular and comprehensive ideology can help us understand the main workings of the contemporary Hindu fundamentalism, both in its self-affirmation and its denunciation of others.

In his book titled *Hindutva: Who Is a Hindu?*, first published in 1923, Savarkar reaches back to India's precolonial identity to reconstitute the Hindu sense of belonging. What are the fundamentals of the essence termed Hindutva (Hindu-ness)? For Savarkar, the term encompasses three elements. First, Hindutva involved an intimate sense of belonging to a sacred geography. He says, "The first image that it [Hindu-ness] rouses in the mind is unmistakably of our motherland, and by an express appeal to its geographical and physical features, it vivifies it into a living Being. Hindustan means the land of Hindus; the first essential of Hindutva must necessarily be this geographic one."[20] The sense of motherland as object of devotion is passionately described in quasi-religious language: unless one "has come to look upon our land not only as the land of his love but even of his worship, he cannot be incorporated into the Hindu fold."[21]

Second, Hindutva binds all those of the motherland together by a common blood. Hindu-ness binds the diverse peoples of India as a race that shares the blessed inheritance of the Vedic ancestor. Again, Savarkar puts this emphatically: "The Hindus are not merely the citizens of the Indian state because they are unified not only by the bonds of love they bear to a common motherland but also by the bonds of a common blood. They are not only a Nation but also a race-*jati*. . . . All Hindus claim to have in their veins the blood of the mighty race incorporated with and descended from the Vedic fathers, the Sindus."[22] Third, Hindutva asserts that as the biological community devoted to this sacred land, all Hindus share a common culture. "We Hindus are bound together not only by the ties of love we bear to a common fatherland and by the common blood that courses through our veins and keeps our hearts throbbing and our affections warm, but also by the ties of common homage we pay to our great civilization—our Hindu culture. . . . We are one because we are a nation, a race, and own a common Sanskriti (civilization)."[23]

Interestingly, though quite predictably, the common culture that binds all Indians together has deep roots in Brahmanism as contained in the sacred scriptures (Vedas) and passed down in the sacred language (Sanskrit). The reclamation of this religiocultural identity—and its use in cementing political power—rests high on the Hindu fundamentalist agenda. One geographic region is made to correspond with one race, and both are part of a religiously and culturally homogenous civilization engendered and developed by the Brahmins, on the basis of the revelation of the Vedas.[24] The religious basis of Hindu fundamentalism unifies sacred land, common blood, and hallowed culture communicated in a primordial vision expressed by the "Vedic fathers." Satish Deshpande captures the religious basis of this self-affirmation of fundamentalism well: "The basic spatial strategy behind Savarkar's notion of Hindutva is the redefinition of the nation as a sacred space: the claim that the nation is, and ought to be, formed in the shape of a *punyabhoo*, a holy land. This serves to invest the Indian nation with a religious essence—an un-analysable, un-questionable sacred value—that 'outsiders' can never experience or comprehend, and which forever and completely defines 'insiders.'"[25]

In addition to affirming the Hindu self, Hindu fundamentalism came to define itself by denouncing the non-Hindu Other. Who are those threatened by this muscular Hindu fundamentalism? The Muslim and the Christian communities, which by the first quarter of the twentieth century were identified as consisting primarily of Dalits and Adivasis, are most explicitly vilified in Savarkar's theory of Hindu fundamentalism. There is little ambiguity that Muslims and Christians do not find a place in the Hindu fundamentalist vision since "they belong, or feel that they belong, to a cultural unit altogether different from the Hindu one. Their heroes and their hero-worship, their fairs and their festivals, and their ideals and their outlook on life, have now ceased to be common with our own."[26] Even though Muslims and Christians may belong to the common nation and the common race, thus fulfilling two criteria of the Hindutva, they do not meet the third and mandatory criterion because they do not participate in the common civilization. Utilizing the cultural alienation of Muslims and Christians as a marker to discount them from a feeling of being bonded to India, Savarkar also represents them as likely to be more loyal to a foreign Holy Land than their own Fatherland. Because "their Holyland is far off in Arabia or Palestine,"[27] Muslims and Christians cannot really be part of the Indian nation in its Hinduized polity since they are misfits within this civilization, and their allegiance to the nation is divided.

The quasi-religious (yet fully political) vision of Hindu fundamentalism was propounded by Savarkar and transformed into a grassroots movement by a disciplined organization named Rashtriya Swayamsevak Sangh (the RSS, often rendered in English as "National Volunteer Corps"). Keshav Baliram Hedgewar (1889–1940), "one of Savarkar's admirers,"[28] founded the RSS in 1925. Hedgewar was wholeheartedly and singularly committed to realizing Savarkar's vision of a nation-state bound together by sacred land, common blood, and the hallowed culture of the Hindus. Two other contextual factors also contributed to the birth and spread of the RSS. The first was the large-scale Christian mission movements that were especially successful among Dalits and Adivasis. The mass movements, which characterized communities of Dalits converting to Christianity, became such a contentious national issue during the 1920s that the National Christian Council of India, Burma, and Ceylon, meeting in 1928 (chaired by V. S. Azariah, a well-known evangelist-bishop of the Anglican Church), commissioned J. W. Pickett to study the phenomenon.[29] His study, published in 1933, pointed to the "mixed motifs" of conversion of Dalits to Christianity but highlighted the social, psychological, and spiritual benefits that it offered communities oppressed by the Hindu caste system.[30] The fear for Hindu fundamentalists was that religious conversion to Christianity would both weaken the unity of the Indian nation and distance Dalits and Adivasis from the Veda-regulated and Brahmin-controlled Hindu civilization. A second factor affecting the region in the 1920s had to do with the wave of "pan-Islamic mobilization" that was galvanizing Indian Muslims around support for the caliph in the reconfigured Ottoman Empire. This led to Hindu-Muslim rioting in some parts of India. These two contextual developments signified renewed momentum in Christianity and Islam in what was being heralded as a nation united under "Hindu-ness." Hindu fundamentalists "cashed in on a new Hindu feeling of vulnerability"[31] to launch the RSS.

The RSS was envisioned as a ground-up organization that tutored the mind and trained the body. It methodically renewed the Hindu mind by inculcating great pride in the Hindu heritage. This included recollection of the Vedic golden age, stories about the heroic battles fought by Hindu warriors, and the obligations of the religious and moral laws governing personal and social life (dharma) for building up the Hindu nation. The aim of such instruction was to cultivate loyalty and forge attachment to the Hindu nation, which "is identified as the 'living God.'"[32] A duly cultivated Hindu mind also requires a well-trained body to serve the interests of the geographically manifest "living God." The RSS took on the challenge of breaking the myth of the weak and self-effacing Hindu body and creating the reality of a muscular and self-assertive one. The male body was on public display in its objective to show the world that Hindu males were muscular, militant, and united. Martha Nussbaum characterizes this spectacle vividly: "We are shown large masses of men with khaki shorts and caps, carrying long sticks over their shoulder, marching along in what is almost goose steps on their way to a huge quasi-fascist rally that whips up violent sentiments."[33] The physical training of the RSS cadre involved developing a healthy and agile body. This also involved wrestling between individuals, which "gave way to games between opposing teams."[34] The idea was to build strong bodies that could work together to defeat other strong opponents.

Even though Hindu fundamentalism gained some traction from the 1920s to the 1940s, it remained mainly confined to the central regions of India and was less appealing to the Dalits and Adivasis. In fact, it was the more pluralistic and inclusive Indian National Congress, symbolized by Gandhi's generous Hinduism, on the one hand, and Nehru's secular humanism, on the other, that captured the imagination of the Indian masses. Furthermore, because Savarkar was accused of plotting Gandhi's murder by his "close colleague and friend"[35] Nathuram Godse (previously a member of RSS), on January 30, 1948, both the ideology of Hindutva and the organizations he inspired came into intense and expansive disrepute. The RSS was banned briefly in February 1948, and many of its leaders were arrested. Even though Savarkar himself was acquitted of Gandhi's murder, the fiery and backward-looking vision of the Hindu fundamentalists was overshadowed by the secular and Western-leaning vision for Independent India propounded by Jawaharlal Nehru (1889–1964). The future seemed to belong to the pluralistic, inclusive, and secular political pundits of the newly formed Republic of India under Prime Minister Nehru. In his speech to the nation on the granting of India's Independence on August 14, 1947, Nehru makes this explicitly clear: "All of us, to whatever religion we may belong, are equally the children of India with equal rights, privileges and obligations. We cannot encourage communalism or narrow-mindedness, for no nation can be great whose people are narrow in thought or in action."[36] The Indian constitution, which was adopted by the Constituent Assembly on November 26, 1949, and came into effect on January 26, 1950, cemented this inclusive and democratic objective of keeping government equidistant from all the religions of India's religiously diverse population.

Resacralizing the Nation, Desecularizing the Society: Hindu Fundamentalism in the 1980s

The thumping majority for the Indian National Congress in the first election of this new democratic nation (1951–52) for a time swept Hindu fundamentalism under a kaleidoscopic carpet. The nation embraced a vibrant pluralism as it moved toward a harmonious interreligious future. The platform of secularism was Nehru's way of building a consensus that would acknowledge India as a land of many religions while refusing to be allied with any one of them. As Nehru stated it, "We call our State a secular one. . . . It does not obviously mean a society where religion itself is discouraged. It means freedom of religion and conscience, including the freedom for those who may have no religion. It means free play for all religions, subject only to their not interfering with each other or with the basic conceptions of our state."[37] This experiment in statecraft was in contrast to Pakistan, which formed a Muslim state after its independence from the British on August 15, 1947, under the leadership of Muhammad Ali Jinnah (1876–1948).

For the next thirty years the Congress Party ruled India with a broad, pluralistic, and secular vision. This did not preclude Congress from stoking Hindu and Muslim communalism when doing so suited the party's interests, nor did it mean that the Hindu fundamentalist movements had given up on the prospects of capturing power in India. After a four-year setback following India's Independence in 1947, the RSS started growing in India: in 1951 it had 600,000 members, primarily in north India, yet by 1979 this figure reached one million.[38] The vision of Hindu fundamentalism spread from the ground up by the systematic teaching and rigorous physical training of its cadres. Although still mainly confined to the central and northern parts of India, the RSS pushed for more national reach under its second leader, Madhav Sadashiv Golwalkar (1906–73). Following Hedgewar, he worked effectively within the RSS to fuse Hindu ideological content into the emerging conception of the nation-state. This he did by reinscribing the myth that Hindus were a united race of indigenous Aryans, who had lived as one nation under the ancient Vedas, until the British, with the help of the Muslims, invaded this embodied civilization of Hindu-ness. Golwalkar's guiding objective "to see the might of the regenerated Hindu nation" ascend by striking down "the enemy's (the British) hosts (the Muslims) with its mighty arm" was at the heart of the RSS's vision and mission till his death in 1973.[39] Built into Golwalkar's xenophobic ethnonationalism was the conviction that the "Hindu nation" ought to emulate the caste-based social order referred to as the *varnashramadharma* (the universal moral law, *dharma*; lived in conformity to one's caste duties, *varna*; and obligations compatible with one's stage in life, *ashrama*), as promulgated by the Vedas. In such an organic society, as Golwalkar professed in 1956, the fours castes (Brahmins or priests, Kshatriyas or rulers and warriors, Vaishyas or traders, and Shudras or artisans and laborers) would "together" and in "mutual interdependence" constitute a noncompetitive and harmonious social order "that, indeed, is the spirit of our land."[40] In much of Golwalkar's thinking, the Hindu nation was visualized as a cooperative organic body (Hindu nation) rather than a competitive synchronized machine (Western state). Such communitarian cooperation, according to RSS ideologues, would be united by the Vedic ideal of Hindu society arranged along caste lines. In some way, such social and economic intercaste arrangements and interrelationships provided an alternative to the competitive and individualistic Western system of capitalism.

For effective expansion into the entirety of nation-space, Hindu fundamentalists needed a much more multifaceted and much better coordinated organization. Working with the Hindu Mahasabha (Hindu Great Assembly), the RSS gradually birthed organizations based on political, cultural, social, and religious objectives to coordinate and consolidate the workings of a national regime pursuing the agenda of Hindu fundamentalists in search of a nation that embodies Hindu-ness. This complex of Hindutva-identified organizations, called "Sangh Parivar" (syndicate or family of Hindu nationalists organizations), was steadily developed by the RSS (Rashtriya Swayamsevak Sangh). Two major branches of the RSS's multifaceted organization have been especially important in promoting Hindu fundamentalism. The Vishva Hindu Parishad (VHP) was founded in 1964 to work toward uniting Hindu religious sects across the nation; while the Bharatiya Janata Party (BJP) was founded in 1980 to provide a political platform to achieve the Hindu fundamentalists' goal of capturing state and national power. The VHP has systematically unified various Hindu sects into a monolithic Vedic-based and Brahmin-centered Hinduism, even as it has riled up its constituents against the past abuses and present wiles of Christian and Muslim conversion plots. The BJP successfully won local, regional, and national elections during the decade after its formation. It managed to rule India through a coalition (National Democratic Alliance) as early as 1988.

During the 1980s the efforts of RSS combined (Sangh Parivar) began to impact the nation as a whole.[41] "Hindu self-assertiveness," Hindu "militancy," and concerted interest in "eternal Hindu values" came to the fore in India during and after the 1980s.[42] The primordial vision of a Hindu nation asserted itself more and more as the defining aspect of Indian identity. This reemergence of the Hindu fundamentalist worldview was in many ways a reaction stimulated by disenchantment with all that was promised for the nation by Nehru's secularism. T. N. Madan, for example, attributes the rise of Hindu fundamentalism in the 1980s to the failure of the secular nature and interpretation of the constitution. This was, he suggests, accompanied by the false hope espoused by the pundits of secularism under Nehru to build a political foundation for India without the resources of religion.[43] On a larger global canvas, Michael Walzer highlights "the paradox of liberation" in which religious counterrevolutions have resulted from secular revolutions in India, Israel, and Algeria. In India, he traces the manner in which early twentieth-century "archaic religious emotions" combined with fundamentalist conceptions of the Hindu nation returned "twenty to thirty years after Independence" to derail the liberation promised by "archaic national emotions" that fashioned a secular nation.[44] Religious fundamentalism is reborn as an alternative to the secular consensus, which even worked its way into the Indian constitution. Deshpande portrays this aptly by seeing India as a spatial organism. Hindu fundamentalism, he suggests, "attempt[s] to reverse the spatial logic of Nehruvianism in order to return to Savarkar's vision of the nation-space. If Nehru claimed that dams and steel plants were temples of modern India, Hindutva stands him on the head and insists that temples are to contemporary India what steel plants and dams were to Nehruvian India."[45]

The symbolic value of sacred temples in a population moving away from Indian secularism toward a Hindu nation can be detected by the electrifying and unifying role of the Ayodhya temple among Hindu fundamentalists from the 1980s onward. Ayodhya is said to be the birthplace of Lord Rama, the ideal king of the Hindu kingdom, purported to have been born here in 5114 BCE.[46] According to Hindu accounts, a temple to Lord Rama stood in Ayodhya from ancient times until it was destroyed by Emperor Babur in 1558, in order to build a mosque known as Babri Masjid (Mosque of Babur). Since 1853 there have been records of Hindu-Muslim violence at this site in Ayodhya. Although the British worked out a settlement whereby both Muslims and Hindus would share the use of this site, a couple years after Independence Day, Hindu devotees installed an icon of Rama. The ensuing dispute between Hindus and Muslims forced the government to close the site beginning in 1949.

The Hindu fundamentalists have used Ayodhya as a symbol to fuel their resurgence. It started in 1984 with the Hindus forming a committee to "liberate" the birthplace of Lord Rama and build a temple in his honor. Emboldened by a court ruling that opened the site to Hindu worshipers in 1986, the VHP and its activist cadre, the Bajrang Dal (literally meaning "the army of monkeys"),[47] intensified the campaign to take back the temple from the Muslims. Although its saffron-clad activists erected the foundation for a Hindu temple adjacent to the mosque in 1989, they also indulged in partially destroying the mosque in 1990. Then in 1991 the BJP was voted into power in Uttar Pradesh state, where Ayodhya is located. At the end of a concerted religious and political buildup over many months, on December 6, 1992, frenzied Hindu fundamentalists (a combination of violent mobs and belligerent devotees) finished destroying the mosque. Munis D. Faruqui narrates a news report of that event, which depicts the mix of Hindu jubilation and Muslim animosity displayed: "A mob danced around the camera crew shouting, . . . 'Descendants of Babur, go to Pakistan or the graveyard!'"[48] The destruction of the Babri Masjid and the threat to replace this with a Ram Mandir led to clashes between Hindus and Muslims in many parts of India, during which more than two thousand people lost their lives.[49]

The ruin of this historic mosque symbolized a violent and victorious strike against "India's religious diversity and the nation's cosmopolitan character" and a renewal of hope in recasting "the nation in explicitly Hindu terms."[50] This event signifies the resacralization of the nation. Originally seen as located within the individual essence of each Indian, Hindu-ness now became constitutive of the sacred geography of the whole nation. There is, however, a second event that stridently and defiantly exploded the myth of India as a peaceable, nonviolent nation. On May 11 and 13, 1998, under the calculating political watch of the BJP, India tested nuclear weapons in Pokhran. This was not unrelated to the aspirations of the RSS and its many fundamentalist allies to light up the skies with both an affirmative display of Hindu *shakti* (energy or power) and with an alerting spectacle of anti-Muslim strength. The BJP prime minister at the time, A. B. Vajpayee, talked about these nuclear explosions as "a new powerful means to 'silence India's enemies and show India's strength.'"[51] A year after this event, Hassan Gardezi and Hari Sharma unveiled the connection between objectives of the syndicate of Hindu fundamentalists (Sangh Parivar) and the tests that blasted India into the prestigious and formidable nuclear club:

> Obviously, the BJP and all the Hindutva forces in the Sangh Parivar had nuclear testing high on their agendas. . . . The Pokhran tests were meant to produce nothing less than a Hindutva weapon. This became pitifully obvious when the leaders of the Vishva Hindu Parishad (VHP) immediately announced their plan to bring "sacred" water to the Pokhran test site from all the major pilgrimage spots in India, thereby turning Pokhran itself into a pilgrimage site. Lest the intimate link between Hindutva and the Nation be missed by anyone, the VHP even announced a plan to erect a monument to national "virility" at the site of the blasts. The tests, then, were meant to legitimize the absurd notion of imagined glories of India's antiquated past.[52]

The idea of the "Hindu bomb," which made its way into public conversation a couple of months after the May 1998 event,[53] is somewhat of an overkill since it overlooks the long and complex commitment to nuclear development that resulted in Pokhran.[54] Yet it took on added relevance when Pakistan followed close on the heels of India by exploding its own nuclear weapons on May 28, 1998. On that day, Pakistan's Prime Minister Sharif began his televised address by stating, "Today, we have settled a score and have carried out five successful nuclear tests."[55] The rivalry between the self-pronounced Muslim state and the Hindu fundamentalist-prone Indian state had now moved to a new level. Both of these nations, which were one community of communities until 1947, were now armed with nuclear weapons. Apart from the national security advantage that the nuclear bomb gave India in relation to Pakistan, and perhaps even China, the Hindu fundamentalists also regained confidence in their own intrinsic communitarian self. I have already sketched how the lack of inner strength was the reason Hindu fundamentalists gave for the Hindu nation's multiple conquests by the Mughal and British Empires. The Nehruvian secular option after Independence further divided and fragmented the strength of the Hindu nation. The nuclear blast, spearheaded by the political party founded by the Hindu fundamentalists (BJP), was thought to have brought back the pride and strength of a resacralized India.

The destruction of the Babri Masjid to build a temple to Lord Rama in 1992 and the nuclear explosion in 1998 were both part of the vision and mission of the Sangh Parivar, the syndicate of Hindu fundamentalists. Political mobilization, religious self-assertion, and an embodied nation-space of Hindu-ness were crucial drivers in these significant events. The twin and entwined processes of resacralizing and desecularizing the nation flowed from above and spread on the ground. Commenting on these watershed events in their interconnectedness, Nanda writes about how "chest-thumping Hindu Nationalists" had already begun to project the reclamation of the Ayodhya temple and achievement of the Pokhran nuclear bomb as "heralding the dawn of the 'Hindu century.'"[56] She thinks of Hindu fundamentalism as a form of "reactionary modernism": "With the Rama temple agitation and the building of the bomb, the country was making a classical choice of all reactionary modernists: modern technology without the ideals of modernity, 'Vedic sciences' without the ethos of science, biceps with the Bhagavad Gita, and bombs with dharma."[57]

A Strident Hindu Fundamentalism for a New Millennium

The transition from the twentieth to the twenty-first century found the Hindu fundamentalists riding high. With the BJP as the ruling party of the coalition in power from 1998 to 1999 and then again for a full five-year term from 1999 to 2004, there was a surge in confidence that the new millennium would see the Hindu nation grow from strength to strength. There were, of course, some restraints on the Hindu fundamentalists' agenda due to the constraints of governing as part of a coalition, the National Democratic Alliance (NDA). Yet along with using the BJP's patronage to expand the Sangh Parivar's activity on the ground across the country, the Hindu fundamentalists also continued their dual strategy of promoting national actualization along the lines of Hindu-ness and of undermining the security and self-advancement of Muslims and Christians. The Hindu fundamentalism that sprouted and developed in the twentieth century thus became a particularly grave threat to the whole of India as it entered the new millennium. Reflecting its long-standing tendency to employ both the carrot and the stick, Hindu fundamentalism turned its energies in the twenty-first century to both the art of persuasion and the drill of coercion. Let us start with the former.

The persuasive approach employed in the new century accelerated what had begun in the old one. Hindu fundamentalism indoctrinated both unschooled Hindus and misguided religious minorities into the all-encompassing Vedic vision of embracing Hindu-ness in a united Brahmanic nation. Among the lower-caste Hindus, as well as Dalits and Adivasis, this was accompanied by well-orchestrated operations to reembrace robust Brahmanic Hinduism. Among Muslim and Christian minorities, this involved well-strategized campaigns to return from their flawed excursion into the religions of the Other. There was also an attempt to utilize both the grassroots organizations of the Sangh Parivar and state institutions to spread the Vedic religious worldview and way of life among all segments of the nation. The fundamentalists were guided by the logic that a unitary consciousness at the heart of the nation would also lead to a uniform practice among all sections of the community. This involved restoring an essentialized Hindu-Indian identity, which had somehow been lost through capture (colonialism), conversion, (Muslims and Christians), and rebellion (Dalits' and Adivasis' self-assertion). Let me lift up two cases of such a state-sanctioned, if not sponsored, undertaking of system-directed ideological persuasion.

A resolute bid to propagate the Hindu worldview as a science into which Indians needed to be assimilated came from the guardians of university education, which had been permeated by the BJP and its Hindu fundamentalist collaborators. The Indian University Grants Commission, the body that credentials, monitors, and regulates all higher education in India, announced in 2001 that it would fund departments of Vedic Astrology in universities. Based on the certainty that the Vedas provide scientific along with religious knowledge, the commission encouraged the future of science to be founded on the revelatory past contained in religious knowledge (the word *Veda* means "knowledge") transmitted to the Hindu seers.

Noticing this decision, the BBC reported on the success of the stratagem: "More than 30 of India's 200 universities have already said that they intend to take part in the scheme which will provide funding for Vedic Astrology courses. These courses will be held at graduate and postgraduate level, with provision made for research at PhDs."[58] In what was hoped to be the Hindu century, the tactic of targeting the academics in the country and tailoring the production of knowledge was a way of transforming thinking from above. While this undertaking involved an overt national strategy "to declare Vedic teachings, which go back 1500 years before the CE, to contain all the advances of modern science," it also entailed a covert way of pitting a Vedic monistic mode of native knowledge against "the [alien] dualistic metaphysics of Abrahamic religions."[59]

The BJP was not content with only reconstituting university education. It also furthered the "saffronization" of education by getting the main central body of education in India, the National Council of Educational Research and Training (NCERT), to infuse the ideology of Hindutva into the curriculum of central board schools. From 2000 to 2004 the NCERT worked vigorously and methodically to rewrite history and reinterpret science to glorify Hinduism, lionize Hindus, and elevate Vedic knowledge. In order to form a common culture of Hindu-ness, the BJP also introduced Sanskrit at the elementary level in public schools and made provision for the Vedas to be learned from primary to higher levels in the school system. Although this educational agenda was weeded out when the Congress Party regained control of the national government between 2004 and 2014, it resurfaced in a big way after the BJP was elected with an absolute majority in May 2014. A 2015 report by a widely acclaimed collective of public intellectuals and social activists details the following in a one-year evaluation of BJP rule:

> They have insistently, steadily, and with increasing success pushed for (a) the complete overhaul of curricula and syllabi, from primary schools to universities, to reflect a more explicitly "Hindu" worldview; (b) the introduction of passages from Hindu religious and quasi-religious texts like the Ramayan and Mahabharat as compulsory reading in moral education; (c) the demand to ban any academic material, at any level, that is perceived to be anti-Hindu and/ or anti-national; (d) the introduction of practices such as Saraswati puja and Surya namaskar as compulsory rituals in schools; (e) the enforcement of Sanskrit learning and the removal of English as a medium of education.[60]

Such official from-above persuading worked in tandem with the Sangh Parivar's on-the-ground machinery to systematically educate all segments of Indian society into the vision and mission of Hindu fundamentalism. They believed that a bottoms-up approach was necessary to successfully invite people from around the country into their Vedic worldview and Brahmanic way of life. The RSS started village-level educational units to enable teachers well versed in the ideology of Hindutva to live with and instruct Dalits, Adivasis, and religious minorities about their nation, heritage, and civilization. Vidya Bharati, which was inaugurated and is managed by the RSS-VHP coalition, has enrolled at least 3.4 million pupils who were taught by 136,231 teachers in 13,514 schools in 2013.[61] Much of the curriculum and ethos being taught in these schools is guided by the aims and objectives of Hindu fundamentalists: "To develop a National System of Education which would help to build a generation of young men and women that is committed to Hindutva and infused with patriotic fervor, fully developed physically, vitally, mentally and spiritually."[62]

Yet fundamentalism rarely, if ever, relies on persuasion alone. The coercive mechanism of the Hindu fundamentalist syndicate complements its apparatus of persuasion. The object of this concerted violence, as we will see toward the end of the discussion on themes that steer fundamentalism, were Dalits who resisted and Muslims and Christians who deserted the Hindu Word-vision and way of life. In the section that follows, we will see how Hindu fundamentalists have used religion to punish and cajole as well as to admonish and entice.

Religious Themes that Steer Hindu Fundamentalism

So far, in the previous sections, we have looked at how historical context, religiocultural transfiguration, and political aspirations have shaped Hindu fundamentalism. In a complexly interconnected manner, the historical impact of Mughal occupation and British colonization induced an innovative reclamation of Hindu-ness as the heart of Indian identity. Purportedly rooted in the Vedas, the movement sought to resacralize and desecularize the nation. In this section, we focus on three religious motifs that animate Hindu fundamentalism.

Strongly Cultivated Scriptural Identity

The role and authority of scripture is crucial for Hindu fundamentalists. It frames a proper way to see the world and trains one in the proper form of human life. While it is tempting to compare Hindu fundamentalism to its Christian and Muslim counterparts at this point, important differences present themselves. After an overview of the idea of scripture in Hinduism, we will see how Hindu fundamentalists shape that idea to achieve their social and political aspirations.

Hinduism confesses to a broad acceptance of the authority of the Vedas as scripture. Traditionally this has been used as the litmus test to distinguish a Hindu from a Buddhist or Jain. The term "Veda," which means "knowledge," refers to the divine wisdom that unites all Hindus, even if they differ on what constitutes this body of revelation. Hinduism differentiates between two kinds of scriptures. *Shruti* ("that which is heard" eternally) is considered to be primary scripture. It captures the echo of truth ringing eternally across the universe. These early scriptures were transmitted orally in Sanskrit with astonishing accuracy between 1500 and 300 BCE. Believed to be authored by the Divine, they were communicated to the Brahmin sages of the Vedic times. *Smriti* ("that which is remembered" reverently) is considered secondary scripture. It compiles the sacred writing of holy men and women who wrote about the Vedic truth contained within the ancient divine wisdom from their own historical contexts. These writings were compiled between 100 BCE and 900 CE from the religious experience of the first three so-called higher castes. Although familiar with the Sanskrit divine revelation, they were written in vernacular or local languages, often outside the control of the priests or Brahmins. There is also the third category of oral scripture that is rarely accounted for by Hindu scholars. I label this form of scripture *jalpita* ("that which is murmured" locally).[63] These regional and informal sacred narratives are mostly unacknowledged in descriptions of Hinduism since they mainly circulate among the lower rung of the fourth caste and Dalits. Operating outside of the Sanskrit tradition, these unofficial Vedas adapt Hindu religious themes and divine figures into the everyday needs and aspirations of marginalized communities. Murmured scripture, as I see it, refers to a much more open-ended body of oral sacred narratives that sustain various local and marginal Hindu communities. Not familiar with Sanskrit, these sacred murmurings traditionally remained outside the domain of the Hindu dominant castes.

How does Hindu fundamentalism invest such confident authority in this large, diverse, and loose array of divine narratives, strewn across a broad subcontinent and gathered down so many centuries? Three strategies play a role in the Hindu fundamentalist construction of a strong idea of scripture. First is the determined cultivation of the homespun belief that absolute and eternal truth, communicated to the Hindus by divine revelation, has been received and preserved by worthy leaders in its pristine form. The Vedas, technically denoting only the first body of early scripture, was projected as a conceptual canon that contains all truths that can be heard eternally for the welfare of all Hindus. Because the Vedas have no beginning and no end, they are said to contain fixed truths that are universally true. Hindus thus are schooled into believing that the Vedas, which are in the possession of Hindu seers, are indeed divine truth for all humanity. Acceptance of the idea that the Vedas are divinely revealed scripture, *even if one does not know what they contain*, undergirds the fundamentalists' aspirations to Hindu unity. This strong concept of scripture becomes the tool that Hindu fundamentalists use to sift and absorb all other ideas of truth into a Hindu worldview and way of life. Nanda points to the power of such a notional acceptance of the supreme authority of the Vedas to delegitimize the truths of others and absorb differing truth into the eternal truth of the Vedas:

> Hinduism has always turned every new idea under the sun into a derivative of the Vedas by refusing to acknowledge that the new idea is actually saying something new, and that it might actually contradict and falsify the old. The "other" is not recognized in its otherness, but simply interpreted as "saying the same thing" within its own limited context, what the Vedas have always known. The Hindu orthodoxy works not by suppressing the heterodox ideas that contradict its "eternal truths," but by relativizing them to their context and then presenting them as deformed, aberrant versions of the higher Gnostic truths always already contained in the Veda.[64]

The problem for the Hindu fundamentalists is how to focus and channel scriptural authority. To do this they deployed a second strategy: promote an across-the-board unifying sacred narrative. The ritualistic, abstract, and metaphysical character of the *shruti* (primary scripture) did not lend itself to offering a sacred narrative that would knit together Indian history, indigenous peoples, and Hindu culture and religion. Therefore, Hindu fundamentalists revived the functional authority of the *smriti* (secondary scripture), mainly the epics of the Ramayana (200 BCE to 200 CE) and the Mahabharata (300 BCE to 300 CE). The glorious rule, military heroism, and the ancient culture of Hinduism encapsulated in these religious epics were fused with the ongoing aspirations of living as a Hindu nation under the universal truth of the Vedas. They used the idea of the Vedas to authorize a way of life grounded in the epics. In this way, contemporary Hinduism rejoined mythical religious history as India reclaimed the communal vocation of living out its divine purpose in the world. The gradual insistence on the authority of sacred book, according to Romila Thapar, is one feature of a transfiguration of robust Hinduism into the likeness of monolithic and uniform Semitic religions like Christianity and Islam. Writing in the mid-1980s, she says, "The kind of Hinduism which is being currently propagated by the Sanghs [Hindutva organizations], Parishads [Hindu councils], and Sammelans [Hindu nationalist assemblies] is an attempt to restructure the indigenous Hindu religions into a monolithic, uniform religion, paralleling some of the features of Semitic religions. This seems to be a fundamental departure from the essentials of what may be called indigenous Hindu religions."[65]

The choice of selecting and embracing the Ramayana as a unifying national sacred narrative has been part of Hindu fundamentalism from the early days of the RSS. This narrative became the core functional scripture in the hearts and minds of Hindu fundamentalists. Lord Rama as an angry, courageous, and just king, who would usher in an ideal Hindu rule (*rama raja*), was part of the Hindu nationalists' imagination for more than a century. The novel mission to propagate the Ramayana through a nationally promoted television series was a project devised in the mid-1980s. A captivating Bollywood-style production of seventy-eight weekly episodes was launched across the nation in 1987–88. It kindled the imagination and reconstructed the religious-cultural memory of the Hindu masses. Reclaiming Rama (and thus the iconic city of Ayodhya) as an ideal divine king, reestablishing the Hindu dharma as a national religious ideal, and reasserting the muscular strength of united Hindu community—all appeared along the path of the nation's progress into its religiously charged future. Notice the progression here: from the *idea* of the Vedas as authoritative the fundamentalists derived the *functioning authority* of the epics. Observe as well the form in which this scriptural authority has been packaged: the oral scripture of the Vedas gave way to the written scripture of the epics, only to see the latter presented in a more compelling aural/visual/electronic form. Yet throughout the goal has been the scripturalizing of Hinduism, in which the Vedas and especially the epics have been granted a more potent authority as the basis for contemporary personal, social, and political life in India.

A third strategy involved absorbing all Hindus, especially those on or outside the margins, into the negotiated authority of sacred scripture, which would also assure some benefits for those who conventionally were not part of the religious elite. This is a more recent tactic of Hindu fundamentalists. Regional, informal, non-Sanskrit, and fragmented religious myths (what I term *jalpita* or that which is murmured locally) were shrewdly and judiciously incorporated into lived scripture for the entire Hindu community. In an effort for local communities, especially marginal Shudras and Dalits, to reinsert themselves into a unified national narrative, Hindu fundamentalism recasts a divine metanarrative under which all Hindus can find a home and defend a homeland. Marginal identities, local myths, and regional divine figures that were important to Shudra and Dalit communities became recognized, rehabilitated, and harmonized into "the meta-narrative to form one unified [sacred] narrative of Hindutva."[66] This process of creative, even if calculating, negotiation of scriptural authority brings traditionally outcaste communities back into the Word-vision of Hinduism in order to be part of an all-inclusive sacred narrative.

Hindu fundamentalism subsumes these previously marginalized communities into its metanarrative by casting them within the conflict with non-Hindus. These previously marginalized communities are made to fit into a united, if hierarchical, Hindu worldview that grants them a heroic past and glorious future, so long as they see themselves in conflict with non-Hindus. Hindutva credits these marginalized groups with having defended against the previous Muslim invasion while urging them to gird for future battles against Muslims and Christians. Badri Narayan states that while "the tactics used" may differ considerably, the "ultimate aim" remained unchanging: "to both unify them [marginal Shudras and Dalits] under the broader Hindu identity and communalise them by separating them from the Muslims, who[m] they portray as foreign invaders who polluted the pure Hindu culture coming down from the Vedic period."[67]

Hindu Fundamentalism and the Body of God

Western conceptions of religious fundamentalism have generally emphasized mind over body. Hindu worldviews, however, hardly work with notions prevalent in Judaism, Christianity, or Islam. The Jewish, Christian, and Muslim idea of a purposively interventionist or persuasive God, vested in the outcomes of a common human history for the whole world, is not what legitimates Hindu aspirations for social, political, and religious order. Hindus do not invoke god as the one desiring, sanctioning, and promoting the restoration or construction of an ideal place, time, or commonwealth. There does not seem to be a great desire among Hindu fundamentalists to take over the world for the sake of a jealous, powerful, and willful monotheistic deity. Thus establishing the kingdom as worked out in the mind of Yahweh, Allah, or Christ is not a religious idea that incites Hindu fundamentalists.

So how is Hindu fundamentalism different regarding the violent transformation of the world? Hindu fundamentalism, I suggest, takes as its critical point of reference the *body* rather than the *mind* of god. In Hindu philosophy there does not appear to be much preoccupation with getting into the mind of god to determine his or her will in order to execute it obediently in the world. Rather, the objective of Hinduism is for human beings to reflect the harmonious order of god's body in the world. Accepting one's place in this harmonious, even if hierarchical, social body and serving out one's station in life with a sense of duty are crucial to fitting into dharma. Manifesting this harmonious order in the world as persons and communities fulfils a religious calling to mirror the material manifestation of the divine. In order to understand the religious underpinnings of this assertion, we need just a bit more to distinguish it from Christianity and Islam.

Hindu worldviews assume positive ontological relatedness between god as creator and human society as god's creation. In contrast to Christian and Muslim theology, which insists on radical ontological separateness between the creator and human creation, Hindu philosophy maintains that human creation emanates from God. Thus material creation, and human society within it, are part of God. They reflect the same ontic nature. The sacred Vedas profess that the four human castes, rather than being created from any other matter, really emanated from god itself (*Brahma*): from his mouth came the *Brahmin*, from the arms came the *Kshatriyas*, from the thighs came the *Vaisyas*, and from the feet came the *Sudras*. The perfection of god is prudently and purposively manifested in the perfectly ordered human social body, which is nothing other than the manifestation of the body of god. Thus the orderly organization and functioning of human society, as designed by god at creation, is what matters to a fundamentalist Hindu.[68] To follow or live according to Hindu dharma is to fit into the material manifestation of the divine in the world in terms of the harmoniously ordered social communal being. It is worth recognizing that Dalits and foreigners are traditionally outsiders to this well-ordered social body.

This concurrence between God's manifest presence as material body and the onus to order the social body of human community to reflect divine orderliness is what drives Hindu fundamentalism. Anderson and

Damle see this goal at the heart of the RSS's ideology and practice: "The corporate Hindu nation is identified as a living God. . . . The metaphor of Divine Mother is used to describe both the nation and the 'sacred' geography where the nation resides. Both are material emanations from the *sakti* [*shakti*, divine energy]."[69] Notably, the social body in some schools of Hindu thought is an eternal and self-sufficient entity along the same lines that Western schools of thought project the individual self. The words of Deensayal Upadhyaya, one of the guiding philosophers of the BJP, are a good case in point. "In our view society is self-born. Like an individual, society comes into existence in an organic way. People do not produce society. It is not a sort of club, or some joint stock company, or a registered co-operative society. In reality, society is an entity with its own 'SELF,' its own life; it is a sovereign being like an individual; it is an organic entity."[70]

The comprehensive framework of the living divine as a social body, held together by a caste-based system of harmonious unity, operates at individual, community, and national levels. It is therefore not difficult to perceive the logical connection between monitoring, maintaining, and perfecting the individual body and containing, controlling, and perfecting the collective social body. Dipankar Gupta makes this correlation clear: "As the caste theory of personhood is extremely biological, it is not at all surprising that the body metaphor should pervade large chunks of our social life."[71] "Good" Hindus must join in the monitoring and maintaining of order reflective of god's material emanation in both the individual and the social body. Herein lies the violence. Hindu fundamentalists must guard the social body, watchfully defending it against all alien members who wish to enter it in order to pollute this sacred entity by endangering its pregiven order. Gupta uses combat language to describe this dynamic: "According to the caste system, the body is a fortress constantly under siege from forces without and hence all opening must be carefully monitored."[72] The divine social corpus must be fortified against and shielded from all foreign elements that may disrupt its orderly working within the logic of the hierarchical caste system. The threat of Muslims, Christians, and rebellious Dalits must be contained at all cost since they become a threat to the efficient functioning of the dharmic social order. Social and political space is claimed with religious justification for preserving a secure and stable sacred geography in the form of the nation-state. Hindu fundamentalists are thus also in the hard-nosed, often violence-ridden, business of monitoring and transforming the land of Hindustan for the purpose of constituting a Hindu social order. They reclaim geography in service to religious politics. "The crux of this project," as S. P. Udayakumar sees it, "is the somatic, the united 'Hindu' body, and the nuclear weapon is the embodiment of modern-day 'Hindu' strength."[73] In a bizarre twist of logic, good violence that is perpetrated by Hindu fundamentalists is rationalized as a sacred duty in the face of projected bad violence that threatens the harmonious order of Hindu caste-based dharma. And the goal of a Hindu nation-state (Hindudom) justifies the systematic erosion of such collective threats to the ideal social body as it seeks to reflect the divine.

A Violent Irony: Hegemonic Politics and Monistic Philosophy

The idea that all living reality is one and really mirrors the body of God is a central Hindu philosophical assertion. Metaphysically, it means that all reality shares in the same essence as God since there is no "twoness" between creator and creation (*Advaita*, or nontwoness); and ontologically, it means that beyond the apparent differences between the divine (*Atman*, or Soul) and human beings (*atman*, or soul) these are actually different manifestations of one eternal substance. One outcome of such a monistic, or Advaitic, religious worldview is that all human beings, indeed all of reality, are intrinsically one—not just with each other but also with the divine, whose essence they share unequivocally. While philosophically fascinating, this religious worldview needs to be useful if it is to animate everyday individual and social living. And here is where our previous discussion enters the picture. By fitting into one's place in the synchronized social body, the individuals fully realize their unity with the universe. The key term that helps in the transition from the ideal of differentiated monism to a working institution of hegemonic holism is Hindu dharma. *Dharma* is a Sanskrit word that cannot be translated since it has no equivalent in other languages. In sum, it refers to the law that governs the moral order of the universe, of which human beings are a part. Hinduism has often been declared to be a religious vision and pathway that teaches human beings to live, both as individuals and as a community, in sync with such universal dharma. As a consequence, often Hindu scholars and sages will use the autochthonous term "*sanatana* [eternal] dharma" as a substitute for the Western label "Hinduism."

In its most basic and practical form, Hinduism exhorts human beings to bind themselves to this universal moral law (dharma) by following the directives of varna (caste) into which they are born and the ashrama (stage of life) within which they find themselves. The first term, "varna," refers to the social stratum of caste through which one is expected to perform the duties of being a member of the Hindu community. "Ashrama," the complementary other constituent, refers to the stages in one's individual journey that maximizes the possibility to live in accordance with dharma. These stages divide an individual's lifetime into four phases of about twenty years each: *brahmacharya* (studentship), *grihastha* (householder), *Vanaprastha* (forest-dweller), and *sanyassa* (renunciant). Each stage requires attaining goals pertaining to that station in life. *Varnashramad-harma* thus grounds and organizes social ethics and individual morality in the Hindu way of life. Since we are dealing with the religiopolitical and social dimensions of life, and cognizant that the obligations pertaining to the four stages in life are largely ignored in contemporary India, let me confine this discussion to the varna dharma.

Convinced that the human community is providentially divided into four castes, and pushed-out outcastes, the varna dharma formalizes inter-relationships between various segments within a hierarchically stratified social system. Since this is quite unique to Hinduism, Hindu fundamen-talists associate this system of human organization and social interaction with what needs to be preserved as Hindu-ness. The caste system pre-scribed duties, rights, privileges, and restrictions for each of the four caste communities and the outcaste community (Dalits). Each one's caste or Varna is determined by birth, hierarchically ordered, and fixed for life. As we have noticed in the previous section, this organically designed system of varna represents the embodiment of god in the world. It is this social interpretation of *dharma* that governs the duties of all individuals accord-ing to their caste and stage in life, which must be maintained to guarantee that the Hindu social body mirrors the body of the divine.

Although beneficial to the first three castes (the Brahmins, Kshatriyas, and Vaishyas as the head, arms, and thighs of the divine respectively), and less advantageous to the fourth (the Shudras as the feet in this same scriptural reference), this system was ruinous to Dalits, who were outside caste society (finding no place in the body of the divine). Dalits have tra-ditionally had very little wiggle room *within* the daily social operations of the community as a whole since they *served* the system as a whole. Cast out of human society and yet appropriated as slaves of the Hindu caste communities, they were traditionally treated as untouchable and unap-proachable because of their polluted status. One can say that Dalits were the most burdened by the weight of the varna system as it functioned to uphold dharma. Their role was to ensure that the four segments of the caste community fulfill their varna (caste) duties by undertaking to do work that none of the four segments could perform. In a way, Dalits' own avarna (outcaste) duties guaranteed the smooth running of the caste community's performance to maintain varna-based dharma. This ambivalent status (most despised outsiders of the caste system and yet most needed to make such a system function for the insiders) made Dalits exceptionally crucial to the traditional Hindu order. Thus, any dissent from Dalits would uniquely upset the harmonious social rhythm of dharma.

But of course human beings do not live forever in a state of unfreedom. Apart from a host of rebellious moves to escape the burdens of the varna dharma, Dalits had also turned to mass religious conversions over the last five hundred years. The fact that Islam and Christianity were attractive options for Dalits throughout the nineteenth and early twentieth centuries was threatening to the forces of Hindu fundamentalism. On the one hand, Hinduism as a religiopolitical and social system was losing a significant proportion of its base. Muslims and Christians, who were and are as a rule from the Dalit communities, threatened to become potently dangerous to the functioning of the varna-based way of life by bleeding numbers. On the other hand, Muslims, Christians, and Dalits consistently reasserted their own religious and cultural difference from the Vedic-governed and Brahmin-interpreted Hinduism that emphasized varna dharma. No wonder that fundamentalists moved Hinduism away from the ideal of philosophical differentiated monism through the system of hegemonic holism. Varna-resisting Dalits and varna-evading Muslims and Christians were projected as antinational, anticultural, and anti-dharmic by Hindu fundamentalism. An aggressive and conflictual politics based on religious adherence to the Hindu Word-vision and way of life led to a twofold class of people in India: those who embraced Hindu dharma based on varna and those who rejected it. Angana Chatterji puts it well: "Hindu nationalists place Christians and Muslims in the liminal in-between, as concurrently internal and external to the nation as enemy."[74] Enemies needed to be violently attacked and overcome. Violence thus was unleashed on minority communities that resist the pan-Hindu identity. What started in the twentieth century continues into the twenty-first. Such violence directed against Muslims and Christians has been escalating, which demonstrates the fundamentalists' heavy-handed approach to contain, thwart, and crush differences of cultural and religious worldviews. Their ascendency to state and national power has become dangerous to these minority communities in the twenty-first century. Let me point to such a threat in a bit more detail.

Violence against Muslims took on new meaning after 2002. In retaliation for the brutal burning of 59 Hindu pilgrims returning by train from a Hindu ceremony in Ayodhya on February 27, 2002, near Godhra railway station in Gurajat, there was a systematic two-month-long deadly onslaught against Muslims in the state. What made this terrifying for Muslims and worrying for those who supported a pluralistic India was the well-thought-out, methodical, and state-complicit nature of the violence. Paul Brass's characterization of the Gujarat riots as a "program," carried out by the ruling BJP government with Chief Minister Narendra Modi in control, may be an overstatement.[75] Yet one cannot deny the fact that "the Sangh *parivar* (the umbrella organization of all militant Hindu organizations) was well prepared and well rehearsed to carry out the murderous, brutal, and sadistic attacks on Muslim men, women, and children."[76] By March 2002, at the end of this riot, the estimate of casualties ranged between a thousand dead (official) and two thousand (unofficial), spread over thirty cities and towns in Gujarat. Apart from the deaths, which occurred at a ratio of 15 Muslims to every 1 Hindu, nearly 150,000 Muslims were driven from their homes while 500 mosques and Muslim shrines were destroyed.[77] These violent attacks against Muslims put fear and anxiety in the hearts and minds of Muslims in a state that was aggressively working to extend Hindu-ness. The violence was curtailed in 2004 when the Congress coalition was returned to national power. However, state governments that elected BJP to rule still kept a watchful eye and firm grip on Muslims, including in Gujarat.

The twenty-first century has also seen Christians become the target of rape, murder, church bombings, Bible burning, and severe beatings. The killing of priests, raping of nuns, and torching of prayer halls and churches are means to terrorize, denigrate, and threaten the different religious and cultural tradition that Christians represent in India. A relatively new phenomenon, violence against Christians, was determinedly incited by the Sangh Parivar, as reported by a Frontline article in August 2000:

> Reports of attacks on priests, nuns, churches and church-goers in Uttar Pradesh, Haryana, Gujarat, Madhya Pradesh, Orissa, and more recently in Andhra Pradesh, Tamil Nadu and Karnataka, continue to appear in the mainstream and alternative media. In most of these cases there is direct proof of the involvement of organisations of the Hindu Right in the attacks. In the two years since open attacks on the Christian community began, the violence has ranged from

gross forms of physical and mental intimidation to murder. Nuns have been abused, spat at and physically attacked, priests have been beaten, churches have been burnt, groups of students engaged in social work have been brutally beaten.[78]

There were other incidences of violence against Christian missionaries and communities in India following 2000. The worst approached the scale of the Gujarat riots against Muslims. It took place in 2007–8 in the District of Kandhamal, Orissa (the state name was changed to Odisha in 2011). Violence directed against Christians had been building throughout this period, due to the false claim that missionaries were converting local Hindus by force or allurement. On August 23, 2008, violence against the Christians broke out on a massive scale in retaliation for the murder of Swami Lakshmanananda Saraswati. He was a Hindu saint killed in his ashram in Kandhamal district along with three others leaders of the VHP. Seemingly directed by well-established Hindu fundamentalist groups in the region, the violence overtook Christians with frightening furor, amazing efficiency, and impressive coordination. In this eruption of violence, houses and institutions belonging to Christians were burned, churches were attacked, and three women (including a nun) were raped. Reports also indicate that by the last week of August 2008, at least fifty-nine persons had lost their lives and thousands were displaced as their homes and villages were burned and destroyed.[79] In this orgy of mass violence, more than 4,300 houses belonging to Dalit and Adivasi Christians were destroyed, mostly by arson.[80] While not as extensive as the riots in Kandhamal, other violent attacks on Christians have been linked to the activity of the Sangh Parivar, especially in Karnataka, where many churches were burned late in 2008.

Systemic infiltration and systematic violence is an acknowledged part of the spread of Hindu fundamentalism all over India. Commenting on the situation in twenty-first-century India, Kalyani Devaki Menon is unambiguous in her judgment: "The Hindu nationalist movement has existed in various forms for over a century, but at no time has it been more powerful in the sociopolitical landscape of India than it is today."[81] Additionally, surmising the overall object of this movement, she suggests, "It is united by the common desire to purge the country of all 'foreign' (i.e., Muslim and Christian) influences and to establish India as a Hindu nation."[82] Its linkage with state machinery in a country that is more than 80 percent Hindu is alarming.

The Future of Hindu Fundamentalism
as a Pan-Indian, Hyper-nationalist Religion

My reading of Hindu fundamentalism leads me to the conclusion that this violent movement does not have transnational aspirations. Thus, because it does not pose a threat to their security, as does Muslim fundamentalism, it is largely ignored by the Western nations This has clearly not helped the Dalits and religious minorities (Indian Muslims and Christians) that have suffered violence from Hindu fundamentalist forces. Let me be clear: I am not saying that a global network of ideologues, promoters, and financiers of the Hindu fundamentalist project does not exist. They do, especially among nonresident Indians in Europe and North America. For example, a study titled "Hindu Nationalism in the United States: A Report on Nonprofit Groups," released in July 2014, found that between "2001 and 2012, five Sangh-affiliated charitable groups (India Development and Relief Fund, Ekal Vidyalaya Foundation of America, Param Shakti Peeth, Sewa International, and Vishva Hindu Parishad of America) allocated over $55 million dollars to their program services, funds which are largely sent to [Sangh Parivar] groups in India."[83] In response, I suggest that all of this international networking is directed toward consolidating and concretizing a Hindu nation in the sacred geography of India. Therwath puts this point across thoughtfully:

> The careful engineering of a changing Indian and Hindu identity by the Sangh for an expatriate audience can be understood as a strategy devised to spread the Hindutva ideology on a global basis, benefit from an international status, and *perhaps most significantly to channel funds aimed at political and sectarian activism in India.* What . . . the Sangh Parivar's foreign networks bring to light is the emergence of long distant nationalism crafted from the center in a give-and-take relationship where material and symbolic wealth is being exchanged.[84]

In concluding this chapter, let me highlight my assertions. Hindu fundamentalism, as I have described its origins in the 1920s, arose out of the trauma of multiple Mughal and British conquests in India. Recovering a supposedly primordial vision of Hindu-ness rooted in the Vedas, Hindu fundamentalism cultivated a concerted regimen of "hyper-practice of cultural dominance"[85] over the sacred geography of India. The Hindu fundamentalists claim their vision derives from the religious and political ideals of the Vedic seers, and they promote it as part of the diverse sacred narratives treasured by all caste communities. More importantly, Hindu fundamentalists aim to turn the mind and tone the body of Hindus in order to bring the sacred land of India under the varna dharma of unitary Hinduism. Dissenting Dalits and nonconforming Muslims and Christians are in jeopardy. Resistance to this shaping of the Hindu social body to mirror the embodiment of God as a kind of "Hindudom" justifies the use of violence. "Through the sacralization and naturalization of Hindu = India = Hinduization guides Hindu militancy, extremism, and nationalism allied to an organized movement for a Hindu supremacist state in India."[86]

The ascension of the BJP to overall political control of India in 2014 brought with it many anxieties, especially in relation to violence against Muslims and Christians. I must not be accused of treating "the wound of my people carelessly, saying, 'Peace, peace,' when there is no peace" (Jeremiah 6:14). So it is important for me to end with a note of caution by quoting the words of a well-researched report that evaluated the BJP's first year in office: "At least 43 deaths, 212 cases targeting Christians and 175 cases targeting Muslims, 234 cases of Hate Speech have been recorded between 26th May 2014 and June 2015, marking almost one year of the National Development Alliance government of Mr. Narendra Modi. The number of dead is other than the 108 killed in Assam in attacks on Muslims by armed tribal political group."[87] The BJP was voted into power until 2019. These statistics, coming so early in a government supported by Hindu fundamentalists, are not good news for religious pluralist and secularists. Many fear that the dual tactics of persuasion through Vedic education and coercion through violence will succeed in uniting Hindu fundamentalism's short-term goals of "intimidation of the minorities, especially Muslims and Christians" with its long-term one, that of "the Hinduization of the whole of India."[88]

Chapter Five

Competing Religious Fundamentalisms

Fundamentalism is not a religion but a way of being religious.
James W. Jones, *The Fundamentalist Mindset*

For more than a generation we have followed scholars and sages down the rabbit hole into a fantasy world in which all gods are one. . . . But the idea of religious unity is wishful thinking, nonetheless, and it has not made the world a safer place. In fact this naive religious groupthink—call it Godthink—has made the world more dangerous by blinding us to the clashes of religions that threaten us worldwide. It is time we climbed out of the rabbit hole and back to reality.
Stephen Prothero, *God Is Not One*

Introduction

The examples of religious fundamentalism that I described in detail over the last three chapters arose out of religions birthed in varying chronological periods and within diverse geographical regions. Hinduism is the oldest, going back to at least the Vedic period (BCE 1500), and it was born in the subcontinent of India. Christianity grew out of Judaism in first-century Palestine. It is founded on the life (birth, death, and resurrection) and teachings of Jesus (BCE 4 to CE 29), who was acknowledged by his follows to be "the Messiah, the Son of the living God" (Matthew 16:16). Islam, which claims to be the final revelation of God, flowed in some measure from the living stream of Judaism and Christianity. Presented as a corrective to their digressions, Islam's origin is attributed to God's final revelation granted to the prophet Muhammad (570–632 CE)

127

in the Arabian Peninsula. Although their births were separated by time and place, an important finding has emerged from this study. Although they are witnesses to longer and more peaceable histories, Christianity, Islam, and Hinduism transformed into violent movements of religious fundamentalism in the United States, Egypt, and India during the first quarter of the twentieth century. In time these movements also shape-shifted from national to international emissaries of religious violence. No doubt there were a host of cultural, political, economic, and psychological factors that stimulated and strengthened this turn to fundamentalism. I have documented the complex historical factors that were at play as these religions of love, peace, and life for all humanity morphed into key promoters of violation and death. Yet, in each of the chapters that described these respective movements, I kept my eye on the *specifically religious* dimension of fundamentalism.

By way of keeping a watchful eye on religion, this chapter revisits the initial challenge that I set forth in chapter 1. While sorting through various theories that explain contemporary religious fundamentalism (cultural, economic, sociopolitical, and psychological versions), I proposed that theologians and religionists step up to their own plate to claim religious ideas and teachings as defining hallmarks of fundamentalism. I tried to shine a light on the overlooked workings of religion in this thing we call fundamentalism. The focus of my analysis then shifted toward making sense of how religious fundamentalism operates on the ground. Through the next three chapters I described and interpreted three specific religions in three different regions in the world (Christianity in the United States, Islam in Egypt, and Hinduism in India) as they metamorphosed into violent movements. Some history was entwined with some geography as collective and violent movements in these three religions were observed through their birthing and development in the twentieth century and their flowering in the twenty-first. Now, by way of sifting through the elements that we have identified within these specific examples, I return to the matter of analyzing the diverse indicators of religion that were sighted in the unfolding of the modern phenomenon of religious fundamentalisms.

Revisiting the Theological Features of Fundamentalism

A substantial part of each of the chapters on Christian, Muslim, and Hindu fundamentalism was dedicated to identifying and elucidating the distinctive religious themes that propped up their theological/philosophical worldview. In revisiting these religious motifs, I mainly bunch together flowers from the three extensive flower beds that the reader has already gazed upon in the previous chapters. Yet my hope is that even while harvesting from these same gardens, I will be able put together a bouquet of flowers that looks genuinely different and feels uniquely fresh for our purpose of understanding the theological architecture of fundamentalisms.

Unwavering Confidence in and Complete Submission to the Word-Vision

What is religious about fundamentalist movements? First is the idea that a true vision of reality has been gifted to human beings through the divine *Word*, which alone offers a blueprint to bind all of humanity to God and to one another. I capitalize the *W* to capture the absolute nature of this revelation, stored faithfully in sacred scriptures and interpreted truthfully by dependable leaders. Let me refer to this foundational religious leitmotif as unwavering confidence in and complete submission to the *Word-vision*. In the name of a universal and absolute Word-vision, religions assert a comprehensive and conclusive true perspective into what reality is, how the universe fits into this reality, and how all of humanity can live in harmony with what is truly Real. In this sense Word-visions are metacosmic frames of all aspects of life that clue human beings into fullness of knowledge and abundance of life. Word-visions, which are received as divine revelation by religiously privileged human beings, present an overall framework of ultimate knowledge from God to human beings for the well-being of all creation. This universal conceptual framework orders and interprets all things in light of the transcendent dimension of reality and with an eye toward the ultimate meaning of life.

Religious fundamentalisms promote unquestioning belief in their Word-visions. Religions become absolutist when they accept the Word-vision categorically, seeing it as applicable to all historical situations and obligatory for all human beings, irrespective of their own religious persuasions. Fundamentalists assert that this meaning-package is normative since it alone encompasses the whole truth, supplementing or supplanting human beings' fragmented insights. This is the logic that legitimizes claims for the incontestable authority of the Word-vision. Word-visions are "fundamental"; they ground and precede all other forms of human knowing. This is why the proposal that religious fundamentalisms are merely reactive movements to tectonic shifts in cultural, political, social, economic, and psychological currents makes little sense. The primordial dimension of this religious metanarrative, steeped in the revelation of scripture, is palpable in the examples of Christian, Muslim, and Hindu fundamentalism we have seen in this study.

We have already highlighted the manner in which the American imperial mission dovetails with the Word-vision of Christian fundamentalism. Two learnings from chapter 2 may be worth recapping. First, national identity derives from God, and loyalty to the state fulfills scriptural mandate. The One True God's divine vision is perceived to be under threat when the United States of America veers away from the Bible-based blueprint that the fundamentalists believe has been thoroughly embraced in the past. Christian fundamentalism in the United States often wants its politicians to manifest a twofold competency. An authentic leader must be well versed with and profess faith in both the Christian Bible (the basis of the Word-vision) and the U.S. Constitution (the vision for the nation). Second, Christian fundamentalists, who live in this one chosen nation under God, must safeguard against other metanarratives gaining ground as an alternative to the Christian Word-vision. We have noticed how Christian fundamentalism is constantly undercutting the legitimacy of a Darwinian-based evolutionary vision and a pluralism-based secular vision.

In theory, the Word-vision's authority for Christian fundamentalists derives from the Bible's comprehensive and objective truth. In practice, however, fundamentalists learned the value of attaching nationalist emotional appeal to claims of biblical truth as means of motivating their followers to build up the chosen nation. This blending of biblical affirmations with nationalist attitudes helps to fend off nonbiblical countervisions. George W. Dollar weaves together affirmations (cognitive beliefs) with attitudes (emotional dispositions) in his portrayal of Christian fundamentalism. "Historical Fundamentalism," he reminds us in referring to the 1970s and 80s, "is the literal exposition of all affirmations and attitudes of the Bible and the militant exposure of all non-Biblical affirmations and attitudes."[1] Specific to the Christian fundamentalist Word-vision, then, are unwavering belief, vested emotional interest, and determination to combat the growth of competing worldviews.

We also encountered this devotedness to Word-vision as the divine frame for making true sense of the world in our study of Muslim fundamentalism in chapter 3. Its absolutist understanding of God, the world, and humanity are grounded in the Qur'an, complemented by the Hadith, and interpreted by authoritative leaders who cultivate an unwavering constellation of beliefs among the faithful. We can think of the Muslim fundamentalists' Word-vision in terms of three concentric circle. At the center of the circle stands the affirmation that "the Qur'an is the literal word of God to Muslims."[2] For Islam the Qur'an, hailed as "the miracle,"[3] represents the full and final revelation of God's will just as the miraculous incarnation of Jesus as God-in-flesh does for Christians.

In the second circle are the Hadith, collections of the sayings and actions of the prophet Muhammad. After admitting that "traditionalists" and "fundamentalists," in spite of "profound" differences in interpretations, "meet in their acceptance of the Qur'an,"[4] Seyyed Hossein Nasr goes on to attest to the fact that "devout Muslims . . . never forget the content of the Hadith."[5]

The third concentric ring around the Qur'an and the Hadith is the authoritative circle of interpreters of the Qur'an and Hadith. As discussed in chapter 3, this involves Islamic interpretations pronounced by a powerful band of male imams, muftis, or mullahs who claim to have authority to determine correct interpretation of true Muslim belief and behavior in today's changing and confusing world. In transnational movements of Muslim fundamentalism, "a variety of answers by a variety of different sources," including "self-taught preachers" and self-appointed resistant leaders, have joined "established sources of religious authorities," such as religious scholars and religious courts, in a zealous effort to define Muslim belief and practice in chaotic times.[6] Scholars who interpret Muslim fundamentalism as a violent cultural, social, and economic movement alone have ignored the deep-seated claim of religion's primordial vision and the concerted power of its leaders to enforce its absolute authority over the lives of its faithful.

The Muslim fundamentalist Word-vision displays another twist: the delegitimizing and even prohibition of other forms of communication like music, art, and song. Thus, to assert a Word-vision rooted in the revelatory words of the Qur'an and the Hadith seemingly requires the violent destruction of creative forms of expression that might foster competing belief systems. Karima Bennoune documents the systematic way in which fundamentalists in Pakistan, Algeria, and Afghanistan demolished theaters where music and dance were performed, often by bombing innocent men, women, and children. In these contexts "enjoying the arts" became a "life-threatening endeavor."[7] Because Muslim fundamentalists were convinced that "it is the devil who makes music," they actually felt justified in their mission of killing artists. Mohamed Ali Allalou, an Algerian artist, puts it graphically: "They [fundamentalists] killed people, they killed artists, because they sing about love, wine, friendship. They assassinate, they cut throats, they cut throats, *ooh la la*."[8] Faithful submission to the Word-vision implied being confined to the medium of writing and speaking, which further privileged Arabic. Other forms of creative expression were dangerous and represented the deceptive charms of modernity and the West; they threatened to undercut the sole authority of the divine message given for the well-being of those who submit to the Word of Allah.

What was remarkable about our discussion of Hindu fundamentalism in chapter 4 is how it also makes full use of the concept of a comprehensive and complete Word-vision to ground Hinduism's historical imagination and mission. Most theorists of religious fundamentalism tend to associate the idea of an authoritative Word-vision only with Judaism, Christianity, and Islam, religions referred to as "people or family of the book."[9] However, I have argued that Hindu fundamentalism cultivates an idea of scriptural orthodoxy among its faithful so as to offer them an authoritative metanarrative with which to bind together a powerful community.

The notion of Word-vision is deeply entrenched in the philosophical memory of Hinduism. In fact, my own use of the term "Word-vision" is influenced by the Hindu concept of Divine darshana (Vision), which refers to the inner-eye's viewing of the Real, gifted to the ancient Seers (the see-ers of the Divine and earthly reality in their true nature and relationship). The metanarrative of Hindu fundamentalism claims to be the primordial vision preserved in the Vedic scriptures. These ancient oral scriptures provided Hindus with the universal principle of order (dharma), which governs all reality and to which human action must conform. Hindu fundamentalists thus insist on the primal (rather than reactionary) character of such a Word-vision.

Utilizing the idea of a primordial divine metanarrative, which tapped into a strong conviction for the authority of the Vedas, Hindu fundamentalists gradually weaved in other forms of regional Hindu scriptures that venerated aggression and legitimized violence. The desired result was to incorporate a more muscular self-image for the whole Hindu community and imagine a more militant collective representation of the Hindu nation. This is why even today the Hindu Word-vision is pitted against the pluralistic vision. The Hindu fundamentalists hope that all Indians, irrespective of their religious identities, will be absorbed into the primordial Hindu vision; the secular pluralists aspire to an India made up of a mosaic of communities living from the richness of their different cultural and religious narratives. With the massive victory of the Hindu nationalists' BJP, backed by the ideological and organizational backing of the RSS, in 2014 the Word-vision of fundamentalism made significant inroads into India. There is thus real danger that the "sustained effort to miniaturize the broad idea of a large India—proud of its heterodox past and pluralist present—and to replace it by the stamp of a small India, bundled by a drastically downsized version of Hinduism,"[10] is gaining momentum and multitudes.

There are two things to notice about the Word-visions of Christian, Muslim, and Hindu fundamentalists. First, they demonstrate little consistency and commonality with regard to what contents of scripture and tradition constitute the Word-vision. Fundamentalists are much more concerned with blind obedience and unwavering assent to the absolute authority of the divinely revealed Word-vision. In spite of the absolutists' claims for scripture as a whole, there is much selective choosing and vested fusing of these components in putting together the Word-vision. Such creativity is portrayed nicely in Jakobus M. Vorster's discussion on the collaborative working of "scripturalism" and "traditioning." Word-visions are metanarratives forged by weaving the warp of more historical and less literal narratives (traditioning) with the woof of ahistorical and literal ones (scripturalism).[11] A fundamentalist mind-set allows the present to be saturated completely by the mythical surety of the past in order to slant completely devoted adherents toward submitting to the Word-vision as the only genuinely true worldview. Second, to be fully authoritative the Word-vision must also tug at the heart. The "emotional and inspirational qualities"[12] of divine metanarratives propel a singular and zealous connection between revealed sacred text and roused sacred heart among religious fundamentalists. Intellectual assent to the text's authority must be cemented by an emotional resonance with the text. Word-visions, though, must also establish emotional bonds with the community of believers, whose heart is invested in their land and their sense of collective identity.

Fixed and Straightforward World-Ways

Upholding and cultivating unwavering belief in a comprehensive and complete Word-vision is one of the theological ingredients that make up fundamentalisms. Strong convictions and emotional attachments must also result in actions; to thrive, fundamentalism must move from the head and heart to the feet and hands. This leads to the second religious motif emerging in all three movements of religious fundamentalism that we analyzed: religious fundamentalisms impose purportedly fixed and seemingly straightforward *world-ways* distilled from the absolute Word-vision revealed to human beings by God. Thus the religiously committed and compliant are charged with living out the ethical implications of the divinely revealed Word-vision in the real world.

Religious fundamentalisms offer rigid and uniform ways of living in the world. Because these ways of living are authorized by the Word-vision, they become mandatory for the faithful. The supposed simplicity of this way of life can be appealing in a fraught and fragmented world. In a world overwhelmed by a giddying diversity of lifestyles and a confusing plethora of ethical choices, religious fundamentalisms carve out a surefire pathway to live the moral life in all its minute detail; they promise wholeness, justice, and liberation for those (s)elect ones suffering a variety of perceived discriminations for living out these God-ordained practices in a God-forsaking world.

The Christian fundamentalism we observed is very concerned that "the moral majority" in the United States can no longer live out the lifestyle of "the chosen ones" in a changing world where modern and secular ideas are growing rapidly and effectively. Opportunities must be created—through struggle, when necessary—for the "biblical" lifestyle to flourish. Tim LaHaye, a godfather among American fundamentalists, sees "an organized attack on this way of life" from "Secular-Liberal-Humanists."[13] Three major shifts, beginning in the latter years of the last century and continuing into this one, are most feared by Christian fundamentalists. First is the attack on the complementary roles carved out for women in families where the husband is head of the household.[14] The success of the family and, by means of this, the thriving of the community and nation depend on this divinely ordained relationship between man and woman. Christian fundamentalists see the patriarchal way of life between a compliant wife and a husband who serves as God's proxy over her as threatened by modern movements that advocate the freedom of women to think and act independently.

The second and third perceived attacks on the Christian fundamentalists' way of life also pertain to the family: same-sex marriage and abortion. Just as men are undisputed heads of the household, so are sexual relationships only to take place between a man and a woman, and women are to cooperate with men to procreate and multiply the race by bearing children that are conceived within such relationships. The struggles of Christian fundamentalism to influence political leadership and legislative decisions in the United States have been directed toward defining marriage as only being between a man and a women and limiting the access of women to abortion. Thus Christian fundamentalists are concerned with a much more clear-cut conventional way of life for the whole nation. In their view, freedom for women, expanding gay rights, and reproductive rights are three currents in contemporary America that have become a threat to a Bible-based and Christ-inspired way of living that secures and extends the Christian lifestyle in the United States. Beverly LaHaye joins her husband in asserting that the future for Christians is threatened by the "anti-marriage, anti-children and anti-man feminism" spirit of the age.[15]

Violence against abortion providers, who make possible another way of living perceived to be contradictory to the biblical idea of morality, has been systematic and widespread. Between 1995 and 2014, in addition to about ten deaths,[16] "there have been a total of 5,147 violent incidents recorded in US abortion clinics . . . [that] include 922 reported incidents of vandalism, 663 anthrax or bioterrorism threats, 354 stalking incidents and 204 reported death threats."[17] Not all violence against U.S. abortion providers derives from Christian fundamentalists in the United States. However, the fundamentalist rhetoric against such public provisions has been vitriolic, even as it is entwined with religious symbols and propped up by biblical warrants. Christian fundamentalists have also perceived that making women responsible for their own reproductive health signals societal shifts toward female empowerment and away from patriarchal authority. That is why safeguarding the Christian family seems to require them to violate the rights of the women, even to the point of violence. My intention is not to place the blame for abortion-related violence solely at the doorstep of Christian fundamentalism. After all, respect for the sacredness of life, which must include the life of the unborn, is a theological position shared by many Roman Catholic, mainline Protestant, and Orthodox Christians in the United States. I am merely pointing to Christian fundamentalism's need to carefully monitor the minds and bodies of women in order to maintain its pro-marriage, pro-children, and pro-man way of life.

Muslim fundamentalism, as we have detailed, is even less ambiguous and even more instructive about the "world-ways" that arise from the revealed Word-vision. A categorical Divine pathway (Sharia) that stitched the Qur'an with the Hadith is presented as an alternative to the secular highway that Muslim-majority nations have traveled in their tainted bond with modern Western powers. Islam, as presented by al-Banna, brought God's vision home to the earth. It demanded "a state, a place of belongingness, a nation and a government" even as it mirrored "the record of creation, of God's power, His mercy and justice."[18] According to Muslim fundamentalists, the Sharia contains the divine vision of "the practical way to reach the glory of Islam and to serve the welfare of the Muslims."[19] The welfare of those who submit (Muslims) cannot be achieved by following human legal and political wisdom. It can only be attained by submitting to Allah's legal prescriptions contained in Sharia, which alone can guarantee a righteous and just human society. The Muslim fundamentalists' project is to make the divine law a possibility on earth. Talk of submission to God must be translated into concrete actions; individuals must conform to a social morality prescribed by a rigid, even if shrewdly interpreted, Sharia.

Establishing an Islamic way of life, alleged to be grounded in the Qur'an and guided by the Hadith, is an important objective for Muslim fundamentalism. The constructive objective of Muslim fundamentalism in various contexts across the world involves instruction and formation of the faithful to submit to the ethical demands of the way of life prescribed by the Sharia. In madrasas the children and youth are coached and formed into a strictly Muslim way of living.[20] Muslim fundamentalist movements, however, aim for much more; they seek to capture the state as well. This ensures a more centralized and systematic way to enforce adherence to the world-ways prescribed by the Sharia. Since the rise of the Muslim Brotherhood in Egypt, the world has seen a concerted effort to resist religious pluralism and establish explicitly Muslim national governments. Yet in the form of the Islamic State we have also seen the ambition to spread fundamentalist Islam around the world in a restored caliphate. Recasting the words of the Iranian sociologist Chahla Chafiq, one might say that Muslim fundamentalism "ideologizes religion to create a totalitarian political [and social] platform."[21] In other words, Muslim fundamentalism creates watertight world-ways, nurtured in educational institutions and embodied in religious and national institutions throughout their territories. This fundamentalist Muslim way of being in the world, and especially its ambition to spread itself, is what unites such disparate movements as the Muslim Brotherhood in Egypt and Wahhabism in Saudi Arabia with Al Qaeda, Taliban, Lashkar-e-Toiba (Pakistan), Islamic State (IS), and Boko Haram (Nigeria).

Those who resist conforming to the Sharia most certainly need to be censured and reprimanded. The objective to publicly and violently discipline those who do not submit to the Divine law is geared toward coercing compliance. Such enforcement is done through a formidable religious and political system bestowed with the moral duty to monitor and punish those who breach Divine world-ways. This theater of punishment set up by Muslim fundamentalists to "shock and awe" has exhibited the rawest forms of violence on the world stage during the twenty-first century. Beheading is an example. A well-established nation-state (Saudi Arabia) and newly declared caliphate (IS), both claiming to execute justice based on Sharia, have used the spectacle of beheading as a form of punishment. "Under Sharia law, there are no crimes that specifically call for decapitation, but it is one of a range of execution methods that may be employed, along with stoning or hanging."[22] Yet these regimes have made the practice of beheading a key part of using violence in the name of applying Sharia. The Western governments escalated "the war against the Islamic State" because of the "widespread revulsion at the gruesome beheading of two American journalists" in August (James Foley) and September (Steven Sotloff) of 2014. "Yet, for all the outrage these executions have engendered the world over, decapitations are routine in Saudi Arabia. . . . In fact, since January [2014 till October 2014], 59 people have had their heads lopped off in the kingdom, where 'punishment by the sword' has been practiced for centuries."[23]

Quite apart from the ruthlessness of beheading, Muslim fundamentalists violently monitor and penalize a whole host of actions and practices that they consider *haram* (forbidden). Muslim fundamentalism keeps a vigilant eye on what men and women wear, what they eat and drink, what they watch and listen to, where and for what purposes women appear in public, what sexual relationships are practiced outside of marriage, and what threats may be brewing against a strong regime of Sharia-proclaiming men. And the retribution for veering from what is *halal* (permitted) is harsh and violent, even deadly. The *quality* of Muslim fundamentalist justice can be seen in such punishments as hanging, crucifixion, public lashing, amputation of hands and/or feet, and stoning; yet the overall *quantity* falls mercilessly on disciplining and punishing Muslim women.

Through their twisted interpretation of Sharia and against the spirit of the Qur'an and the example of the prophet, Muslim fundamentalists deny women the right to take formal education, impose strict laws on veiling when women leave the house, and perpetuate a Muslim family law developed in the Middle Ages. They feel a constant need to "place females under the authority of male kin, and wives under the control of husbands,"[24] and to punish them when they flirt with unconventional ways of life (modern education, Western dress, outdoor sport, work outside the home, and the like). Bennoune is blunt in her indictment of the fundamentalists' aim to control women even as they seek to promulgate and legalize Sharia: "Muslim fundamentalists aim to control the womb, the unmentionable areas of the body—what the Qur'an class 'the unseen parts.' Sometimes those are even said to include the faces of women. Fundamentalists also seek to restrict women's movement, space, being."[25] Bennoune is also meticulous in documenting horrendous violence against women in Muslim-majority countries where fundamentalists "want to police and judge and change behavior, appearance, and comportment of people of Muslim heritage, . . . sharply limit[ing] women's rights, though this is sometimes couched in the soothing language of protection and respect and difference."[26] She also catalogs the various ways in which these strategies of Muslim fundamentalists are courageously and creatively resisted by individual and collective women who yearn for freedom, liberty, and life.[27]

Hindu fundamentalism may not have as reliable a sense of all that constitutes the revealed Word-vision of the Vedas. That does not mean, however, that promoters of fundamentalism in India do not know the practices that such a Divine vision mandates for living in their world. Hindu fundamentalists, as already demonstrated, are keenly vested in reinforcing specified ways of living in the world, reflecting their understanding of the ideal social organism constitutive of the body of the Divine. Theirs is not a scheme of being directed by the *mind or will of God*, as understood by Christian and Muslim fundamentalism. Rather, Hindu fundamentalism pays much more attention to the necessity of each human being fitting into the harmonious *body of God*. The emphasis lies in the right manner by which one acts as an individual body (human person) through fitting into the divinely ordered social body (human society) so as to reflect the integral body of God. For Hindu fundamentalism, unwavering adherence to obligatory world-ways trumps unquestioning assent to revealed Word-vision. Contemporary Hindu fundamentalism maintains a keen scrutiny on correct behavior, while turning a lazy eye toward dogmatic belief.

Hindu fundamentalists have passionately committed themselves to a set of fixed world-ways for each human being based on that person's caste and gender. Traditionally such caste-centered and gender-based dharma, including the ostracizing of Dalits and containment of women, was locally managed effectively within self-contained communities. Exclusion based on caste and suppression based on gender were successfully administered within self-governing local communities. Within the logic of complementarity, certain ways of living in the divinely organized world were assigned to certain castes and specific genders. Hindu fundamentalists from the early twentieth century, however, reimagined the nation-state as the theater for working out a pan-Hindu dharmic community of communities.

The election of the Hindu Nationalist BJP as the governing party of India from 1998 to 2004 and then again in May 2014 was a dream that became reality for Hindu fundamentalism. It could now protect and promote an organic sociopolitical body within which the prescribed caste-based and gender-regulated world-ways can flourish through a combination of tough legal measures and brutal lawless means. The former is done through a highly organized network of politicians, bureaucrats, and religious leaders bound together by the ideology of Hindutva. The latter is carried out by passionate and violent local foot soldiers who discipline and punish all those who are a threat to the well-ordered and hierarchical Hindu way of life. Muse and muscle work together, even if they are not conspiring with each other as functionaries of Hindutva. On their way to consolidating a Hindu nation, Hindu fundamentalists have adopted three strategies targeting specific segments in India for special scrutiny and exemplary violence: rooting out religiocultural practices considered anti-Hindu, fencing in religious adherents to prevent crossover into non-Hindu religions, and keeping women within their proto-Hindu traditional place. Let us turn our attention to each of these three strategies as they operate in India today.

First, Hindu fundamentalists are united in stridently stamping out practices that are considered anti-Hindu and exist within non-Hindu (Muslims in particular) and semi-Hindu (Dalits and Adivasis in particular) communities. One curious example of purging India of anti-Hindu practices is eliminating beef eating. Yet eating beef is part of the way of life of Dalits and Adivasis in India. Even though the media has interpreted banning cow slaughter as being anti-Muslim, since they have a large stake in the business of meat sales and tanning leather, one must not overlook the fact that Dalits have conventionally been treated as being impure also because they ate beef and cured the hide of cattle. While the protection of the cow has been written into the Indian Constitution from 1949,[28] the expansion of the idea that this must be a yardstick to measure the religious character of the nation-state is certainly a hallmark of Hindu fundamentalism since it assures Hindus of the purity of the social body's practices. It is thus not surprising that "24 of the 29 states in India have imposed restrictions and penalties of varying degrees on the slaughter of cows and other bovine cattle."[29] This has led to bold legal measures in Hindutva-inspired state governments to impose "a beef ban, making slaughter of cows and possession of beef a criminal offence."[30] Kancha

Ilaiah reports that the pro-Hindu world-ways promulgated by numerous states were emboldened by a BJP-led national government after the 2014 elections; he highlights the violation against other ways of life, especially against the Dalits and Adivasis: "Large number of tribes, Dalits and Backward Castes have a historical food culture of beef. The anti-beef agenda has been in the Brahmanical fold. . . . If beef eating is bad for Brahmins or Baniyas or certain upper castes, then the state is imposing that on the rest of the society. So the state is actually becoming a theocratic state. This is how the RSS ideology is being pushed [onto the nation]."[31]

The forcible left hand of violence is also unleashed by the foot soldiers of Hindu fundamentalism to warn communities not to indulge in such anti-Hindu religiocultural practices. Two well-publicized incidents have shocked the world and yet effectively warned nonconforming Indians about how serious an offense consuming beef is in a nation controlled by Hindu fundamentalists. On September 28, 2015, "a 50-year-old man, Mohammad Akhlaq, was beaten to death and his 22-year-old son severely injured . . . in Uttar Pradesh's Dadri, allegedly by residents of Bisara village, after rumours spread in the area about the family storing and consuming beef."[32] A few months later in another state (Jharkhand), "Mazlum Ansari, 32, and Imteyaz Khan, 13, . . . [were] allegedly lynched and hanged from a tree by a mob in Balumath."[33] The lynching and public hanging emphasize that this punishment was also intended to serve as a warning that anti-Hindu practices would be dealt with ruthlessly by Hindu fundamentalists building a Hindu nation. Notice the cooperation, then, between two developments. On the one hand is the well-planned-out ban on beef, although beef is important to Dalit, Muslim, and other non- or semi-Hindu communities. On the other is the less reflective mob violence toward those simply suspected of consuming or supplying beef. Together these two phenomena transform figments of an imagined Hindu organism into the cohesive regions of a sociosacred geography in which Hindutva reigns.

Second, Hindu fundamentalists impose tight controls on backsliding or forward-gliding Hindus (esp. Dalits and Adivasis), preventing them from freely embracing the Word-vision and world-ways offered by non-Hindu religions (esp. Islam and Christianity). Hindu fundamentalism uses religious reasoning to secure a dharmic community of communities. In order to do this they need to stem the growth of Muslims and Christians on the one hand and prevent the crossover of rebellious Dalits and Adivasis from Hinduism to non-Hindu religions on the other. The threat of expanding Muslim and Christian communities and deserting Dalits and Adivasis must be contained at all cost since they become a threat to the efficient functioning of the dharmic social order.

Thus far much of the legislation placing hurdles on religious conversion has been introduced at the state level. Such state-level interventions were needed to contrive impediments for the fundamental right enshrined in the Indian Constitution, which states that "all persons are equally entitled to freedom of conscience and the right freely to profess, practise and propagate religion" (article 25.1).[34] Already over the last few decades six states (Maharashtra, Madhya Pradesh, Chhattisgarh, Odisha, Gujarat, and Himachal Pradesh) have passed such constraints on religious conversion through what is absurdly termed the "Freedom of Religion Acts." It is dangerous that all these acts make the State responsible for attesting to the validity of conversion. In an unprecedented move the Central Government led by the BJP explored putting in place an anticonversion bill for the whole country. Rajnath Singh, Union Home Minister, said in April 2015 that "the unanimous enactment of an anti-conversion law would be the best way to put an end to oft-repeated questions on communal harmony and 'ghar-wapsi'"[35] (literally meaning "homecoming," referring to Hindu reconversion efforts that supposedly bring Muslims and Christians back to their original Hindu faith). He added, "No country can countenance a change in its demographic profile through conversions." Apart from manifesting the amazing lack of confidence in the power of Hinduism to hold its own, this comment also expresses Hinduism's need to maintain a stable and secure communal order.

While the elitist Hindu fundamentalists worked resourcefully to draft and introduce legislation to ring-fence Dalits and Adivasis within the Hindu fold by making religious conversion cumbersome, the foot soldiers of fundamentalism unleashed violence against Muslim and Christian communities. I have already described the rise in violence in India against Muslims and Christians. As of this writing there has been no letup in violence against these religious minorities during BJP rule. One study by the Evangelical Fellowship of India estimates that "more than 40 people have been killed in 600 violent attacks on Christians and Muslims in India" between May 2014 and March 2015.[36] Taking note of the scores of violent attacks against Muslim and Christian communities, places of worship, and religious leaders, John Dayal has thus evaluated BJP's actions against minorities: "The pungent mix of supremacist religious and nationalist rhetoric, and the accompanying demonizing [of] the Muslim and Christian minorities raising the bogey of demographic threat to Hinduism in

India, polarized the electorate. The obvious hatred was against Muslims. Much of the ground action was against the Christians."[37]

Third, Hindu fundamentalists strive to keep women from straying too far from the traditional and stable Hindu order. Other ideologies and theologies must not derail the quintessential role women must play to keep reproducing a caste-based Hindu society. Emphasizing the difference between "Bharat" and "India" is a useful means of valorizing the role of women in the view of Hindu fundamentalists. "Bharat" is the indigenous term for the nation-state, preferred by Hindu fundamentalists because it is rooted in Hindu ways of life, as different from "India," the meaning of which has been sullied by Western, modern, and pluralist ideas. Mohan Bhagwat, chief of the Rashtriya Swayamsevak Sangh (RSS), confidently stated in January 3, 2013, that "rapes are an urban crime shaped by westernisation, and are not a matter of concern in rural India where traditional values are upheld." In a move to find honor and respect for women in a Hindu dharmic order, Bhagwat went on to decry "India" and idealize "Bharat." Tapping into a long nationalist tradition of referring to "Bharat" as the land of Hindu-ness in opposition to India as infiltrated by westernization, he was suggesting that rape happens when Hindu-ness is forsaken for foreign values and culture. Bhagwat went to declare that "Indian values and culture should be established at every stratum of society where women are treated as 'mother.'"[38]

This lifting up of motherhood as the paradigm for the Hindu way of life for women was not unintended. "The ideals of motherhood and women's role as mother intersect with the nation-building process" by bearing children who will "become the citizen soldiers ready to defend the nation," "socializ[ing] future warriors by passing on culture, rituals, and nationalist myths to the next generation," and "shaping political rhetoric aimed at bringing women into the nationalist conflict."[39] Women must be assured of the bonds of marriage and the badge of mother within a patriarchal family and kept within the bounds of the Hindu community. Women are needed to keep the complementary order of dharma going eternally. Education for girls and women pursuing public work has been encouraged by Hindu fundamentalists. Significantly, however, "differences between men and women were emphasized in defense of the existing lower status of women"[40] so that "westernized 'liberation' was irrelevant within the traditional [Hindu] family structure," which lionized the "dutiful" wife and "self-sacrificing" mother.[41]

Let me make two comments on this discussion of religious fundamentalisms' grounding in purportedly fixed and apparently clear-cut world-ways. The first stresses the inextricable link between orthodoxy and orthopraxis. Promise of shelter, consolation, and healing are important motifs in the Word-vision of religious fundamentalisms, but they are tied securely to ways of living in the world. Fragmented, exploited, marginalized, restless, and wrecked individuals and communities appear to seek out such professedly simple, clear-cut, and empowering expressions of living out their deep-seated convictions. This assurance of providing a divinely given way of life to accompany the divinely revealed vision of reality is what religious fundamentalists utilize to recruit and retain their members. Fundamentalisms thus offer a curative way of life to communities struggling to make sense of the modern world. Interpretations of fundamentalism that focus on it as a belief system often miss this fact. For the fundamentalists this positive therapeutic effect of practicing one's religion justifies short-term destructive aggression. Violence simply creates a space in which to live one's own way in a hostile world.

Second, fundamentalisms are inevitably masculine and patriarchal. Although drawing from her research in Muslim-majority countries, Bennoune is willing to offer a more global assertion when she says, "Subordinating women—in the family, in the street, in the bedroom—is central to most fundamentalist society around the world."[42] This patriarchy requires violence. First, it requires the systemic violence of laws and social mores that enhance male freedom while shrinking its female counterpart. Second, it requires the day-to-day violence used to control women in fundamentalist communities, making them conform to patriarchal expectations and curtailing expressions of independence and resistance. The former watches out for attempts to promote lifestyles alternative to traditional marriage and the secular socialization of children. The latter tries to limit the spread of those women's rights that threaten the authority of men in the family and the church/ummah/Hindu nation (family of God).

Global Order in Conformity to an Absolute Word-Vision and in Compliance with Fixed World-Ways

Strong-headed belief in an absolute Word-vision (as if this picture of reality were unsullied God-speak), craftily fused with strong-armed enforcement of unbending world-ways (as if it were possible to translate transcendent vision into immanent practice), would be less harmful if this tight pact of faith and action were not meant to be played out on the world stage. Religious fundamentalism has become much more dangerous over the last several decades as it has projected its ambitions onto a global screen. The world stage is the platform on which the religiously vested Word-vision and its allegedly clear-cut world-ways come together to replace human dominions with God's reign over the whole of humanity. We can see a third characteristic common to Christian, Muslim, and Hindu fundamentalisms: they take as their object the establishment of a global order in which their respective Word-visions can dictate the world-ways of all humanity.

Religious fundamentalisms envision the whole human race as the focus of the Divine vision and all of human history as the theater of such saving world-ways. In other words, fundamentalists aim to control and govern the world for a kingdom-seeking and kingdom-forging Divine being or principle. Religion's propensity to operate out of such a divinely given imperial vision becomes invaluable to violent movements that want to claim and shape the world. Explanations of fundamentalism as movements of *resistance* (whether that be cultural, political, social, and psychological) fail to see that they are better understood as movements of global *mission*. Undoubtedly "all of these religions [Christianity, Islam, Hinduism, and Buddhism] influence the politics of their members."[43] But more importantly the religious fundamentalisms that we have examined also strive to shape the politics of the world. It is to this expansion of a divine Word-vision seeking to impose fixed world-ways on the whole world that I wish to turn our attention.

For Christian fundamentalism, saving souls and controlling bodies go hand in hand. But this religious worldview is vested in much more than just individual souls and bodies. Apart from encompassing communities, bodies of land and nations were brought under the province of God. The universal dominion of the Lord is grounded in Psalm 22:27–28, which proclaims, "All the ends of the earth shall remember and turn to the LORD; and all the families of the nations shall worship before him. For dominion belongs to the LORD, and he rules over the nations." The global reach of this universal "dominion" and "rule" for Christian fundamentalists is presided over by the exalted One at whose name "every knee should bend, in heaven and on earth and under the earth, and every tongue should confess that Jesus Christ is Lord, to the glory of God the Father" (Philippians 2:10–11). Christian fundamentalism requires the whole world to be the terrain on which God establishes Christ's kingdom to bring wholeness to all of humanity.

Christian missions, when designed and carried out by those in possession of worldly power, tend to wed expansion of global dominion (the world for Christ's own) and promotion of God's reign (Christ over the whole world). Spearheaded by the United States of America, as described in chapter 2, an aggressive political and military expansion over the world is inextricably intertwined in Christian fundamentalist thinking with another grandiose desire that such a world be ruled by God. In our analysis of Christian fundamentalism, I have argued that three threads contribute to its tightly woven narrative within the United States: (1) the jealous God who alone is Great in the whole world (2) elects the "Chosen" nation of the United States to live out its vocation (3) as a "redeemer" nation among the nations of the world for the purposes of establishing the Lord's will for all. In an ironic and twisted way, it takes the Lord's flexing of "a strong hand and an outstretched arm" (Psalm 136:12) through God's chosen and redeemer nation to usher a Christian Word-vision of "peace on earth" as an attestation of the "glory to God in the highest heaven" (Luke 2:14). This enigmatic logic largely explains the fundamentalists' support for the United States' spread of global violence after 9/11.[44] Pax Americana (global peace superintended by the United States of America) was all about ushering in pax in terra (peace on earth).

Without subscribing to conspiracy theories, let us notice the common objective between the nonviolent and persuasive "soft power" of global mission, exerted by a wide range of Christian evangelicals, and the violent and coercive "hard power" of world domination, wielded by a more select section of Christian fundamentalists in the United States. The evangelical camp, well-versed in persuasive proclamation, is a loose assortment of mission-driven churches and organizations that overflow with passion to win all souls in the world for Christ, often by a certain projected year. These well-meaning, often apolitical or marginally political, entities are inspired by the Great Commission. Obedient to Jesus, they take to heart his instruction to missionize the whole world: "Go therefore and make disciples of all nations, baptizing them in the name of the Father and of the Son and of the Holy Spirit, and teaching them to obey everything that I have commanded you" (Matthew 28:19–20a). While they make exaggerated claims of bringing individual souls and entire communities to Christ and offer excessive promises of what Christ can do for the welfare of these individuals and communities, the grandiose objective of these agents of Christian mission is to "make disciples of all nations" so that the whole worlds may live under the lordship of Christ.

The fundamentalist camp, well-acquainted with the power of coercive statecraft, is much more political. They share the desire to disciple "all nations," but this end can be achieved by strong-arm means that include the power of U.S. military and political expansion. The hope of the United

States to be the greatest nation, which claims to dominate the world for the well-being of all the inhabitants of the earth, is fused with the objective of Christian mission, which works toward Christ's rule of peace and prosperity on earth. The commission taken to heart by Christian fundamentalists embraces their blessed role as a chosen nation put to service for the welfare of the whole world. George H. W. Bush was the one who ignited the United States with the idea of being chosen agents to usher in a "New World Order." In a speech made on March 6, 1991, to the joint session of the U.S. Congress, he articulated the following imperial vision: "Until now, the world we've known has been a world divided—a world of barbed wire and concrete block, conflict and cold war. Now, we can see a new world coming into view. A world in which there is the very real prospect of a *new world order*."[45] Reminding his countrymen and women that the nation's role is both local and global, President Bush Sr. urged them to take pride in the violent interventionist victory they had won in the Persian Gulf War. Let me quote his words: "We're coming home now—proud, confident, heads high. There is much that we must do, at home and abroad. And we will do it. We are Americans. May God bless this great nation, the United States of America."[46]

Even if there was much retraction of the language of New World Order, the marriage of the imaginations of a global empire presided over by the United States of America and a world unified in Jesus as Lord envisioned by the Christian fundamentalist came together in a powerfully new way after the September 11, 2011, attack by Muslim fundamentalists in New York and Washington, D.C. As we have already seen, George W. Bush, with much support from fundamentalists, used the colossal tragedy to spur an angry, confounded, and humiliated nation to take the violent fight against Muslim fundamentalists onto the global stage. On the one hand, there was a perception that the attack symbolized a Christian nation under siege by warriors of Allah. On the other hand, this judgment was matched by a belief that the Christian God unified and aided the United States against the mostly Muslim Middle East. Against this backdrop it was easy for Christian fundamentalists to interpret the ensuing violence in the Middle East as a cosmic war between good (represented by a Christian U.S.A.) and evil (represented by a Muslim Middle East). The global reach of the United States and the worldwide scope of this divine mission necessitated the carrying out of "just war." One may even talk of a "smart" coalition of soft and hard power emerging in the twenty-first century as Christian fundamentalism from the United States reached out to establish a "new global order" for the God in whom America trusts![47]

More than just a nationalist project, for Christian fundamentalists a strong United States of America prepares the world for the imminent return of Christ. Christian eschatology (the doctrine of last things) thus offers another justification for the use of coercive force against the enemies of the nation and its God. The Christian fundamentalists espouse aggressive military action in the world to facilitate the glorious return of Jesus Christ. This long-expected event brings history to its blessed end: Christ returns as king to reclaim, judge, and rule the world for one thousand years (the millennium).[48] Based on a literal reading of the end times from allegorical biblical writings, especially the books of Daniel and Ezekiel (Old Testament) and the book of Revelation (New Testament), there are two conditions that must be protected and promoted in the unfolding of human history in accordance with God's design. Both of these involve the United States in its role as redeemer nation asserting global influence and forceful intervention. First, as both divinely gifted land and divinely elected people, Israel must be defended. It represents the axis mundi of history and geography for Christian fundamentalists. Both people and place are crucial in God's end-time scenario. Israel functions as the literal patch of land on which Christ will return and the principal site from which Christ will rule the earth. Second, every adversary considered a threat to this holy land and elect people must be destroyed as an impediment to the return of Christ. This idea reinforces the perception among Christian fundamentalists that Muslims are agents of the antichrist. The plot puts Christians and Muslims on either side of the unfolding end-times showdown. The return of Christ must be preceded by a cosmic battle between the forces of good and evil. Especially since 9/11, Muslims have come to occupy the latter role, and Christians the former.

The teaching of John Hagee (televangelist, author, and megachurch pastor from San Antonio, Texas) and Rod Parsley (televangelist, author, and megachurch pastor from Columbus, Ohio) have contributed to this understanding of the end times. They represent "two of the most prominent fundamentalist leaders in the early 21st century,"[49] pushing a political role for religion in the United States, especially as it affects the interests of Israel. Their theological interpretation, which dictates a call for global political action in the Middle East, is influenced by the "claim to have the ability to discern the true meaning and interpret 2,500-year-old utterances from Ezekiel or 1,900-year-old symbolic language from the book of Revelation, as though the Bible were a big collection of coded messages and puzzles."[50] An imperial vision encompassing all of human history, according to Christian fundamentalism, is revealed in Scripture and must direct political action in the whole inhabited world. More-over, in embracing its role as chosen by God to be a redeemer nation, the United States is indispensable for furthering God's purposes in the world.[51]

Muslim fundamentalism also has a trove of religious resources to construct a global imperial vision. We noticed in chapter 3 that this expansionist feature of Islam can be traced back to the time of the prophet. The political future of Islam from its inception involved growing people, gaining land, consolidating territory, and ruling subjects through "the straight path" for the glory of Allah. From its beginnings in the seventh century to this very day, Islam, just as Christianity, has traveled from the Middle East to gradually spread to the ends of the earth, proclaiming itself to be the universal revelation from God that can bring peace to the whole of humanity. Similar to the above description of Christian fundamentalism, the global vision and expansion of Muslim fundamentalism also involves both persuasion to submit and coercion to surrender to the only God (Allah). As a religion that integrates private devotion and community practice in an all-encompassing political order, Allah rules over the cavern of the heart, the dynamics of the hearth, and the welfare of the whole earth.

Muslim fundamentalists assert that the universal vision of an Islamic global order stems from the Word-vision revealed by God for the well-being of humankind. The following Qur'anic passage sets up the domination of "the religion of truth" against Judaism and Christianity on the one side, and other idolaters on the other side:

> They have set up their religious leaders and scholars as lords, instead of GOD. Others deified the Messiah, son of Mary. They were all commanded to worship only one god. There is no god except He. Be He glorified, high above having any partners. They want to put out GOD's light with their mouths, but GOD insists upon perfecting His light, in spite of the disbelievers. He is the One who sent His messenger with the guidance and the religion of truth, and will make it dominate all religions, in spite of the idol worshipers. (9.31–33)[52]

The point is not whether the guarantee of world dominion is an accurate exegesis of the Qur'anic text. In reality, it does involve a huge leap of faith to turn a promise that Islam will "dominate all religions" into an assurance that it will entail the domination of the global order. Yet, as we have detected, through the process of "traditioning," fundamentalism creatively fuses the real and mythic to make Scripture authoritatively speak to the immediate everyday realities of the present as though this is an absolute Word for all time.

I must not obscure the long-standing debate about whether Muslim fundamentalism seeks to establish a religion that spreads Sharia across the face of the earth or merely wants to push back the expanding Christian/Western cultural and political hegemony infiltrating the whole world. The former would make it a world-conquering movement while the latter would secure pockets of enduring religiopolitical Islam. There is much merit on either side of this argument. However, based on my description of religious fundamentalisms as grounded in an absolutely true picture of reality revealed through Scripture (Word-vision), and growing out of a commitment to fashion a corollary pattern of world-ways among all within its reach, I have underscored the consistent all-encompassing feature of Islam that spreads and rules over individual, community, and nations. Sayid Qutb (1906–66), whom we encountered in chapter 3, unquestionably professed global ambitions for Islam:

> Indeed, Islam has the right to take the initiative. Islam is not a heritage of any particular race or country; this is God's religion and it is for the whole world. It has the right to destroy all obstacles in the form of institutions and traditions which limit man's freedom of choice. It does not attack individuals nor does it force them to accept its beliefs; it attacks institutions and traditions to release human beings from their poisonous influences, which distort human nature and which curtail human freedom. It is the right of Islam to release mankind from servitude to human beings so that they may serve God alone, to give practical meaning to its declaration that God is the true Lord of all and that all men are free under Him.[53]

Efraim Karsh (b. 1953) is well acquainted with this trajectory of interpretation as represented by the Muslim Brotherhood's intellectual heavyweights and draws attention to the long history of this macrovision for Islam's mission.[54] He underscores a narrative thread of Islam that I have also identified in Christianity: the idea of a primordial Word-vision that frames the working out of historical events in the world for fundamentalists. Using the rhetoric of empire, Karsh warns us that the imperial religious vision of present-day Islamists is much more global and political than that of the caliphs of yesteryears:

The quest for Allah's empire thus passed from monarchs to political activists and ideologues, or Islamists, as they are commonly known, who set their sights much higher than their predecessors. For the monarchs, the caliphate meant little more than adding legitimization of their ambitions for a regional empire. They had little interest in the deeper inculcation of Islam's precepts in their Muslim subjects. The Islamists, by contrast, modeled themselves on Islam's early conquers, and aspired to nothing less than the substitution of Allah's universal empire for the existing international system.[55]

There is much hype, I admit, in projecting theological coherence and organizational synchronization among disparate groups of Muslim fundamentalists. Yet such a consolidation of all Muslims into a united political community is partly embedded in the imagination of fundamentalists as they envision a rule for Allah over all of God's creation. A pivotal religious theme shared by the universal expansion of the ummah must not go unstated: the arc of God-ordained history is bent toward a final cosmic showdown, which heightens the need to marshal all the faithful in preparation for a duel between Allah and his adversaries. Contemporary Muslim fundamentalists draw upon this apocalyptic end-time projection to justify the violence that accompanies their present-day operations.

The Islamic State (IS/ISIS/ISIL) offers the best example of this Muslim apocalypticism. It represents the twenty-first century convergence of political order, global ummah, and violent expansion with the close-approaching apocalyptic conflict of end times. As a summary of his widely circulated essay on "What ISIS Really Wants," Graeme Wood suggests: "The Islamic State is no mere collection of psychopaths. It is a religious group with carefully considered beliefs, among them that it is a key agent of the coming apocalypse."[56] Reflecting a version of the eschaton similar to that visualized by Christian fundamentalists, the ISIS version of the end times has the cosmic battle being fought between "the armies of Rome" and "the armies of Islam," in which "Islam's final showdown with an anti-Messiah will occur in Jerusalem after a period of renewed Islamic conquest."[57] The caliphate represents the global Muslim ummah that is ready for the divine cosmic end times. "Global jihadism, epitomized by the Islamic State and al-Qaeda," states Barak Mendelsohn, "seeks more than change in particular countries, promoting as a central goal the destruction of the existing order and its substitution by a universal Islamic one."[58] The worldwide scope of this looming end times; the preparation, inclusive of violent combat, that it involves; and the promise of victory for God as Lord over all creation—these become interwoven themes as the faithful marched with complete faith toward this divinely ordained global order.

Hindu fundamentalism is not as focused and fervent about establishing a global religiopolitical order that encompasses the whole world. As we have noticed, Hindu fundamentalism has mostly been used as a cognate for Hindu nationalism. Thus the objective of Hindu fundamentalism is to transform India into a nation saturated by Hindu-ness (Hindutva) and fit all individual expression and social interaction into the universal dharma. As made clear in chapter 4, the purification of the Indian enclave rather than the privilege of ruling the whole world is the main objective for Hindu fundamentalism. Unlike Christian and Muslim expressions of religious fundamentalism, Hindu versions do not aim to tame and train the whole family of creation. Hinduism is not a world-conquering religious movement that wants the entire globe to submit to the Hindu dharma. Rather it seeks to establish this religiopolitical and social order only within the borders of India.

Yet two interesting aspects of contemporary Hindu fundamentalism, pointing to vague aspirations of spreading beyond the borders of India, present themselves. The first of our two contemporary suggestions of Hindu global dominance is highly rhetorical, attributable perhaps to the elated mood of the Hindu Nationalist party's 2014 sweep of the polls. In July 2015 Ashok Singhal, one of the influential leaders of the Vishva Hindu Parishad (VHP: World Hindu Council),[59] reported on a conversation with a godman (Sai Baba) and declared, "By 2020 the entire country will be Hindu and by 2030 the entire world will be Hindu." He also asserted, "This revolution [that] has started . . . will not remain confined to India but [will] present a new ideology before the world."[60] Singhal was a veteran spokesperson for Hindu fundamentalism. He served as the international working president of VHP for two decades and was a key leader in organizing Hindu fundamentalists to raze the Babri Masjid in 1992. The hope of Hinduism becoming a dominant religion, which will involve converting the whole world, may simply be an extravagant declaration to egg local Hindu mission workers on as they stay determined in the goal of reconverting Christian and Muslim Dalits and Adivasis back into what is claimed as the original fold. Yet such a vision is consistent with the notion that Hinduism is a revealed vision given to all humanity from the womb of India.

Another example of reaching for a Hindu global order stems from the firm belief by Hindu fundamentalists that the divine vision and way of life revealed to the Indian seers is *sanatana* dharma. This is the Sanskrit terminology employed by Hindu proponents as a substitute for the Western concept of religion. When translated into English, the expression emphasizes the eternal duties or practices consonant with the complete law of the universe. Consistent with such a totalizing view of sanatana dharma, India's Prime Minister Narendra Modi, himself a proponent of Hindutva, has become an icon for uniting India around this universal Word-vision and world-ways across the whole world. The BJP chief Amit Shah touted this image for the ruling party headed by Modi on February 8, 2016: "The Modi government had taken measures to preserve and promote 'Sanatana dharma,'" he stated, "while politics in the country had earlier got 'detached' from religion.'" He went on to claim that "the BJP government will not only make India a prosperous nation, but also spread its spiritual message worldwide."[61] The lurking aspiration for the world to be ordered by universal dharma may not rest within the realm of possibility, but this does not mean that its claim to universal truth will not be globally embraced in the future.

In spite of these fanciful and impassioned yearnings for Hindu fundamentalism's influence over the global order, from our study we can only assert with certainty that this expression of strong religion remains altogether national. Hindu fundamentalism is not a threat to world stability. It minds its own Indian business. The focus of terror for Hindu fundamentalists is turned inward to discipline and disciple those who live in the subcontinent of India. Yet its predisposition for violation and propensity for violence is as intense and wide-ranging as its fundamentalist transnational religious cousins. Therefore, the world cannot stand by and act as if this is an internal matter for the nation-state of India alone. Human rights abuse is a moral attack on human beings the world over.

Let me conclude this section on fundamentalism's intent to establish a *global order* with two observations. First, the political dimension of religious fundamentalisms demands that religions spill over from the realm of the head and the heart into that of the hands and feet. It first must transform (1) the way individuals behave, then (2) the way societies are formed and nations governed, and finally (3) the way the world is ordered. Part of the challenge for fundamentalists thus is to ensure that beliefs and emotions produce practices. But the other part of the challenge is to consolidate this transformation over all the earth. This move from local to global, we have noticed, eventuates in cosmic dualism that demands violent combat. We have found this true of the rationalization for violence in Christianity and Islam. Aslan is mainly addressing these two religions in declaring, "Religions' ability to sanction violence, to declare it permissible and just, to place it within a cosmic framework of order versus chaos, of good versus evil, is indispensable to the success of social movements."[62] However, even at a national level we have found this legitimization of violence against Christianity and Islam in place as Hindu fundamentalist muscle their way toward a political nation-state infused with Hindutva (Hindu-ness).

Second, although on the one hand the Christian and Muslim fundamentalists envision the rule of God versus the Evil One on a global scale, and on the other hand the Hindu fundamentalists envisage the rule of dharma versus adharma (that which threatens the harmony of universal order) on a national scale, both of these groups posit their own respective geographical locations as the epicenter for a universal display of triumphant human order. For Christians and Muslims, the Middle East, with Jerusalem as the fulcrum, hosts the sacred battlefield in which God will overcome Evil once and for all, whereas the subcontinent of India with either Varanasi (devotional) or Ayodhya (political) as the center serves as the sacred geography for the conflict between universal order and disorder for Hindu fundamentalists. While Christians and Muslims have to fend off each other to proclaim victory over the other on the sacred Middle Eastern stage of the world, Hindus have to fend off Muslims and Christians who seek to pollute the purity of the land of dharma with their own disharmonious Word-vision and world-ways. Drawing on James W. Jones, we might say that "a discernable constellation of beliefs, emotions, and schemas of self and world" played out on a sacred geographical stage characterizes "fundamentalism wherever it exists."[63]

A Definition of Religious Fundamentalism

Throughout this work I have tried to resist interpretations of fundamentalism that overlook and discount religion. I have argued that this severe and worldwide spread of violation and violence cannot be deciphered and explained solely as a pushback against Western or modern or neocolonial forces gaining control over the world. Such reductionist explanations fail to account sufficiently for the vested Word-vision and clear-cut world-ways of religion. Some distinctive religious motifs have risen to the top in this lengthy sifting-through of concrete manifestations of religious fundamentalism. Absolute religious worldviews were fused with exacting ways of living out such a system of ideas in everyday practice. Furthermore, we also ascertained that religious fundamentalisms generate immense passion and imaginative strategies as convinced believers saturate the world with their particular worldviews and ways of life.

Therefore, let me briefly remind us of the principal traits of fundamentalism and use those features to propose a definition. First, religious fundamentalism is a *communal mind-set* that is unwaveringly committed to a revealed Word-vision. It requires an unconditional surrender to its vision of reality, received through divine revelation. To declare that the Divine has given this Word-vision means to claim that it is true, certain, and comprehensive. Thus an uncritical and deferential demeanor accompanies fundamentalisms. Second, religious fundamentalism provides a *clear-cut ethical system*, closed and straightforward world-ways. Those who have received the Word-vision are obligated to live out these world-ways. Third, religious fundamentalism insists on a *creative imperial global vision*; while requiring loyalty from the local group and the nation-state, its end goal is to spread its influence across the planet.

Integral to fundamentalism is the need to challenge other worldviews (be they secular, religious, or other fundamentalist). Certainly we can see connections between the rigidity of fundamentalists' Word-vision and world-ways and the radicalism of their tactics for taming and shaping the world. Thus religious legitimization accompanies concrete and colossal violence, and theological authorization undergirds various violations of human rights. Based on this extended discussion, let me offer this definition: *Religious fundamentalism is a communal mind-set steeped in a revealed Word-vision, corroborated by a definitive ethical system of world-ways for human living, and calibrated by an aggressive movement that labors toward the goal that such a global order will govern the social, political, economic, cultural, and religious lives of all human beings.*

The Competitive Spirit of Fundamentalisms

While describing in detail the three religious characteristics of fundamentalisms, I have also been conscious of an overarching spirit that forms and binds them. The spirit of competition, so much a part of our historical context, is the impetus from which religious fundamentalisms proliferate and escalate. Such a "competition for souls," Micklethwait and Wooldridge remind us, was a central component of "the old wars of religions in the Seventeenth Century." In striking similarity, they suggest that "the background for the new wars of religion" in the twenty-first century also "includes a fierce competition for souls—this time largely between Christianity and Islam." This study has shown Hinduism as having joined in this aggressive competition for the soul, even as bodies and minds, along with peoples and lands, were added as targets by all three religions. What makes matters worse for the current century is that "the battlefield this time is global."[64]

Our study shows the limitations of the well-intentioned but naive viewpoint that all religions harmoniously mediate their differences through some kind of deep wisdom that God is one, and consequently that these families of religion are moving toward organic unity under their shared Creator. Stephen Prothero observes this sentiment among soft-hearted and liberal-minded religionists even while he points to the imprudent nature of such a stance. "One purpose of the 'all religions are one' mantra is to stop this fighting and this killing. And it is comforting to pretend that the great religions make up one big, happy family. But this sentiment, however well-intentioned, is neither accurate nor ethically responsible."[65] Using the term fundamentalism loosely and sardonically, he insists, "Faith in the unity of religions is just that—faith (even a kind of fundamentalism). And the leap that gets us there is an act of the hyperactive imagination."[66]

Rejecting the romantic myth that religions mirror the concord that they attribute to God is one part of the learning from this study. The other part is much more distressing, even scandalous: religions compete with each other to violently disestablish others even as they seek to rule over all. Rather than shift the blame to economic, political, social, and psychological considerations, I have tracked the religious features that explain the detrimental effects of fundamentalisms in the world. I believe I have established the truth that "the pathologies of religious zealotry . . . do not derive from an inconsistent application of Hindu, Jewish, [Christian,] or Muslim doctrine but rather from a passionate consistency."[67] And yet much of the working out of these religious themes, as we have studied them, take place within the spirit of aggressive competition that marks our age. "Predatory corporate globalization," which percolates into most aspects of our twenty-first-century world because of the possibility of expansion and the actuality of compression, "breed[s] violent confrontation."[68] Globalization, however, also simultaneously generates "transnational social movements," which often vehemently challenge both the homogenizing absolutisms and "hegemonic masculinities" seeking to rule our age.[69] Globalization as a process, age, and spirit is contentiously effusive. It can be said to be powered by the interaction between the competition of "market globalism," the contestation of "justice globalism," and the confrontation of "jihadist globalism."[70] In the last category I include Christian "crusades" and Hindu "battles." In the rest of this section, I intend to look into three aspects of the spirit of competition, which functions like oxygen, supplying religious sources with the verve to propagate violation and proliferate violence locally, nationally, and globally. Through such a description I wish to draw attention to the sustained dynamics of competing religious fundamentalisms in our twenty-first century.

Intrareligious Competition

Religious fundamentalisms compete with other claims concerning what it means to be religious *within* each particular religion. The fundamentalist option is only one version of what it means to be faithful within a specific religion. Recognizing that there are factions vying to represent the fullness of their own religious tradition in the world helps us see the imprudence and error of identifying any one religion as the embodiment of religious fundamentalism. Grace Davie warns against "a slippage in meaning [of the term "fundamentalism"] which implies that all members of one particular faith group might come into this category."[71] Within each religion there is competition as to which version of the religious Word-vision and world-ways will be represented to the world. Each fundamentalism is one version that claims to represent the whole of religion in its most pristine form to the world.

The scope of this study has prevented me from attending to the competing factional claims of what is genuinely Christian, Muslim, or Hindu. I did, however, cover in broad strokes the internal struggle between major divisions within these religions. In Christianity, as I have reported, there has been a long-standing debate about the relationship between softhearted evangelicals and hardheaded fundamentalists in the United Sates. Similarly, in Islam there are ways to delineate the violent extremists in both Sunni and Shia camps from the majority of faithful Muslims spread all across the world. In the same vein, there is the distinction in Hinduism between the muscular Hindutva side and the amiable Pluralist side of being religiously Hindu in India. In each of these traditions, religious fundamentalists are feverish competitors who are often violent against their own opponents within the community. Aligned more with conservatives than with progressives (Christianity), more with jihadists than with mainstream Muslims (Islam), and more with militants than with universalists (Hinduism)—fundamentalists have gathered up and galvanized a closed, aggressive, and communal interpretation of their respective religions to advance an absolutist form of thinking and a political way of living in the world. Because they envisage an infallible, fixed, and universal worldview, religious fundamentalisms vie to emerge as the sole representatives of their religions by undermining and dismantling alternate portrayals. For example, a 2011 report by the National Counterterrorism Center of the United States states, "In cases where the religious affiliation of terrorism casualties could be determined, Muslims suffered between 82 and 97 percent of terrorism-related fatalities over the past five years."[72] The main victims of violence emanating from Muslim fundamentalists are other Muslims who are thought of as having departed from "the straight path."

The fuel from the internal religious sources is ignited by the zeitgeist of coercive competition spread through the process of globalization. In an odd but destructive way, the zealous internal drive of religious fundamentalism has effectively joined with the external spirit of competition that is forcefully taking over the world. In fact, one might even suggest that the prevalent mind-set of combative competition of our age has been responsible for exaggerating the potency and reach of religious fundamentalisms, even as it obscures the capacities and impact of those faithful Christians, Muslims, and Hindus who cultivate tolerance and build peace. The politics of competing for representation within specific religions reveals an area of mission that needs to be undertaken within one's own faith communities in the twenty-first century: each religion's devotees and resources need to be shielded from becoming infected by the ethos of clashing antagonism. This calls for the difficult in-house work of taming the spirit of vicious competition, which seeks to transform resources of shalom, salaam, and shanti into battles for righteousness. On the one hand, faithful devotees within the religious family are vulnerable to being agents of the belligerent spirit of the world within the house of religion. Thus encounter, exchange, and engagement with those who live within one's own religious boundaries, even if one thinks of them as religious extremists and knows them to be psychologically draining, cannot be surrendered. Charity toward aggression best begins at home.[73] On the other hand, the intrareligious competing nature of fundamentalism also forces us to own up to the fact that there are resources within one's own religion that give fundamentalists' version of religion a chance to be successful within an ethos of competing representation. Religious fundamentalists are navigated from within by their own religious resources. As McTernan puts it, "The political and social milieu may be a trigger, but the roots of the religious intolerance and militancy are embedded in the history and the sacred texts of each of the world faiths."[74] I shall turn our attention to both of these challenges in the next chapter.

Interreligious Competition

Religious fundamentalisms are energized by the fact that each religion finds itself competing against other religions in an ever-shrinking world under the weight of an aggressive and contentious global market system. In this sense religious fundamentalisms illustrate a larger phenomenon within our contemporary global era. This century has heralded the global truth that "the world is flat."[75] Thus every religion that wants to remain or become a world religion is competing against other ideologies and theologies in a level playing (battle)field. Suggesting that the twenty-first century can best be comprehended by thinking of globalization as "the superstory" within which to understand other narratives, Thomas Friedman goes on to talk about this process as involving three superagents "bumping up against" each other: "You will never understand the globalization system . . . unless you see each [bump] . . . as a complex interaction between all three of these actors: states bumping up against states, states bumping up against Supermarkets, and Supermarkets and states bumping up against super-empowered individuals—many of whom, unfortunately, are super-empowered angry men."[76] Even if he does not address religion as another superactor, we have observed the way in which Christian, Muslim, and Hindu fundamentalisms also bump up against each other, often with an intent to knock the others down. Like commodities, services, and people moving stridently across the globe through somewhat open borders, religions too have become aggressive and robust as they compete for convinced and loyal consumers in the market of religious exchange. Other religions have thus become intimate rivals: potential threats to the existence and spread of one's own religion in our contracting, competing, and flat world. There are new opportunities in our present century for forceful religion to be disseminated and operationalized. Religious fundamentalisms march forth to capture religiously uncommitted or partially committed persons and territories to their own religious worldview in an aggressive world of competing, fully globalized markets.

Again, one must not attribute all the blame for the aggressive and even violent competition between religions to the bullish rivalry set loose by the forces of globalization. As I have demonstrated, such bloody competition has long been part of the history of Christianity and Islam. They not only competed with each other but also undercut the authenticity of the other. In the words of Bernard Lewis, "Though Christendom and Islam were rivals, indeed, competitors, for the role of world religion, and though both shared so many traditions and beliefs, so many purposes and aspiration, neither was willing to recognize the other as a viable alternative."[77] I have also described in detail the zealous and universal missionizing objectives of Hinduism. But doubtlessly much of the aggressive global expansion is still carried out by the traditional two missionary faiths. Huntington, usually silent on religion, makes this point: "The two great missionary religions, Islam and Christianity, are competing worldwide for converts and gaining them, most notably in Muslim fundamentalist movements and Evangelical Protestantism, which has had a tremendous impact on Latin America and is now influencing Africa, Asia and the former Soviet world."[78] Hinduism may be less global in its scope, and yet there is this same aggressive spirit of competition that we have detected in its expansion in India.

Religious fundamentalisms aggressively promote tightly packaged, meaningful, and compelling worldviews through ruthlessly competitive and open-to-all global networks and organizations. They appear to feed off the passion and energy of religious communities that are vested in taking the ways of the world seriously and shaping the world according to their particular religious convictions. This combination of strong and passionate religion with aggressive globalization expanding across our flat world animates conflict. One can see why violence is generated and justified in such a competitive interreligious global context. Faith in God, a disposition of competition, a desire for market share, aggressive border crossing, and a search for territory—all these summon and train loyal adherents in the service of establishing a kingdom of God on earth, for the sake of human flourishing and Divine glory. Tisaranee Gunasekara from Sri Lanka points to this competing dimension among religions and links it to violence both among and within religions: "The manifestation of one type of religious fundamentalism encourages and fosters fanatics of every other religion, creating a vicious cycle which will lead to not just wars between religions but also wars within religions."[79]

The Common Enemies: Secularism and Modernity

The spirit of competition finally ties religious fundamentalisms to a concerted struggle against their common external challengers. Robert Wuthnow and Matthew Lawson have drawn our attention to this aspect of religious fundamentalism in the fading years of the twentieth century.

"Fundamentalism," they propose, "cannot be understood adequately as a single social movement. Instead, it must be considered as part of a wider field of competing movements. It exists in dynamic tension with its various detractors and competitors."[80] Throughout our study of all three brands of religious fundamentalism, we have seen the emergence of a pair of common antagonists. Christian, Muslim, and Hindu fundamentalisms are consumed with fending off the twin ideologies of secularism entwined into modernity. Religious fundamentalisms represent a cluster of fierce and furious movements that beef up their respective religions in order to stave off the seemingly successful and amazingly robust expansion of secularization. As Peter Herriot states, "Fundamentalisms are unashamed grand narratives, competing against other grand narratives as secular humanism and religious pluralism. Their key characteristic is their hostility to modernity."[81] Religious fundamentalisms manifest an imitative strategy in defending against and defeating these influential processes. As we have seen in this book, religious fundamentalisms invoke strong belief, prescribed behavior, and a global vision. They use each as weapons in the struggle against (what they see as) the irreligious, hegemonic designs of secularism and modernity. The following quotation from three noted scholars writing on religious fundamentalism sketches the historical trajectory of this argument:

> The concept fundamentalism . . . refers to specific religious phenomena that have emerged in the twentieth century, particularly in the last several decades, in the wake of the success of modernization and secularization. For much of the nineteenth century and for the first half of the twentieth, the Western world was in the grip of a "culture of progress," the spreading confident belief that humanity, through the power of reason, the triumphant discoveries of science, the magnificent inventions of technology, and the secular-rational transformation of the traditional institutions, was on a clear course toward the mastery of the evils of the human situation. In much of the contemporary world, religious communities and elites had been put on the defensive, retreating into cultural ghettos, or adapting to and compromising with the spreading secular world. Fundamentalist movements are the historical counter-attacks mounted from these threatened religious traditions, seeking to hold ground against this secular "contamination," and even to regain ground by taking advantage of the weaknesses of modernization.[82]

What these fundamentalists share in common is the fear of threats from outside of religion. There is a certain commonality that binds such religionists as they turn their ideological and institutional power against the malevolent forces of secularization and modernization. I have systematically addressed how Christian, Muslim, and Hindu fundamentalisms feared secularism and modernity making inroads into world religions. But comingled with this fear was the disillusionment of all that secularism had promised in the twentieth century. Addressing "Resurgent Religion and Global Politics" in our present "God's century," Toft, Philpott, and Shah conclude that "one of the major causes of religious resurgence was a crisis in secular ideologies."[83] Keeping in mind the mutual support observed between angst of and disillusionment with secularism, we might say that twenty-first-century religious fundamentalisms offer strong schemata of belief and stable ways of life through a global system, against the background of the sure-to-fail promises of human-invented and God-displacing regimes.

Two brief comments must suffice to bring this discussion to a close. First, let me reiterate that fundamentalisms only draw on select strands from the larger religious narratives to which they belong, and always solely those that suit their context and purpose. Due to fears about threats from within and without, fundamentalists weave these fragments into a tight and seemingly seamless religious narrative. Grace Davie suggests that this inventive crafting of secure narratives in uncertain times is what produces "competing fundamentalisms" in the globalized twenty-first century: "Fragments, however, can be rebuilt into certainties, artificial ones perhaps, which provide a bulwark against the corrosiveness of perpetual change. Such certainties can be described as competing fundamentalisms—the plural is important. . . . They provide coping mechanisms in times of uncertainties."[84]

Second, fundamentalists tap into the currents of modernization to further their own ideological, organizational, and religiopolitical agenda, just as they do with globalism. Thus, in the end, one must be careful not to suggest that these movements are being antimodern in all aspects. Rather, "religious communities have benefited from cooperation with modern forces like democracy, globalization, and technological modernization."[85]

Conclusion

Religious fundamentalisms compete with other versions of the same religion in order to engage the world. They also overflow their own boundaries, ending up in active competition with other religions and with the worldviews of secularism and modernity. They try to establish themselves as the singular representatives of their own religious traditions even as they seek to extend the reach of those traditions around the world. In service to their Word-visions and divinely ordained worldways, they show little aversion to violence, using it to cement their own communities and dissuade dissenters and deserters. In a sense competing religious fundamentalisms are their own species. It is a contentious interpretive force within specific religions today, baptized into the aggressive spirit of contemporary globalization and inventively shape-shifting to zealously confront the perceived threat of expanding modernization and secularization. In an attempt to distinguish competing religious fundamentalisms as a modern creation, which must be separated from any one religion and yet which seem to be attractive to religious actors from several religions, we might even designate it as *surrogate religion*. As surrogate religion its conception is possible only because of the resources within religion, and yet it is incubated and brought to maturity in the less organic environment of aggressive capitalism and by more belligerent religiopolitical actors. Thus resources of religions, clothed by some extrareligious ends, are fused with the forces of globalization to forge competing fundamentalisms, which are both harmful to particular religions and hurtful to the whole world. Such a surrogate religious phenomenon is a modern and composite invention, which must be separated from any one religion per se.

Competing religious fundamentalisms are both proactive and reactionary: proactive, in that they advance across the world to promote their fixed beliefs and unwavering practices; reactionary, in that they shout out their creeds ever more loudly to compete with the siren melodies of the modern and the secular. Even while aggressively fending off secularism and modernity, fundamentalisms cannot take their eyes off other religions, since each religion seeks to establish its own mind-set and body politic in the world. They justify violence by explicitly dredging up centuries of intra- and interreligious conflict, implicitly engaging in the aggressive ethos of hardnosed marketing in a shrinking flat world. Competing religious fundamentalisms thus creatively combine proactive allegiance to advance Divine metanarratives with reactionary momentum to dismantle other competing metanarratives through offensive maneuvers in our mostly aggressive and ruthless globalized world.

Chapter Six

Countering Violence and Nurturing Peace amid Competing Religious Fundamentalisms

Do not repay anyone evil for evil, but take thought for what is noble in the sight of all. If it is possible, so far as it depends on you, live peaceably with all. . . . Do not be overcome by evil, but overcome evil with good.

Romans 12:17–21

Christians are called to reject all forms of violence, even psychological or social, including the abuse of power in their witness. They also reject violence, unjust discrimination or repression by any religious or secular authority, including the violation or destruction of places of worship, sacred symbols or texts.

Christian Witness in a Multi-Religious World:
Recommendations for Conduct (June 28, 2011)[1]

Introduction

Fundamentalism is an inherently religious reality. Its violence derives from religious beliefs and motivations. Focusing attention, not on the sociological, psychological, or economic roots, but rather the religious roots of fundamentalism has been the central task of this book. Yet this intention to unmask religious violence is not intended to demonize religion. In fact, it is motivated by an obligation to accentuate the influential, even if ambivalent, nature of religion in our globalized twenty-first century. I wholeheartedly agree with John Kerry when he says, "Religion is a multivalent force, not reducible to good religion and bad religion." "Still," as he counsels, "we must take seriously those instances when actors seek to justify violence through religion. Rather than talking about building a school, creating a community, or providing health care, these actors sometimes promote destruction—occasionally, sadly, in the guise of religion."[2]

Let us look back at the argument propounded thus far. After chapter 1 described the theories that deem cultural, political, economic, and psychological factors primarily responsible for the bloody sins of religious fundamentalists, I sought to refute all reductionist narratives that pay no heed to the substance and agency of religion. Next, I examined the particulars of fundamentalist movements arising from the world's three largest religions: Christianity, Islam, and Hinduism. Through the next three chapters (2–4), focusing on historical twists and turns as well as geographical incursions and extensions, I described in detail the religious themes that ignite and fuel the vision and mission of Christian, Muslim, and Hindu fundamentalisms from the early twentieth century to the present. In chapter 5, I sought to categorize anew the theological motifs that propel these movements into the twenty-first century. Three shared and distinctive themes rose to the top: unwavering confidence in and complete submission to the *Word-vision*; purportedly fixed and seemingly straightforward *world-ways*; and the mandate to establish a *global order* in conformity with the divine Word-vision and in compliance with its fixed world-ways. Quite cognizant that the dynamics of religious fundamentalisms flow from the head to the hand and feet before impacting the world, I concluded with the submission that the spirit of fierce competition, which has saturated the whole world through the process of globalization, has also played a decisive part in stoking competing religious fundamentalisms. So, at the end of this analysis of violent religion, we are left with the ensuing question: What can other believers do to contain and remove those expressions of religious devotion that injure and kill in the name of God?

Since fundamentalism is a religious issue, it requires a religious solution. Religious persons and groups must occupy the center of any response to the violence that fundamentalists have perpetrated in the name of their religion. Associating religious fundamentalism only with culture, politics, economics, and psychology diverts the energies of qualified religious personnel away from addressing the fundamentalist problem. It prevents Christians, Muslims, and Hindus of goodwill and compassionate outlook from deploying their most treasured religious ideas and practices to foil the rise and spread of religious fundamentalism. My sense is that dated economic tools, simplistic political models, and reductionist psychological lenses have contributed all they can to the struggle against fundamentalism. It is time for scholars and practitioners of religion alike to bring the resources of their traditions to bear on this problem.

Let me be clear. I am not saying that religion can be compartmentalized out of the organic complexity of the world. Zeroing in on religion thus does not mean becoming unconcerned with the cultural frameworks, social yearnings, political ambitions, economic interests, and psychological motivations that undergird fundamentalism. Rather, by focusing on the religious sources, apparatuses, and systems complicit in the rise of fundamentalism, we both admit to the culpability of religion in engendering violent fundamentalism, and we point to religion's potential to overcome its fundamentalist offspring. Lloyd Steffen has carefully explicated this ambivalence within the power of religion: "As religion can incite violence [a demonic dimension], so too does it offer responses to violence [a life-affirming dimension]."[3] My point is simply that just as much as religious resources and mechanisms are vulnerable to being captured for destructive ends, they are also available for the enrichment of human life. This conviction in the dual potential of religion is sufficient for the faithful from various religions to both critically evaluate and constructively utilize their resources for de-escalating violence and fostering peace in our world.

Unleashing Religion's Constructive Power

Before getting to the task at hand, which involves looking into ways to counter, contain, and cure violent religious fundamentalisms, I must attest to the fact that much is already being done to accomplish these goals. Christian movements against modern violent fundamentalism in the United States are consistently represented by historic peace churches, such as the Mennonites (including the Amish), the Church of the Brethren, and the Religious Society of Friends (Quakers). These pacifist churches are actively joined by legions of other communities committed to the nonviolent Jesus and his call to dismantle the destructive gods of wealth, war, and world domination. In the last decade of the twentieth century, Walter Wink declared, "Violence is the ethos of our times," "the spirituality of the modern world," and is "accorded the status of a religion"; he also announced that "it, and not Christianity, is the real religion of America."[4] To confront this "ethos" and "spirituality," Wink's concerted biblical interpretation, along with John Howard Yoder's classic theological reconstruction,[5] successfully circulated a pacifist option for Christians as a third way. Such a way of life lies between "submission or violence, flight or fight." It involves imitating the nonviolent way of Jesus, who in resisting the brutally competing spirit of his own age reveals the true nature of both God and humanity.[6]

In spite of the spread of Hindu fundamentalism's mind-set and operation across the nation of India over the last decades, with Hindu nationalists in the driver's seat after 2014, there has been broad resistance to the hegemony of one religion at the expense of others. Drawing from the widely popular nonviolent movements initiated by M. K. Gandhi and B. R. Ambedkar (both of whom clashed with Veda-touting orthodox Hindus through differing modes of mediation and rejection respectively), a plethora of pluralistic voices have sought to carve out a more generous form of Hindu belief and practice, one that celebrates all religions. To this day the more inclusive option represents the religious and political vision of the majority of Hindus in India. In a March 2016 statement, the president of the Catholic Bishops' Conference of India (CBCI), Baselios Cleemis Cardinal Thottunkal, expressed the sentiment of more than just the Christians in India. "If the entire Hindu community in India had decided to be communal," he stated publicly, all the religious minorities "would not have been safe." He then said, "Thanks be to God, . . . the majority of Hindus in India are secular."[7] The invoking of secularism as a political virtue in India, I must restate, assumes the refusal to promote the religion of the majority community at the expense of others. Instead, secularism guarantees all religions the right to freely participate in the public sphere in equal measure. Pluralist Hindu movements are trying to expand the philosophical meaning of *ahimsa* beyond "merely not hurting or not killing others." This ancient ethical and religious concept is coming to include "giving up concepts of 'otherness,' 'separateness,' 'selfishness,' and 'self-centeredness,' and identifying oneself with all other beings."[8]

Similarly, movements to stand up to the violence perpetuated by Muslim fundamentalism are plentiful in our times, even if they largely escape the eye of the international media. While admitting that "globally, the danger of fundamentalism is now [in the 2010s] even greater than it was then [the 1990s]," Karima Bennoune is able to capture rays of hope in the "unstoppable chorus of all the people" she interviewed who were "fighting against Muslim fundamentalism" because they "love their religion and are completely against violence."[9] These courageous men, women, and children scattered all over the Muslim world suffer retribution in the harshest forms. Yet they continue bravely and creatively to birth new life in the shadowy valleys of death. Bennoune offers many examples of

Muslim individuals and collectives pitting their bodies and minds against the repressive beliefs and practices of Muslim fundamentalists. But she does not restrict her dream of the swelling of resistance to fundamentalism to one religion alone. "This solidarity," she urges, "needs to be extended across the spectrum to those believers and nonbelievers, practicing Muslims as well as atheists, agnostics, and freethinkers of Muslim heritage, and the religious minorities who live with them, who work together against fundamentalism."[10] A "community of communities," bound together by love of their own particular religions and by revulsion toward violence in all its religious manifestations, is creating a new religious spirit of hope.

In the discussion that follows, I resist the temptation to offer advice about what other religions ought to do about their violent co-adherents. Instead I confine the discussion to Christianity, since that represents my own religious commitments. I venture into two areas through which to contain, counter, and cure violent religious fundamentalisms. First, taking seriously the role of Word-vision in fueling violent fundamentalism, I candidly deal with what we might responsibly do in Christianity to disarm Scripture (esp. its "toxic texts") and redeploy its resources to serve the well-being of the whole family of God. This key religious source has been used to justify destruction; it can also be deployed in the search for harmony and peace. Second, I explore avenues to shape Christian believers in the ways of peace and nonviolence.

Detoxifying Scripture

As we have seen, violent sacred scriptures engender lethal theologies founded in a vengeful God. Even a generous reading of the Bible, the Qur'an, and the Mahabharata cannot overlook the link between the Divine, the associated faithful ones, and violence. Violence seems to be "baked into" the sacred texts. Christian Scripture testifies to people as chosen and commissioned to violently carry out the purposes of a sometimes jealous and oftentimes aggressive God. Jack Nelson-Pallmeyer is blunt about this matter. "Religiously justified violence," he reckons, "is first and foremost a problem of sacred texts and not a problem of misrepresentation of the texts. The problem in other words is not that people take passages out of context and twist them in order to justify violence."[11] "The problem," he concludes, "is actual violence at the heart of these texts that can be reasonably cited by people to justify their own recourse to violence."[12] The violation and violence authorized by God in the Bible, I concur, is not simply a matter of misinterpretation, as though one can overcome such passages by a more pious interpretation. We need to squarely face the issue of violence in the Bible as a whole since violent fundamentalism ascribes absolute authority to the entire revealed Bible.

Any perspective on what to do about violence emanating from the Bible will have to address two issues. First, one has to deal with the Bible as a whole. While composed of many texts written across hundreds of years, Christian belief insists that the Bible is authoritative *in its unity*. Complicating any answers to the question of biblical violence is the fact that Christians are emotionally attached to the *idea* of the Bible, beyond their intellectual assent to the truth of its content. Second, one also has to work creatively with and around specific texts in the Bible that legitimize and sponsor violence. Dealing with the Bible as a whole addresses the normative viewing of the sacred Bible in the context of violent religious fundamentalism; interpreting specific texts pays attention to practical strategies of delegitimizing violence in Christian teaching emerging from the Bible.

Reading Scripture as a Whole

Let me begin by posing the question bluntly. How does one embrace the Bible as life-giving while at the same time rejecting its divinely sanctioned violence? To put it differently, how do you take the cannon fire out of the canon?

Apart from the fundamentalist approach we've already seen, there are at least three Christian responses to the problem of violence in Scripture. The first uncouples the Christian Bible from all social significance and community import. It confines Scripture's application to individual salvation alone, understood in terms of successful living in this temporal realm and the attainment of heaven in the eternal domain. Such an approach to sacred Scripture referred to as "biblicism" highlights the private appeal of the Bible to one's personal journey. Daniel Migliore maintains that biblicists approach the Bible as "a private devotional text whose authority is located in the saving meaning it has for the individual."[13] This interpretive tactic considers the Bible as absolute, mainly in terms of pointing to the ultimate means by which individuals can negotiate all the complexities of this world on their way to being secured in God and safe for a future with God. Violence that appears in the Bible is mostly ignored as being irrelevant to the rigorous journey of the individual disciple, seeking fellowship with Christ in the present world and communion with God in the life after this one. Even if violence is noticed and acknowledged in sacred Scripture, it is interpreted as representing the metaphorical conflict between the things of God and the things of the world. The individual believer needs to wade through these conflicting forces to get to personal salvation, which is marked by deep inner peace, love, and joy. In this approach, which no doubt accepts the whole Bible as authoritative, the "public realm" and communitarian bearing of Scripture, including its entanglement in violence, is discarded for a much safer "private realm" and individualist reading.[14] While this approach does not actively justify religious violence, neither does it do anything to challenge and curb that violence.

The second approach involves sculpting a nonviolent "canon within the canon." Marcion of Pontus (ca. 85–ca.160 CE) was both the best known and most vilified figure in the history of early canonization of the Bible.[15] His version of the Bible, compiled around 120–25, is notorious for drastically expunging the whole Old Testament. Thus he cuts the God of Jesus Christ free from the God of the Old Testament. Less known is Marcion's heavy redaction of the Gospels and Epistles. He presented a radically edited Bible that only draws on segments from the Gospel of Luke and the writings of the apostle Paul. Central to guiding his surgical knife on both what preceded Jesus in the Old Testament and what followed Jesus in the Gospels and Epistles was Marcion's rationale to save the "God of mercy and love" revealed in Jesus Christ from the "God of justice and law" that seeped in before and after him. One might say that the texts had to suffer violence, in Marcion's view, for merciful love to overcome violent justice.

A variety of both conservative and liberal Christians employ a modified version of this strategy to redact or edit the violence out of the Bible. While such canonical rescues may stoop to the theologically sloppy and biblically unjustifiable maneuver of pitting the Old Testament against the New Testament, Eric A. Seibert speaks for many in our age when he admits, "Clearly, the Bible's troubling legacy is not confined to the Old Testament. The New Testament is problematic as well."[16] So how does one redact the whole Bible in order to hand over authority to a reconstituted canon that delegitimizes violence?

Hector Avalos, a secular humanist biblical scholar, is best known for making just such a daring deconstructive proposal. He advocates that religion scholars "eliminate any scripture that contains religious violence . . . as a whole genre of religious experience."[17] Along these lines, Avalos invites biblical studies "toward helping humanity wean itself off of the

Bible and towards terminating its authority completely in the modern world."[18] In a more constructive mode, Avalos invites Christians interested in alleviating violence to join in "the principled decanonization of violent texts."[19] His constructive approach both suggests general guidelines for refashioning a "principled" master narrative and recommends actual biblical texts as candidates for ejection in a redacted nonviolent Christian canon.[20] The radical redaction approach uses the theological or philosophical notion of "zero-tolerance" of "any endorsement of violence in our scriptures" to come up with a Christian narrative that is beneficial, minimally, for the survival of all humanity, and optimally, for the well-being of all humanity. In our context of competing fundamentalisms, cleansing the Bible of violent texts, claims Avalos, can "serve as a signal to Islam and other non-Christian religions that Christians are serious about eliminating violence from our sacred texts."[21]

In spite of the logic of this plea to extricate violence-justifying texts from the Bible and construct a truncated canon through "principled" appeal to zero tolerance of violence, the radical redaction approach has very little appeal. I perceive two reasons for the lack of enthusiasm for this proposal. First, Christians all across the world are not ready to trust a call from Western academics in the United States to dump large portions of the Bible. At a time in which churches are losing their members in the global West and North and gaining adherents in the global South and East, there is little appeal for such lofty North American wisdom. Second, the emotional connection between the Christian Book and the Christian community is not easy to sever. Although there are many different ways to identify the "core" of the Bible, little agreement exists as to which portions of Christian Scripture actually account for Christians' attachment to it.

The third approach in dealing with violent sacred Scripture as a whole puts the Word-made-flesh at the center of the metanarrative of scriptural words and places authority on "the biblical vision of God's nonviolent distributive justice"[22] that Jesus embodied. In this school of thought, the Christian Bible is accepted in its complex fullness. Much like a library of sacred writings, which is embraced by Christians through a long process of collecting, selecting, and collating, it honors the unity of the Word of God as it is gently cupped in the hands of men and women. Even though collectively honored as the Word from God, however, the multiple strains of the narratives about God, the world, and human beings are acknowledged to contain the fingerprints of human wisdom and folly. But how can one get to the wisdom of God, which leads to life, through the mixed testimonies of human beings who transmit life and death? The answer to this question lies in thinking of the Word-made-flesh (Jesus Christ) as the key to unlock the complicated vault of sacred literary treasures. The Bible thus is authoritative only insofar as it witnesses to Jesus Christ. As Jerome Creach puts it, because the Christian Bible is "a testimony to Jesus Christ,"[23] whose life and ministry embodies nonviolent love, "the whole scripture may be understood rightly as a grand testimony *against* violence."[24] In this line of thinking, Christian identity and mission is thought of not as people formed in the world by the sacred Book (Revealed Word-vision) but as people set free for the world by the God-Man (Word-version in flesh) testified to in Scripture. Even though Martin Luther (1483–1546) was much more conservative in reclaiming the authority of the Bible and played a part in justifying the use of violence to put down the German Peasants' Revolt (1524–25), he is well known as advocating for the central role of Jesus Christ in interpreting the Christian Bible. He likens Christ to the "star and kernel" of Scripture, "the center part of the circle" around which everything else revolves.[25] Invoking poetic license for creatively using Luther's words to address Bible and violence, we might think of violent texts as "hard nuts" that resist cracking. Following his lead, this approach invites Christians to throw such toxic texts against Christ the Rock so that they would release their "delicious kernel."[26]

But which version of Jesus Christ—among the historical, the evangelical, and the apocalyptic models—determines the key to unlock the Christian Bible? Following the well-paved pathway of liberation theology and the stepping-stones laid by John Dominic Crossan, I find the turn to the historical Jesus the most suited for holding on to the Bible while denouncing violence in and for God. Even if there are drops of violence oozing from the evangelical Jesus and a flood of violence pouring forth from the apocalyptic Jesus, the historical Jesus exemplifies the nonviolent affirmation of God's peace with justice and the courageous nonviolent insurrection against human regimes of repressive order.[27] Resonant with Walter Brueggemann's influential work, which concedes that the Old Testament contains both strands of "royal Consciousness" (false consciousness) vested in consolidation of power and of "prophetic imagination" (consciousness of hope) invested in God's rule,[28] Crossan admits to a similar set of themes evident in the Christian Bible. Building upon the soft metaphor of the heart rather than the steely one of a train on parallel tracks, Crossan suggests, "There is a recurrent rhythm between the biblical vision of God's nonviolent distributive justice and God's violent retributive justice."[29] In spite of these two contending streams in the Bible, the historical Jesus (here I rephrase Crossan) both fully "asserts" the biblical heartbeat of God's nonviolent vision to bring about embracive peace with distributive justice and also demonstrably "subverts" the forces that promote God's violent vision to establish retributive justice with global order. In continuity with the "prophetic imagination," Jesus represents the radical and inclusive nonviolent version of ushering in God's vision for the world that subverts the contending vision of God pursued by the elite establishment, which depends on violence.

I believe that this third approach, with its emphasis on embracive peace with "distributive justice," offers up a credible conception of sacred Scripture as a whole that both delegitimizes violence and validates nonviolent action on behalf of the well-being of all human beings. It manages to keep the traditional canon as a mark of respect for the centuries-long process of its historical and emotional connection with the Christian community without ignoring the contest between violent and nonviolent strands woven into the metanarrative. In an interesting twist this approach transfers the emotional attachment of the community from the Word-vision to the enfleshed Word. Along with chipping away at the fundamentalists' vision of a God who seeks justice through retribution, this third option offers in Jesus a God with an inclusive vision of peace with distributive justice. When we envision God in these broader, more universal terms, then even such divisive ideas as "chosen people," "promised land," and "elect nation" must take on more inclusive meaning.

But let us not paper over the drawbacks of this approach. For starters, it allows for some trivializing of many narrative threads in the Christian Bible that cannot be woven into Jesus Christ. Thus the integrity of historical particularity is sacrificed for preserving the centrality of the Word-made-flesh. Also, it fails to adequately account for the way we come to know the historical Jesus only in the living testimony of the community of faith, the church.[30] But most importantly, it undercuts the freedom of the Holy Spirit to lead us into truth that may not be contained in Jesus Christ: "When the Spirit of truth comes, he will guide you into all the truth" (John 16:13).

Yet simply focusing on God's vision of nonviolent peace with distributive justice will not get the job done. Christian scholars and church leaders must also reinterpret and rework those violent texts within the canon that fire up the fundamentalist base. These toxic texts (also referred to as "texts of terror") fund the fundamentalists' dangerous Word-vision.

"Restorative readings"[31] of biblical texts are part of what is needed to overcome violence and cultivate peace. Derek Flood suggests that this is the manner in which Jesus "disarms Scripture." Instead of glossing over these toxic texts, he proposes working through these passages "like Jesus did" to recover the gospel through dismantling and disarming toxic texts.[32] Now let us turn our attention to transforming these literary swords into prosaic plowshares.

Disarming Exclusive and Explosive Texts

One hand must courageously darn nonviolent threads of the Christian Bible, from the beginning of Genesis to the end of Revelation, to fashion a garment that adorns all of humanity. The historical Jesus, as declared, becomes the manifest texture of this peaceful and just scriptural narrative. At the same time, the other hand must reinterpret the Bible's toxic, violent texts. The latter task will need to account for the way the historical Jesus has become entwined with the evangelical and the apocalyptic Jesus. In what follows, I explore ways of reinterpreting toxic biblical texts by neutralizing the violence stowed within them and animating peace by mining in and around them.

In Scripture the fundamentalists discover two types of toxic texts as they construct an absolutist Word-vision, which informs violently imposing rigid world-ways en route to establishing an imperial global-order. The first are *exclusivist texts* that demonize individuals and groups perceived to be a threat to God's chosen people in the world. The second are *explosive texts* that authorize violence against individuals and groups conceived to be a threat to God's special purpose for the world. Of course, these categories are not watertight since in the Bible they often overlap and frequently seep into each other. But for purposes of clarity, let us treat them separately.

Exclusivist texts in the Christian Bible are those passages that privilege the community of the faithful and debase communities that are a threat to the flourishing of God's elect. In the Old Testament, these narratives promise protection to the people of Israel, yet at the expense of violating the rights of other communities around them, only because Israel has been drawn into a covenantal relationship with the living God. As the Lord says to Abram, "I will bless those who bless you, and the one who curses you I will curse; and in you all the families of the earth shall be blessed" (Genesis 12:3). In the New Testament such exclusivist narratives are directed at assuring the eternal security of "believers," promising them everlasting life while pronouncing destruction to those who do not confess and have faith in Christ. Jesus makes such a pronouncement in the Gospel of John: "Whoever believes in the Son has eternal life; whoever disobeys the Son will not see life, but must endure God's wrath" (3:36). Throughout this Gospel those who do not believe in Christ are associated with darkness and assigned death; those who acknowledge Jesus as "the light of the world" enjoy life (8:12). Clearly, in both Testaments of the Bible one community's elevation by God becomes a threat to another community's security. Exclusivist Bible texts contribute to divine assurance of being favored by God and divine disfavor of religious others, which gives room for violence both in God and through God's chosen. Drawing on Jack Nelson-Pallmeyer's categorizations of divine violence in the Bible, I submit that "God's liberating violence" was what makes exclusivist texts justify the violence of God in protecting the elect ones at the cost of disgrace, even utter ruin, of other peoples of the world.[33] The narrative of the liberating violence of God, according to him, weaves together texts from the Old and New Testaments that bespeak the exodus, the exile, and apocalypse.

Explosive texts are much more potent at instigating and justifying violence against those religious others who threaten the divine purposes of God in the world. Often these are sacred texts that authorize and enact terror. Perhaps we might even label them "t[error]exts": texts that in error spread terror. These texts legitimize the injuring or even killing of individuals and communities that are conceived of as being enemies of God's perfect will for God's creation. In the Old Testament the divine purposes of God are narrated through an unfolding story of election, exile, and restoration. All those who oppose God's perfect design to choose Israel as God's covenant community thereby dishonor Israel's journey from exile into the promised land; they refuse to be impressed with the glory of the living God, who makes Israel a blessing to all nations, and thus become targets of God's wrath. In this story line of the Old Testament, says Nelson-Pallmeyer, "God is powerful, violent, and partial. [The narrative] . . . identifies the Israelites as God's chosen people, who, depending on which passages are cited, are destined by God either to be *the* vehicle through which God blesses all the nations, or to dominate the nations of the world."[34]

The New Testament papers over some of this raw violence in Scripture by offering a nonviolent historical Jesus. Yet there is much symbolic violence contained in Jesus' teaching, and more real violence is connected with the apocalyptic end times, where Christ will destroy evil and rule in righteousness. I do not go as far as Nelson-Pallmeyer's conclusion that "God's liberating, punishing, or apocalyptic violence is the named or unnamed assumption behind nearly every passage, story, and theological claim in the New Testament."[35] However, based on the discussion of end-times violence in the chapter (2) on Christian fundamentalism, I am convinced that apocalyptic interpretations of Jesus Christ point to the goal of a final violent showdown between "the kings of the whole world" and "God the Almighty" at a place called "Armageddon" (Revelation 16:14–16 KJV). Charles B. Strozier puts it this way: "The violence of the Book of Revelation is quite astonishing. . . . Destruction is everywhere. . . . The violence is exterminatory, or totalistic in nature, . . . a kind of biblical genocide, . . . with an agency from a very angry God."[36]

Creative interpretation of exclusivist and explosive texts must be a major part of educating Christian communities amid spreading violent religious fundamentalisms. Simply put, we need to retell the story in ways that promote peace, not violence. Let me suggest two ways to do this.

First, restorative interpretations diligently search for and deploy the metanarrative of peace with justice to strengthen the overarching story line of Jesus' vision and mission. In doing so, the contra-texts that speak of the violent expansion of Christ's global order are weakened, if not edged out. Let me give an example. The competing narrative threads between a violent, expansive mission of God and a peaceful and just one can be seen in the Gospel of Luke.[37] The first happens when Jesus sends disciples on the Samaritan mission, while the second appears when Jesus sends other disciples out to the Gentiles. In Luke 9:51–56 Jesus sends his messengers to a Samaritan village asking that he be welcomed to stay there on his way to Jerusalem. The Samaritans refuse to receive Jesus. In this narrative the refusal "is not related to Jesus' racial background. He is rejected simply because he is on his way to Jerusalem."[38] Mount Gerizim rather than Jerusalem was the center of religious cultic life for the Samaritans. So they refuse to accept Jesus' resolve to journey toward Jerusalem. The reaction of James and John is "to command fire to come down from heaven and consume" those who do not receive Jesus (Luke 9:54b). Jesus, though, rebukes his disciples for getting the vision of God's mission wrong. He aborts the retributive, violence-driven mission and starts anew by immediately sending out "seventy others" on another mission (as seen in Luke 10). This time Jesus rejects the shock-and-awe model of God's violent retribution and instead chooses to send peace-bearing messengers "like lambs into the midst of wolves" (10:4). If self-giving love fuels Jesus's vision and mission throughout the Gospel of Luke, then Luke 10 reveals peace as its accompanying gift (10:5–6).

Second, human experience can help disarm violent texts. Experience can be creatively utilized to make Scripture more porous so that it can breathe life into human beings—which explains why the authority of the Bible and the authority of experience are often in conflict. Let me return to Luke 10 to use my own experience as an experiment for disarming symbolic violence in the Bible. In a strange twist, the mission of peace instituted by Jesus culminates in a less-than-gracious ending. Those who disagree with the emissaries of peace in Luke 10 are threatened with destruction. This tilt toward violence seems out of sync with the thematic progression of peace, hospitality, and healing. Moreover, it is uncharacteristic of the compassion with which Jesus sent his emissaries into the world as sheep among wolves. Yet the symbolic violence against those who do not welcome them is unmistakable. "Even the dust of your town that clings to our feet, we wipe off in protest against you. . . . I tell you, on that day, it will be more tolerable for Sodom than for that town" (Luke 10:11–12). The shock-and-awe character of destruction that Jesus rebuked in James and John reemerges. As a form of "acted parable against those rejecting them,"[39] this anticipates an actual incidence of God's fiery retributive violence.

How can one reclaim the nonviolent God who energized Jesus from this text of terror? Let me source experience creatively to defuse violence emanating from the text. From working in India, where evangelists and social activists often journey barefoot, I can attest that it is not easy to gather enough dust onto one's feet. Thus, while one can remove dust by using water and/or a towel, one will find it hard to demonstrably shake off dust from one's feet. This experience may offer us an alternate interpretation that disarms this text. The emissaries are commissioned to work long and hard enough in the town so as to be able to gather dust on their feet, which in a manner of speaking means infinitely. Even if Jesus' emissaries leave a town in frustration, thus, they can only take symbolic action against the inhabitants of the town. These peace emissaries know full well that this action will not be effective since realistically and perceptibly dust cannot be shaken off one's feet. It remains merely an ironic symbolic charade. Additionally, the "on that day . . . for that town" (Luke 10:12) may indeed imply a future continuous sense. My restorative interpretation of this toxic text through creatively inserting my experience resonates with Tannehill, who underscores the notion that rather than thinking of this as "prediction of the future," here the use of "forceful language" was "meant to crack the complacency of these towns."[40]

"Stewards of God's Mysteries" and Proclaimers of "the Gospel of Peace"

Countering violence and nurturing peace in the face of competing fundamentalisms necessitates defusing violence in God and disabling violence exercised by God's agents, which is embedded within the Bible. But undercutting violence and fostering peace involves more than just advancing strategies of disarming and restoring Scripture. Training and transforming human beings who can de-escalate violence and advance peace is also needed. Surely the best examples of the theological truths and ethical ideals of any religion are its "living letters" (cf. 2 Corinthians 3:2–3). Such embodied expressions of truth are the most authentic witnesses of religious claims that are hidden in Scripture and embedded in theology. The mantra that our religion is not violent but has peace at the core is trite and misleading when acts of hate, anger, and violence radiate from the actions of its adherents. Christians thus need to be formed in body, mind, and spirit to be peacemakers in this world of competing violence.

Civic responsibility often appeals for tolerance. For religions in the world that breed passionate faith, though, tolerance is not enough. It is far too passive a disposition. Tolerance no doubt helps prevent the conception and development of violent thoughts and deeds against adherents of other religious faiths and those within one's own faith tradition who are different. But much more is required of Christians, who are called and commissioned to transform the broken world that God loves so much. The "re-habitation" of Christian disciples to exemplify God's nonviolent vision of relational peace and distributive justice in the world is an important part of doing something about curing violence and generating peace. I use this concocted term to highlight the need to transform the habits of disciples ("re-habit") in order to assemble a dwelling place ("habitation") of peace for all human beings. In the remainder of this section I elaborate on two dimensions of re-habitation that can help Christian disciples become peacemakers. The first entails preparing Christians to cultivate their mind to be faithful "stewards of God's mysteries"[41] by living into a spacious God; and the second involves inviting Christians to consecrate their feet to trek on the way of Jesus as emissaries of "the gospel of peace."[42]

Cultivating the Mind to Be "Stewards of God's Mysteries"

The monarchial God—jealous of other Divine challengers, in an exclusive relationship with a chosen people, and opposed to other peoples who do not acknowledge his sovereignty—has dominated the vision and mission of Christian fundamentalism. Cherry-picking the Bible allows them to fuse a brawny God with an imperial Christ. A vision of the universal God whose care and concern encompasses all human beings needs to ground Christian disciples if they are to be groomed into a more hospitable relationship with other members of the human family. There is a commonsense appeal to cure this problem of parochializing an all-encompassing God. In his book aptly titled *God Is Not Christian: And Other Provocations*, Archbishop Desmond Tutu frees God from being narrowly confined to any one religion. Addressing Christians, he writes, "To claim God exclusively for Christians is to make God too small and in a real sense blasphemous. God is bigger than Christianity and cares for more than Christians. He has to, if only for the simple reason that Christians are quite late arrivals on the world scene. God has been around since even before creation, and that is a very long time."[43] This may be a good start. Christianity, however, does possess a much richer theological tradition from which to formulate a more inclusive and embracive conception of God as an alternate to the narrow and exclusive God who is grounding the worldview of Christian fundamentalism.

Counterfundamentalist theology must offer a God who looks like the historical Jesus, one who generously embraces the well-being of the whole human family. The Christian doctrine of the Trinity, I believe, helps us mine a spaciousness within God that embraces all while lifting up the love of God as revealed in Jesus Christ. The words of the apostle Paul in 1 Corinthians 4:1 are pertinent: "Think of us in this way, as servants of Christ and stewards of God's mysteries." Christians must discover more fully what it means to be servants of Christ and stewards of God's mysteries. One part of this statement highlights the particular vocation of being faithful to Jesus Christ, which I shall address later. The other part points to the calling of being stewards of God's mysteries, which I take to celebrate the capaciousness of the Trinity.

The most ancient, orthodox, and ecumenical affirmation of the Christian global family has been the belief that God is Trinity. It serves as the "grammar" or template for Christian reflection on God. This declaration, which underscores that God is communion rather than singular, produces infinite space within God. Leonardo Boff puts it thus: "Christianity's most transcendent assertion may well be this: In the beginning is not the solitude of One, but the communion of Three eternal Persons: Father, Son, and Holy Spirit. In the remotest beginning, communion prevails."[44] This notion of a God in three persons, modes, or movements presents us with a more fluid and yet quite orthodox model for God. The mysteries in this relationship of Divine communion are open, dynamic, loving, and overflowing. Adapting Bevans and Schroeder's language, I think it wise to think of Divine communion as holding together both the flow of movement into each of the three persons in love and also the overflow of such a movement of love to all of God's creation. "God is a Movement, an Embrace, a Flow," they suggest, "more personal than we can ever imagine—who is always and everywhere present in God's creation."[45] God as communion is spacious God in Godself, whose capaciousness can embrace all creation. Let me invoke Christian terminology. The Trinity represents God as the universal creator, a parent of all humanity; Jesus Christ as an embodiment of the concrete love of the Divine communion; and the Holy Spirit as continued immanence available to every component of diverse creation. It is because of such spaciousness in the One-in-Three that Christians are also emboldened to be in awe of the mysteries of God, whose traces appear in strange locations among different peoples all over the world.

This is not the occasion for an extended commentary on the Trinity.[46] For our purposes it is sufficient to stress that Divine Communion opens up infinite space in God, lifts up love as the characteristic that binds Divine unity, and celebrates difference in the Divine communion of persons or movements. The spaciousness of God captures the abundance of mystery, and the copiousness of love is signified by difference. The Trinity communicates the inexhaustible riches hidden in the fullness of God, riches that spill over from the Abba God to Jesus Christ and onto God as Holy Spirit. And this spacious hospitality in God overflows into all of creation through Christians in relationship with other communities. Christians are called to be stewards of this mystery of God in interreligious relationships in the world of God's diverse human family. Rowan Williams, leaning heavily on Panikkar, argues that the Trinity demonstrates "a practical pluralism [that] can be unconditionally faithful to the gospel, . . . warning us away from the lust for religious Grand Theory."[47] He also emphasizes the mystery built into God that can be witnessed through the process of interreligious engagement. Such dialogue, he suggests, "is one of the many means that God gives us to sink more deeply into the infinity of God's work, presence, and purpose."[48] There is some similarity between the idea of "*the infinity* of God's work, presence, and purpose" that Williams emphasizes within God's inexhaustible abundance and my own contention for the spaciousness that is contained within the inter-being and interaction of the Trinity. Theodore Friend does well to put together the more commonsense approach for the universality of God with the spacious understanding of God in most religions, including in the "three Christian Persons." Let me quote him as I end this segment on the spaciousness of God as requiring graciousness from Christians in the world of providential difference:

> A more open Islam [also Christianity and Hinduism] will think of God as . . . a universal, benevolent, and forgiving god, intimate with humans drunk or sober, wrong or right, errant or correct. This need not rule out a God that is passionately just and eternally accurate in justice; but it does exclude a vengeful, maiming, or murdering divinity. God may have three Christian persons, or thirteen Talmudic attributes, or ninety-nine names, or infinite Hindu avatars, or no Buddhist meaning. But God may be shared as our planet must be shared—and our universe, or pluriverse, if that it proves to be.[49]

Apart from the spaciousness and graciousness built into the affirmation of God as Trinity, such an orthodox and ecumenical credo also sets in motion a model of God that subverts imperialistic theologies and ideologies desiring the reign of singularity (absolutism) and yearning for the eradication of difference. The idea of God as Trinity refutes and rebukes fundamentalism's intention to bring the whole world under the divine rule of the sovereign One. Jürgen Moltmann has contributed much to differentiating between the monotheistic Almighty who models and legitimizes ruthless monarchism and the trinitarian God who reveals and authorizes self-emptying love. Similar to the singularly absolute God of violent Christian fundamentalism, the former singular Deity rules by domination in heaven, thus extending monarchism through the political and church leaders all across the world. The counter to such a God, according to Moltmann, is revealed for Christians in the self-giving of the Trinity, which represents not almighty power but passionate self-emptying love expressed by suffering, pain, and solidarity on the cross in the figure of Jesus Christ.[50] As he puts it, "The shortest expression of the doctrine of the Trinity is the divine act of the cross, in which the Father allows the Son to sacrifice himself through the Spirit.'[51] The Trinity presents us with a self-*expending* God of love, rather than a self-*expanding* absolute divine monarch. *This* is the God whom Christians are called to follow. It is in this same vein that Panikkar points to the doctrine of Trinity as "an irritant" to all forms of monarchism. This relationship model of Divine communion "is an irritant to any monarchic ideology, be it religious (monotheism), political (imperialism and colonialism), economic (global market), academic (*pensée unique*), or even of lifestyle (technology)."[52]

Consecrated Feet and the "Gospel of Peace"

Stretching the mind to encounter the mysteries of a spacious God is one way of countering submission to the parochial, singular, and even violent deity who enlists agents to rule the global order. But peacemaking in the way of Jesus requires that this graciousness in the head makes its way down to the feet. I am reminded of something that a student of Shin Young-Bok (1941–2016) shared with me at Sungkonghoe University, Seoul, in July 2014.[53] Professor Young-Bok was a renowned social activist, philosopher, calligrapher, and emeritus professor at Sungkonghoe, who spent twenty years in prison for criticizing the repressive policies of the government. During one of his classes, the professor was reported to have asked his students the following question: "What is the longest journey you will ever undertake?" Many thought through this and mentioned hopeful trips they might undertake from one major city in Korea to another exotic city in a distant country, many thousands of miles away. He waited for all of them to finish. Then looking at them with an element of pity, he said: "No. The longest journey you will undertake is getting your ideas to flow from your head to your heart and then on to your hands and feet."[54]

Let us spend a moment with the long and needed journey of connecting the head with the feet, since this is what grounds the path of Christian disciples. The feet are, most vividly, what it takes to traverse the way. I am struck by the irony surrounding much discussion about Jesus' declaration, "I am the way, and the truth, and the life" (John 14:6). Christians often forget that the way must be walked upon rather than merely shouted out. And, as we have noticed in the historical Jesus, this way that is truth and leads to life is intimately tied up with embracive peace and distributive justice. Christian discipleship as walking with feet on the Jesus way toward "the gospel of peace" is suggested by the Epistle to the Ephesians. The author of Ephesians writes, "As shoes for your feet put on whatever will make you ready to proclaim the gospel of peace" (6:15). The long but necessary journey required for formation of Christian disciples in the context of violent competing fundamentalisms involves connecting the graciousness of the mind fixed in the spacious Trinity with feet that are consecrated for the spread of "the gospel of peace."[55]

What does it mean to walk faithfully in the way of Jesus as we become proclaimers of the gospel of peace in the context of violent fundamentalisms? Let me start with deconstructing Ephesians and then return to the teaching of Jesus in the Gospel of Luke to offer a few suggestions. Ephesians 6:15, we must note, is part of a larger discourse that urges Christians to become spiritual warriors, preparing for battle against the kingdoms of this world by becoming outfitted with the full armory of the children of God. The shoes of readiness for the feet are included to complement the belt of truth, the breastplate of righteousness, the shield of faith, the helmet of salvation, and the sword of the Spirit (6:13–17). Of course, this passage must be read through the perspective of Pauline thought, which embraces nonviolence in all its fullness, including the constant requirement for Christian disciples to be faithful in imitating the suffering of Jesus. The author in this epistle thus was drawing from the imagery of the Roman Empire even as he was spiritualizing such military symbolism by infusing it with the ethic of nonviolent resistance of the people on the Jesus way. If the Greek is rendered literally, it simply translates, "and having shod your feet with the readiness of the gospel of peace." What is the readiness for the proclaimer of peace?

The feet consecrated for the task of proclaiming the gospel of peace commissioned by Jesus are not preparing for a march (shoes or boots of the Roman soldier) nor protected on an expedition (fancy sneakers of joggers). Rather, like the emissaries of Jesus sent out for mission in Luke 10, they are to "carry no purse, no bag, no sandals; and greet no one on the road" (10:4). Most Bible commentators have concluded that this merely instructs Jesus' disciples not to carry an extra pair of sandals. However, one might even suggest a much more radical demand: to go into the communities devoid of footwear. On the one hand, this is consistent with the instruction that the disciples are not to carry "purse" and "bag," which signifies the extreme simplicity needed for the immediate mission journey. On the other hand, the feet are mentioned without sandals at the end of this passage. It is "the dust" of the "town" that "clings" to the "feet" (rather than dust gathered on the sandals) that represents a protest against those who reject the messengers (10:11). This presents us with the image of vulnerable, barefoot peace emissaries walking swiftly through the streets, looking for welcome in homes where they can rest. Notably, the passage from Isaiah 52:7, surely familiar to Jesus and the writer of Ephesians, retains the simple "feet" of the messenger of peace: "How beautiful upon the mountains are the feet of the messenger who announces peace, who brings good news, who announces salvation, who says to Zion, 'Your God reigns.'" One cannot miss how various themes bind the text from Isaiah with that from Luke: the feet of the messenger, an announcement of peace, the proclamation of good news, and the promise of salvation are tied together to construct a nonviolent vision of God's mission.

The barefoot or barely shod messenger of the gospel of peace reveals insights relevant to the task of forming nonviolent Christian disciples in a world rife with religious violence. First, the authority to pronounce peace as the first word comes to the messengers of the gospel from Jesus. He is quite categorical: "Whatever house you enter, first say, "Peace to this house!" (Luke 10:5). Peace is the good news, and the nonviolent vulnerable presence of the proclaimer of peace witnesses to this gospel. One can say that Christian disciples receive Jesus' peace before they offer it to those who welcome them into their communities. It is the peace embodied by Jesus. Terrance J. Rynne does a convincing job of sketching the manner in which, beginning from Augustine, Christian theology veered away from the radical, active nonviolence expounded and embodied by Jesus.[56] He presents "a new theology of peace [that] starts with the gospel portraits of Jesus." Such a vision for peace, like the early Christians, follows Jesus' "way of nonviolent resistance to evil and love for enemies [real or imagined, religious or not]—even in the teeth of overwhelming violence."[57] I have sketched the core plot of this nonviolent narrative earlier as embracive peace that works alongside distributive justice for all. Consecrating the feet of disciples involves walking the way of peace because we have been commissioned as agents of this gift by Jesus. This alone is our confidence even if we take it into the world in simplicity and vulnerability.

Second, announcing peace is accompanied by actually making peace. In Matthew 5:9 Jesus affirms the vocation of peacemaking: "Blessed are the peacemakers, for they will be called children of God." In Luke 10 the word of peace is proclaimed publicly by the barefoot or barely shod messengers, and all the deeds that follow this pronouncement are acts that nurture peace. The proclaimer of peace becomes the peacemaker. In this passage, peace is not simply the absence of hostility; it is truly a positive state of well-being for a social unit. To reiterate: the peace that Jesus gives his disciples is not simply an absence of hostility, a tranquility that presumes inactive maintenance of calm for the sake of concord. Real peace embraces a social, physical, and spiritual sense of relational well-being. In this case the household is the site of peace where there is table hospitality, healing of the body, and freeing of the mind through forgive-ness. Throughout the rest of Luke, the entire community is invited to live into this relationship of wholeness that gives, forgives, feeds, and heals. It is striking that in Luke 10 the good news of peace does not eulogize Jesus, nor does it make pious God acclamations. It starts with announcing peace and ends with the pronouncement that the reign of God is available here and now through God's gracious gifts of mutual hospitality among differ-ent persons, through table fellowship and generous healing. Peace that is announced becomes God drawing close at hand through the practice of peacemaking. This is the risk of hospitality, symbolized by the barefoot peacemaker crossing into others' intimate spaces to announce and then make peace, based on the authority given by Jesus. Martin Marty situates such a vocation of mutual hospitality as a form of risky peacemaking. "Faiths will continue to collide," he concurs, "but those individuals and groups that risk hospitality and promote engagement with the stranger, the different, the other, will contribute to a world in which measured hope will survive and those who hope can guide."[58]

Finally, in our world of competing violent religious fundamentalisms, peace *is* salvation. The barefoot or barely shod Christian peacemaker may indeed need to cast aside the boots of militant absolutism and the cleats of religious exclusivity in taking peace into the world for the well-being of all God's creation. Raimon Panikkar's submission that religions think of themselves as receptors and transmitters of peace rather than salvation may have some merit in our twenty-first century of competing funda-mentalisms. Some of his theological interpretation of the conception of "peace" as shalom (Jewish) combined with "shanti" (Hindu) enriches the term "salvation." "Peace," for him, "becomes the present-day homeo-morphic equivalent for all those earlier interpretations of 'salvation.'"[59] Panikkar puts the invitation thus: "The traditional notion of religion was that it was a way to salvation. It is a fact that most wars in the world have been religious wars. We are witnessing today a transformation of the very notion of religion, and it may be expressed by saying that religions are various ways of approaching and acquiring that peace, which is today one of the few universal symbols."[60]

Conclusion

Religions simultaneously (if ambivalently) function as tents for convivial dwelling and fortresses for strategic battle. They assemble an array of resources into a cogent and compelling system to serve the communities that seek shelter beneath their particular tents. This includes inviting the world to gather under what they take to be a universal canopy. Religious fundamentalisms, as we have seen, reconceive the soft metaphors of tent and canopy into much more robust ones. "Fortress" and "garrison" are more apt metaphors to describe these "strong religions." The self-appointed task of religious fundamentalism is to transform the infinitely diverse and supple resources of a given religion into an inflexible, rigid, and simplistic belief system. In a complex way, religions are blessed with an excess of sources that can be put together creatively by human beings. "Religion," Reza Alan opines, "with its familiar yet infinitely malleable supply of symbols, offers a trove of words, phrases, and images that can be interpreted and reinterpreted as often and as innovatively as one likes to invest a movement's message with meaning and significance."[61] For this reason, religious sources can be both soft as bread and hard as stone.[62]

Religious fundamentalisms' absolutist alchemy takes the lavish and supple sources of religions and renders them categorical and hard. Propping up such robust symbols to support their own strong religion has involved deliberately locating, collating, and circulating a host of resources in Christianity, Islam, and Hinduism. These hardy religious resources play a substantial role in building up strong and violent religions that aspire to stand firm, grow effectively, and victoriously overcome competitors in the shrinking global world order. We have seen the way in which absolutist scripture, unbendable ethical practices, and imperial global mission fund these movements of religious extremism. Perhaps ironically, my own appreciation of the abundance and sponginess of religious resources motivates this creative endeavor to seek miracles in the reverse direction. In this chapter I have thus ventured to transform my own religion (Christianity) from fortress and garrison back into tent and canopy to show how it (and other religions) might serve as a convivial abode for nurturing peace and well-being in the universal human family.

With this book I have sought to promote the counternarrative of embracive peace and distributive justice as a cure for the violence-spawning narrative of imperial Divine global order seen in competing religious fundamentalisms. I have tried to ground a narrative of peace in the Christian Scriptures, using a more flexible and constructive approach to the Bible to testify to a much more spacious and gracious God. This peaceful narrative seeks to honor the peace and justice advocated by the historical Jesus. It is a nonviolent narrative, grounded in the spaciousness of the triune God, which encompasses the whole human family, shows grace to other cultural and religious worldviews, and honors difference.

Let me end with a metaphor. The difference between fundamentalist religion on the one hand, and peace-embracing religion on the other, can be seen in the *competing* propensity of the battlefield and the *completing* possibility of the flower garden. On God's behalf, violent fundamentalisms are competing in a battle to take over the world. Much violence emanates from the absolute Word-vision, stringent world-ways, and imperial global order of competing religious fundamentalisms, which are in a battle for God and intend to take over the world for a retributive Divine imperial rule. Other religious loyalties are an affront to the singular God who demands homogenous belief and homologous practice. Competing names, competing peoples, competing lands, and competing lifestyles are all needed in this cosmic dualistic struggle to make the One God to be Lord over all. By contrast, the nonviolence implied in the restorative Word, inclusive ethical practices, and all-encompassing world of *completing* religions serves to make room for God's overflowing plenitude. God is the richer communion into which the whole human family is made free to enter. Names, peoples, lands, and lifestyles complete each other in this divine-human communion of abundant life. Other religious identities and contributions complete Christian witness and offerings. Islam, Hinduism, and the other religions of the world are not threats to be obliterated. They become instead indispensable companions along the way toward embracive peace and distributive justice for all creation.

Notes

Introduction

1. John Kerry, "We Ignore the Global Impact of Religion at Our Peril," September 14, 2015, http://www.americamagazine.org/issue/religion-and-diplomacy. Thanks to Jennifer Gillyard for drawing my attention to this blog by Secretary John Kerry.
2. Ibid.
3. "Restrictions on Religion: Religious Hostilities Reach Six-Year High," Pew Research Center: Religion and Public Life, January 14, 2014, http://www.pewforum.org/2014/01/14/religious-hostilities-reach-six-year-high/.
4. While the terms "fundamentalism" and "extremism" are often used interchangeably, I shall confine myself to speaking of "religious fundamentalism or fundamentalisms."
5. Published by Chicago University Press, they are the following: *Fundamentalisms Observed*, 1991; *Fundamentalisms and Society*, 1993; *Fundamentalisms and the State*, 1993; *Accounting for Fundamentalisms*, 1994; and *Fundamentalisms Comprehended*, 1995.
6. Martin E. Marty, "Hindu Nationalism," *Sightings: Religion in Public Life*, May 19, 2014, http://divinity.uchicago.edu/sightings/hindu-nationalism-%E2%80%94-martin-e-marty.
7. For more than a decade I have studied the impact of Hindu fundamentalism on marginalized Dalits and minority Christians in India, as shown in my writings: "The Promise of Religious Conversion: Exploring Approaches, Exposing Myths, Expounding Modalities," in *Religiöse Grenzüberschreitungen: Studien zu Bekehrung, Konfessions- und Religionswechsel = Crossing Religious Borders: Studies on Conversion and Religious Belonging*, ed. Wolfgang Lienemann and Christine Lienemann-Perrin (Wiesbaden: Harrassowitz, 2012), 590–610; "Dalits and Religious Conversion: Slippery Identities and Shrewd Identifications," coauthored with Philip Peacock in *Dalit Theology in the Twenty-First Century: Discordant Voices, Discerning Pathways*, ed. Sathianathan Clarke, Deenabandhu Manchala, and Philip Peacock (New Delhi: Oxford University Press, 2010), 178–98; "Dalits Overcoming Violation and Violence: A Contest between Overpowering and Empowering Identities in Changing India," *Ecumenical Review* 54, no. 3 (July 2002): 278–95; "Viewing the Bible through the Eyes and Ears of Subalterns in India," *Biblical Interpretation* 10, no. 3 (2002): 245–66; and "Hindutva, Religious and Ethnocultural

Minorities, and Indian-Christian Theology," *Harvard Theological Review* 95, no. 2 (2002): 197–226.

Chapter One: Religious Fundamentalism in the Twenty-First Century

1. Anthony J. Parel, introduction in *Religious Fundamentalism in the Contemporary World: Critical Social and Political Issues*, ed. Santosh C. Saha (Lanham, MD: Lexington Books, 2004), 1.
2. See the introduction by Charles B. Strozier and David M. Terman in *The Fundamentalist Mindset*, ed. Charles B. Strozier, David M. Terman, and James W. Jones, with Katherine A. Boyd (New York: Oxford University Press, 2010), 3–7, emphasis original. "The one word never mentioned in all of the five volumes of The Fundamentalism Project is terrorism" (5). Moreover, they add, "even a discussion of violence was skirted in the Marty project" (221n5).
3. R. Scott Appleby, Gabriel Almond, and Emmanuel Sivan, *Strong Religion: The Rise of Fundamentalism around the World* (Chicago: University of Chicago Press, 2003).
4. Raimon Panikkar, *The Experience of God: Icons of the Mystery* (Minneapolis: Fortress Press: 2006), 111.
5. Samuel P. Huntington, "The Clash of Civilizations?," *Foreign Affairs* 72, no. 3 (Summer 1993): 24.
6. I am aware that there is a substantial group of scholars who argue that in spite of the eight civilizational paradigms set forth by Huntington, there is an inner dynamic that presupposes a West-versus-rest frame, or West versus Islam. See, for example, Edward Said, "The Clash of Ignorance," *The Nation* (October 22, 2001), http://www.thenation.com/doc/20011022/said.
7. Samuel P. Huntington, *The Clash of Civilizations and the Remaking of World Order* (New York: Simon & Schuster, 1996), 29.
8. Donald C. Freeman, "Old American Myths; New World Realities," in *Civilizations—Conflict or Dialogue?*, ed. Hans Kochler and Gudren Grabher (Vienna: International Progress Organization, 1999), 83.
9. Samuel P. Huntington, *Who Are We? The Challenges to America's National Identity* (New York: Simon & Schuster, 2004), 62.
10. Ibid., 356.
11. Akbar Ahmed and Brian Forst, "Toward a More Civil Twenty-First Century," in *After Terrorism: Promoting Dialogue among Civilizations*, ed. Akbar Ahmed and Brian Forst (Cambridge, UK: Polity Press, 2005), 8.
12. Parag Khanna, *The Second World: Empires and Influence in the New Global Order* (New York: Random House, 2008), xiv.
13. See esp. these works by Edward W. Said: *Orientalism* (New York: Pantheon, 1978); *Covering Islam: How the Media and the Experts Determine How We See the Rest of the World* (New York: Pantheon, 1981); *Culture and Imperialism* (New York: Random House, 1993).
14. See esp. these works by Michel Foucault: *The Archaeology of Knowledge* (New York: Pantheon Books, 1972); *Power/Knowledge: Selected Interviews and Other Writings, 1972–1977* (New York: Pantheon Books, 1980); *The Order of Things: An Archaeology of the Human Sciences* (New York: Vintage Books, 1994).
15. Reza Aslan, *How to Win a Cosmic War: God, Globalization, and the End of the War on Terror* (New York: Random House, 2009), xvii–xviii.

16. Ashis Nandy, *Time Warps: Silent and Evasive Pasts in Indian Politics and Religion* (New Brunswick, NJ: Rutgers University Press, 2002), 100.

17. Ashis Nandy, "Cultural Frames for Social Transformation: A Credo," *Alternatives* 12, no. 1 (January 1987): 113–23.

18. Gandhi used this term *sanatana dharma* instead of "Hinduism." He felt that this brought all communities in India, in spite of their religious differences, into one large family under God.

19. M. K. Gandhi invoked the idea of the Ramarajya, which is, literally, "kingdom of Lord Ram," as found in Hinduism, and he reconfigures this to stir a more interreligious community of resistance fighters. "By Ramarajya I do not mean Hindu Raj. I mean by Ramarajya Divine Raj, the Kingdom of God. For me Rama and Rahim are one and the same deity. I acknowledge no other God but the one God of truth and righteousness. Whether Rama of my imagination ever lived or not on this earth, the ancient ideal of Ramarajya is undoubtedly one of true democracy in which the meanest citizen could be sure of swift justice without an elaborate and costly procedure. Even the dog is described by the poet to have received justice under Ramarajya" (*Young India: A Weekly Journal*, 14 vols. [Ahmedabad: Navajivan Publishing House, 1919–31], for September 19, 1929, http://www.mkgandhi.org/momgandhi/chap67.htm.

20. Benjamin R. Barber, *Jihad vs. McWorld: Terrorism's Challenge to Democracy* (New York: Random House, 2001), 9.

21. Benjamin R. Barber, *Fear's Empire: War, Terrorism, and Democracy* (New York: W. W. Norton, 2004), 26.

22. Ibid., 221.

23. This can be a separate section. Yet since I will interact with this school through various segments of this book, a paragraph under this heading ought to suffice at this juncture. The section, if worked out separately, might have been titled "Theories of Postcolonial Religious Nationalism: Our Native Kingdom, Right Here, Just Now."

24. Mark Juergensmeyer, *The New Cold War: Religious Nationalism Confronts the Secular States* (Berkeley: University of California Press, 1993).

25. For an excellent source on the various scholarly voices engaged in this debate, see Atalia Omer and Jason A. Spring, *Religious Nationalism: A Reference Handbook* (Santa Barbara, CA: ABD-CLIO, 2013).

26. Juergensmeyer, *The New Cold War*.

27. Tariq Ali, *The Clash of Fundamentalisms: Crusades, Jihads and Modernity* (London: Verso, 2003), xiii and xi.

28. Parag Khanna, *The Second World*, 338.

29. Scott W. Hibbard, *Religious Politics and Secular States: Egypt, India, and the United States* (Baltimore: Johns Hopkins University Press, 2010).

30. Ibid., 11.

31. Ibid., 12.

32. Larry Witham, *Marketplace of the Gods: How Economics Explains Religion* (New York: Oxford University Press, 2010), 6.

33. Ibid., 8.

34. Ibid., 7.

35. Larry Witham, "Was Adam Smith an 'Economist of Religion'?," paper presented at Association for the Study of Religion, Economics and Culture, Arlington, VA, April 8, 2011, 9–10, http://www.thearda.com/asrec/archive/papers/witham_adam_smith.pdf.

36. Oliver McTernan, *Violence in God's Name: Religion in an Age of Conflict* (Maryknoll, NY: Orbis Books, 2003), 10.

37. Paul Collier, *The Bottom Billion: Why the Poorest Countries Are Failing and What Can Be Done about It* (New York: Oxford University Press, 2007), 17–37.

38. Interview with Paul Collier published by *One Earth Future* on February 5, 2015, "Peace in the Twenty-First Century," https://www.youtube.com/watch?v=9xJLJef2r5A.

39. Jeffrey C. Alexander, "Analytic Debates: Understanding the Relative Autonomy of Culture," in *Culture and Society: Contemporary Debates*, ed. Jeffrey C. Alexander and Steven Seidman (Cambridge: Cambridge University Press, 1990), 2.

40. Laurence R. Iannaccone and Eli Berma, "Religious Extremism: The Good, the Bad, and the Deadly," *Public Choice* 128 (2006): 124, where they also distance themselves from the "economics really" position while stating how economic factors truly matter in any explication of religious extremism: "Lest we appear to have arrived at the secularist view that religious terrorism is "really" about economic deprivation, we must remind readers that we are addressing a subtle interaction between religion and economics."

41. Safiya Aftab, "Poverty and Militancy," *Conflict and Peace Studies* 1, no. 1 (October–December 2008): 8–9, http://san-pips.org/downloads/20.pdf.

42. Jessica Stern, *Terror in the Name of God: Why Religious Militants Kill* (New York: HarperCollins, 2003), 284.

43. James W. Jones, *Blood That Cries Out from the Earth* (Oxford: Oxford University Press, 2008), 27.

44. Ibid.

45. Ruth Stein, *For Love of the Father: A Psychoanalytical Study of Religious Terrorism* (Stanford, CA: Stanford University Press, 2010), 18.

46. Sudhir Kakar, *The Colours of Violence: Cultural Identities, Religion, and Conflict* (Chicago: University of Chicago Press, 1996), 186.

47. See ibid., 87–185.

48. Farhad Khosrokhavar, "The Psychology of the Global Jihadists," in Strozier et al., *The Fundamentalist Mindset*, 144.

49. George M. Marsden, *Understanding Fundamentalism and Evangelicalism* (Grand Rapids: Wm. B. Eerdmans Publishing, 1991), 1.

50. Barber, *Fear's Empire*, 26.

51. Martin E. Marty, *When Faiths Collide* (Malden, MA: Blackwell, 2005), 19.

52. Stern, *Terror in the Name of God*, 30.

53. Kakar, *The Colours of Violence*, 238.

54. As quoted in Stern, *Terror in the Name of God*, 136–37.

55. Aslan, *How to Win a Cosmic War*, 136.

56. One could even say "masculine" religion. I am aware of the scholarship that connects religious fundamentalism with the gender anxiety of men. Violence thus is a public symptom of masculine pathology worked out by religious fundamentalists. There can be no denying that much of the violence that is planned and executed in the world derives from male chambers and male brigades. The aggressive actions of taming the world also arises from a need and desire to take the world back to a paradise that is lost, one in which there would be less confusion about the roles of men and women, a place and time where order will be maintained by patriarchy. Violence is man's way of taking the world back to where it will be safe, secure, orderly, and perfect. Religious conceptions of

such a paradise mythologically put men at the center of such a rule. This lost kingdom may be taken back violently since its objective is to herald original order where God's rule and man's reign are restored. Juergensmeyer suggests the manner in which violence connects individual male anxiety with collective patriarchal pathology. "Nothing is more intimate than sexuality, and no greater humiliation can be experienced than failure over what one perceives to be one's sexual role. Such failures are often the basis for domestic violence, and when these failures are linked with the social roles of masculinity and femininity, they can lead to public violence. Terrorist acts, then, can be forms of symbolic empowerment for men whose traditional sexual roles—their very manhood—is perceived to be at stake" (Mark Juergensmeyer, *Terror in the Mind of God: The Global Rise of Religious Violence* [Berkeley: University of California Press, 2003], 198–99).

57. Ibid., xi.
58. From the news article "Israel Is Clamping Down on Jewish Terrorists," *The Economist*, January 8, 2016, http://www.economist.com/news/middle-east-and-africa/21685727 -what-prosecution-two-settlers-says-about-relations-between-israeli-jews-and-arabs.
59. Juergensmeyer, *Terror in the Mind of God*, 210.

Chapter Two: Christian Fundamentalism

1. Paul's self-confession of "violently persecuting" religious communities other than his own is found earlier, in Galatians 1:13.
2. This slogan, which is the name of a super PAC, represents the Democratic party's mantra for opposing Trump and promoting Hillary Clinton in the 2016 presidential election.
3. Although associated with Donald J. Trump's presidential campaign of 2016, this slogan was first used by Ronald Reagan during his 1980 presidential run.
4. The demographic study—based on analysis of more than 2,500 censuses, surveys, and population registers—finds 2.2 billion Christians (32% of the world's population), 1.6 billion Muslims (23%), 1 billion Hindus (15%), nearly 500 million Buddhists (7%) and 14 million Jews (0.2%) around the world as of 2010: "The Global Religious Landscape," *Pew Research Center: Religion and Public Life*, December 12, 2012, http://www .pewforum.org/2012/12/18/global-religious-landscape-exec/.
5. Harvey Cox, *The Future of Faith* (New York: HarperOne, 2009), 147.
6. Marty, *When Faiths Collide*, 57.
7. Ibid.
8. Fisher Humphrey and Philip Wise, *Fundamentalism* (Macon, GA: Smyth & Helwys, 2004), 26.
9. Ibid.
10. The five fundamentals of fundamentalism were based on a 1910 statement of the General Assembly of Northern Presbyterian Church that framed the identity of this movement in conformity to the following core doctrinal affirmations: The inerrancy of Scripture; the virgin birth and deity of Christ; the substitutionary view of the atonement; the bodily resurrection of Christ; and the historicity of miracles. The last of these was substituted in the 1920s by belief in the imminent return of Christ. Referred to as premillennialism, it professed that Christ is returning soon and on his return will rule on earth for a thousand years after defeating the devil in the great battle of Armageddon. For a summary of these five fundamentals, see ibid., 43–56.

11. Karen Armstrong, *The Battle for God* (New York: Ballantine Books, 2001), 369.
12. Humphrey and Wise, *Fundamentalism*, 28.
13. Ibid., 29.
14. Ibid.
15. Cox, *The Future of Faith*, 150–51.
16. In this case, John Scopes, a substitute science teacher, was found guilty of teaching the theory of evolution prohibited by state law and fined accordingly. "Fundamentalism won the battle in Dayton, but they lost the war," according to Humphrey and Wise, *Fundamentalism*, 29.
17. For more details, see Noah Adams, "Timeline: Remembering the Scopes Monkey Trial," *National Public Radio*, July 5, 2005, http://www.npr.org/2005/07/05/4723956 /timeline-remembering-the-scopes-monkey-trial.
18. Richard T. Hughes, *Christian America and the Kingdom of God* (Urbana: University of Illinois Press, 2009), 151.
19. "Region and Country or Area of Birth of the Foreign-Born Population: 1960 to 1990," *U.S. Bureau of the Census*, March 9, 1999, http://www.census.gov/population/www /documentation/twps0029/tab03.html.
20. Drawn from ibid.
21. Richard T. Antoun, *Understanding Fundamentalism: Christian, Islamic, and Jewish Movements*, 2nd ed. (Lanham, MD: Rowman & Littlefield Publishers, 2008), 85–116.
22. Ibid., 108.
23. In 1989 Bob Jones III wrote that his university "is proud to be known as fundamentalist. . . . We oppose all atheistic, agnostic, and humanistic attacks on the Scripture"; Mark Taylor Dalhouse, *An Island in the Lake of Fire: Bob Jones University, Fundamentalism, and the Separatist Movement* (Athens, GA: University of Georgia Press, 1996), 1.
24. Ibid., 2–3.
25. Gregory A. Boyd, *The Myth of a Christian Nation: How the Quest for Political Power Is Destroying the Church* (Grand Rapids: Zondervan, 2005), 80.
26. Michael Hardt and Antonio Negri, *Empire* (Cambridge, MA: Harvard University Press, 2001), 147–48.
27. Pat Robertson, *The New World Order* (Dallas: Word Publishing, 1991), 218.
28. Ibid., 227.
29. James Ciment, ed., *World Terrorism: An Encyclopedia of Political Violence from Ancient Times to the Post-9/11 Era* (New York: Routledge, 2015), 211.
30. K. N. Panikkar, afterword in *The Concerned Indian's Guide to Communalism*, ed. K. N. Panikkar (New Delhi: Viking Press, 1999), 230.
31. See Ibid., 230–39.
32. Charles B. Strozier and David M. Terman, introduction in Strozier et al., *The Fundamentalist Mindset*, 3.
33. George Marsden, *Militant Christianity: The Rise of Fundamentalism in American Culture* (Online: Now and Then Reader, 2012), http://www.nowandthenreader.com /militant-christians-the-rise-of-fundamentalism-in-american-culture/preview/.
34. Hughes, *Christian America*, 156.
35. Steve Bruce, *Fundamentalism*, 2nd ed., rev., updated (Cambridge, UK: Polity Press, 2008), 9. He also suggests somewhat sweepingly that such a vision binds Christian and Muslim fundamentalists. According to him, "Both in general terms and in many specifics the fundamentalist agenda in the USA is much the same as it is in Islamic counties.

Religious rightists first and foremost wish to reestablish the public primacy of their culture. Secondly, they wish to remove obstacles to the successful transmission of their culture to their children" (75).

36. Hans G. Kippenberg, *Violence as Worship: Religious Wars in the Age of Globalization* (Stanford, CA: Stanford University Press, 2011), 182.

37. George W. Bush, "Remarks by the President upon Arrival, The South Lawn," *The White House*, September 16, 2001, http://georgewbush-whitehouse.archives.gov/news/releases/2001/09/20010916-2.html.

38. Ibid.

39. David Domke, as quoted in Hughes, *Christian America*, 166.

40. Charles B. Strozier, "Opening the Seven Seals of Fundamentalism" in Strozier et al., *The Fundamentalist Mindset*, 119.

41. I am aware of other approaches to Christian fundamentalism that suggest many more features. Three examples of such approaches, arising from scholarly work that examines Christian fundamentalism in the context of other global fundamentalist movements, are especially pertinent. The first is a fascinating though older book by Gabriel A. Almond, R. Scott Appleby, and Emmanuel Sivan (*Strong Religion: The Rise of Fundamentalism around the World* [Chicago: University of Chicago Press, 2003]) that looks back and summarizes aspects of these religious movements as interpreted in the five volumes published in 1991–95 by the Fundamentalism Project (see Introduction, n. 5). Differentiating between ideological and organizational categories, the collaborators on this project posit *nine* "characteristics of fundamentalism." The *five ideological* characteristics are reactivity to marginalization, selectivity of Scripture, dualistic worldview, absolutist character of sacred text or tradition, and miraculous culmination of history. The *four organizational* characteristics of religious fundamentalism, according to these scholars, are election of members, sharp boundaries, authoritarian leadership, and strictly regulated behavioral requirements.

The second is a widely circulated book by Charles Kimball from the United States that points to *five* religious "warning signs" exhibited by religious fundamentalism. Writing as an ordained Baptist minister, he suggests that the following *five religious* marks lead to a corruption in religion causing that which is good to become evil: absolute truth claims, blind obedience, establishing the "ideal time," the end used to justify any means, and the authority to declare holy war; see his work *When Religion Becomes Evil: Five Warning Signs*, rev., updated (New York: HarperOne, 2008).

The third scholarly contribution is a comprehensive and meticulously researched essay by Jakobus M. Vorster from South Africa on the *seven* "core characteristics" of fundamentalism. With an eye toward Christian fundamentalism in the U.S.A., he offers the following seven motifs that propel this movement: literalist use of religious texts, traditioning, casuistic ethics, reactionary prejudicial intolerance, in-group frame of mind, reliance on strong leadership, and inclination to violence; see his "Perspectives on the Core Characteristics of Religious Fundamentalism Today," *Journal for the Study of Religions and Ideologies*, 7, no. 21 (Winter 2008): 44–66. In my own analysis of religious marks of Christian fundamentalism, I tend to collapse some of the categories discussed by scholars such as Almond et al., Kimball, and Vorster, even as I consciously confine myself to the more ideological aspects of these sources.

42. Douglas Pratt, "Terrorism and Religious Fundamentalism: Prospects for a Predictive Paradigm," *Marburg Journal of Religion* 11, no. 1 (June 2006): 8.

43. Antoun, *Understanding Fundamentalism*, 37.

44. Ibid., 41.

45. Harriet A. Harris, *Fundamentalism and Evangelicals* (Oxford: Oxford University Press, 2008), 313.

46. Robert P. Jones, *Progressive and Religious: How Christian, Jewish, Muslim, and Buddhist Leaders Are Moving beyond Wars and Transforming American Public Life* (Lanham, MD: Rowman & Littlefield Publishers, 2008), 85.

47. Chuck Baldwin, "Our Politically Correct Theologian-in-Chief," *The Covenant News*, December 13, 2002.

48. Kevin Sieff, "Florida Pastor Terry Jones's Koran Burning Has Far-Reaching Effect," *The Washington Post*, April 2, 2011, http://www.washingtonpost.com/local/education/florida-pastor-terry-joness-koran-burning-has-far-reaching-effect/2011/04/02/AFpiFoQC_story.html.

49. Via Rebeccah L. Ratner, "A Small Church Pastor Provokes the World: Positioning Theory Unravels the Quran Burning Controversy," MA thesis, Georgetown University, April 23, 2012, https://repository.library.georgetown.edu/bitstream/handle/10822/557550/Ratner_georgetown_0076M_11780.pdf;sequence=1, 7.

50. Hardt and Negri, *Empire*, 147.

51. Philip Jenkins, *Laying Down the Sword: Why We Ignore the Bible's Violent Verses* (New York: HarperOne, 2011), 6.

52. Kimball, *When Religion Becomes Evil*, 80.

53. It is important to reiterate that allegiance to the absolute authority of the Bible is intertwined with other social, economic, and political factors in the overall working out of Christian fundamentalism. Thus, even while asserting that "the literalist use of Scripture can be regarded as the most important characteristic of fundamentalism," Vorster is quick to include "nationalism and patriotism combined with self-centric ideals" as elements creating "violence for the sake of furthering a holy agenda" (Vorster, "Core Characteristics of Religious Fundamentalism," 49).

54. Jenkins, *Laying Down the Sword*, 75.

55. Ibid., 76.

56. Charles B. Strozier and Katherine Boyd, "Definitions and Dualisms," in Strozier et al., *The Fundamentalist Mindset*, 14.

57. As quoted in Juergensmeyer, *Terror in the Mind of God*, 160.

58. Raimon Panikkar, *The Rhythm of Being: The Gifford Lectures* (Maryknoll, NY: Orbis Books, 2010), 215.

59. Karen Armstrong points to this othering of Muslims from 2001 onward. In a 2003 interview, she says, "I am also worried about the rise in religious intolerance in the West. Immediately after 9/11 there was a window of opportunity, and many Americans were eager to learn more about Islam. But recently the mood seems to have hardened. The Christian Right, for example, seems to have been fanning the flames of hatred and misunderstanding" ("The Freelance Monotheist: An Interview with Karen Armstrong," *Tricycle: The Buddhist Review* 12, no. 4 (Summer 2003): 113.

60. Sabrina Siddiqui, "Americans' Attitudes toward Muslims and Arabs Are Getting Worse, Poll Finds," *The Huffington Post*, July 29, 2014, http://www.huffingtonpost.com/2014/07/29/arab-muslim-poll_n_5628919.html?utm_hp_ref=religion.

61. Ibid.

62. "How Americans Feel about Religious Groups," *Pew Research Center: Religion and*

Public Life, July 16, 2014, http://www.pewforum.org/2014/07/16/how-americans-feel
-about-religious-groups/.

63. Jürgen Moltmann, *Sun of Righteousness, Arise! God's Future for Humanity and the Earth* (Minneapolis: Fortress Press, 2010), 144.

64. James W. Jones, "Eternal Warfare: Violence in the Mind of American Apocalyptic Christianity," in Strozier et al., *The Fundamentalist Mindset*, 94.

65. "To date [2009] the Left Behind series has sold more than 65 million copies, which means they've sold as many Left Behind books as copies of *Catcher in the Rye*. . . . They've even sold 10 million more copies than *Merriam-Webster* dictionaries, and that's been on sale since 1898! Commenting on the first book in the series, Reverend Jerry Falwell said, 'In terms of its impact on Christianity, it's probably greater than that of any other book in modern times, outside the Bible'"; Rachel Maddow, "Tim LaHaye and Jerry B. Jenkins Sit Down with MSNBC's Rachel Maddow," summary plus video of February 25, 2009, *NBC News.com*, aired February 27, 2009, http://www.nbcnews .com/id/29496421/ns/msnbc-rachel_maddow_show/t/full-video-left-behind-authors-join -maddow/#.VO-M_fnF-nE.

66. Moltmann, *Sun of Righteousness*, 143.

67. As quoted in Stein, *For Love of the Father*, 20. See Michael Ignatieff, *The Lesser Evil: Political Ethics in an Age of Terror* (Princeton, NJ: Princeton University Press, 2004).

68. Pratt, "Terrorism and Religious Fundamentalism," 13.

69. Lloyd Steffen, *The Demonic Turn: The Power of Religion to Inspire and Restrain Violence* (Cleveland: Pilgrim Press, 2003), 25.

70. Ibid., 15–25.

71. Moltmann, *Sun of Righteousness*, 98.

72. "War and occupation directly and indirectly claimed the lives of about a half million Iraqis from 2003 to 2011," according to a groundbreaking 2013 *PLOS Medicine* journal survey led by public health expert Amy Hagopian of the University of Washington in Seattle. Apart from this huge figure, "some 4,804 U.S., British, and other coalition armed service members died in the invasion and occupation of Iraq." This is reported in a news article by Dan Vergano, "Half-Million Iraqis Died in the War, New Study Says: Household Survey Records Deaths from All War-Related Causes, 2003 to 2011," *National Geographic*, October 16, 2013, via http://news.nationalgeographic.com /news/2013/10/131015-iraq-war-deaths-survey-2013.

73. Jerry Falwell, "God Is Pro-War," *WND.com*, January 31, 2004, http://www.wnd .com/2004/01/23022/.

74. "If you take out Saddam, Saddam's regime, I guarantee you that it will have enormous positive reverberations on the region" (Benjamin Netanyahu). This is recounted by several in response to a similar appeal Netanyahu made to the U.S. Congress on March 3, 2015. For an excellent critical response to this collaborative ploy of Christian and Jewish fundamentalist worldviews, see Rabbi Michael Lerner, "The Fantasy World of Benjamin Netanyahu: Responses to His Talk to Congress," March 3, 2015, http://www .huffingtonpost.com/rabbi-michael-lerner/the-fantasy-world-of-benj_b_6796216.html.

75. Jürgen Moltmann, *The Coming of God: Christian Eschatology* (Minneapolis: Fortress Press, 1996), 170.

76. "Manifest destiny" is a phrase that invoked the idea of divine sanction for the territorial expansion of the United States. It first appeared in print in 1845, in the July–August issue of the *United States Magazine and Democratic Review*. The anonymous author,

thought to be its editor, John L. O'Sullivan, proclaimed "our manifest destiny to over-spread the continent allotted by Providence for the free development of our multiplying millions"; via http://www.u-s-history.com/pages/h337.html.

77. Ibid.

78. In coming with these categories, I am influenced by Julie Scott Jones's work on contemporary Christian fundamentalism: *Being the Chosen: Exploring a Christian Fundamentalist Worldview* (Farnham, UK: Ashgate Publishing, 2010).

79. Ibid., 24–25.

80. Ibid., 25.

81. Jones suggests that this conviction is the fulcrum on which Christian fundamentalism oscillates: "The sense of being 'chosen' is the base on which the rest of the worldview is built, without this belief the other elements would cease to be as important or more importantly make sense; why worry about the end of the world or of taking political action against so-called 'enemies,' if you did not consider yourself to be chosen" (ibid., 27).

82. David Domke and Kevin Coe, *The God Strategy: How Religion Became a Political Weapon in America* (New York: Oxford University Press, 2010), 47.

83. Ibid., 19.

84. Hibbard, *Religious Politics and Secular States*, 177.

85. Ibid.

86. Geiko Müller-Fahrenholz, *America's Battle for God: A European Christian Looks at Civil Religion* (Grand Rapids: Wm. B. Eerdmans Publishing, 2007), 18.

87. Marty, *When Faiths Collide*, 58.

88. Armstrong, *The Battle for God*, 369.

89. In a blog for University of South Carolina on August 6, 2012, titled "Christian Terrorism Comes to Milwaukee," Mark Juergensmeyer continues to argue his case: "Like the Oklahoma City bomber, Timothy McVeigh, and the Norwegian militant, Anders Breivik, Page thought he was killing to save white Christian society. Though there is no evidence that Page was a pious Christian, that is true of many religious terrorists. If the hard-talking, swaggering al Qaeda militants can be called Muslim terrorists, certainly Page can be called a Christian terrorist." See http://religiondispatches.org/christian-terrorism-comes-to-milwaukee/.

90. To my surprise, almost horror, I discovered the following on a Web site named for Scott Roeder, who is in prison on a 50-year jail sentence: "On Sunday morning of May 31, 2009, Scott Roeder entered Reformation Lutheran Church and shot George Tiller in the head. Scott had an assignment from Almighty God. He knew he had right-standing with God, not because of anything he had done, but only because of what Jesus Christ had done for him. Since Jesus died on the cross for us and rose again, we too can have right-standing with God and fulfill our God-given purpose": http://www.scottroeder.org/.

91. Daniel Hill, "Fundamentalists Faith States: Regulation Theory as a Framework for the Psychology of Religious Fundamentalism," in Strozier et al., *The Fundamentalist Mindset*, 87.

92. Susan Friend Harding, *The Book of Jerry Falwell: Fundamentalist Language and Politics* (Princeton, NJ: Princeton University Press, 2000), 270.

93. Hibbard, *Religious Politics and Secular States*, 256.

94. See Ernest Tuveson, *Redeemer Nation: The Idea of America's Millennial Role* (Chicago: University of Chicago Press, 1968).

95. Walter Wink, *The Powers That Be: Theology for a New Millennium* (New York: Doubleday, 1999), 53.

96. Also see Robert Jewett and John Shelton Lawrence, *Captain America and the Crusade against Evil: The Dilemma of Zealous Nationalism* (Grand Rapids: Wm. B. Eerdmans Publishing, 2003).

97. Jack Nelson-Pallmeyer, *Saving Christianity from the Empire* (New York: Continuum, 2007), 168.

98. Juergensmeyer, *Terror in the Mind of God*, 255.

Chapter Three: Muslim Fundamentalism

1. Ayisha Malik, via Callie, "My Story through Faith: Paris," November 14, 2015, http://mystorythroughfaith.blogspot.com/.

2. Analysis by the Gallup Center for Muslim Studies, "In U.S., Religious Prejudice Stronger against Muslims, *Gallup*, January 21, 2010, http://www.gallup.com/poll/125312/religious-prejudice-stronger-against-muslims.aspx.

3. "Islamophobia: Understanding Anti-Muslim Sentiment in the West," *Gallup*, January 2013, http://www.gallup.com/poll/157082/islamophobia-understanding-anti-muslim-sentiment-west.aspx. Copyright © 2013 Gallup, Inc. All rights reserved. The content is used with permission; however, Gallup retains all rights of republication.

4. Peter Gottschalk and Gabriel Greenberg, *Islamophobia: Making Muslims the Enemy* (Lanham, MD: Rowman & Littlefield Publishers, 2008), 5, emphasis original.

5. Ibid., 5.

6. N. C. Asthana and Anjali Nirmal, *Urban Terrorism: Myths and Realities* (Jaipur: Pointer Publishers, 2009), 23.

7. John Esposito, *The Future of Islam* (New York: Oxford University Press, 2010), 23.

8. "The Global Religious Landscape," *Pew Research Center: Religion and Public Life*, December 18, 2012, http://www.pewforum.org/2012/12/18/global-religious-landscape-exec/.

9. "The Global Religious Landscape: Muslims," *Pew Research Center: Religion and Public Life*, December 18, 2012, http://www.pewforum.org/2012/12/18/global-religious-landscape-muslim/.

10. Stephen Prothero, *God Is Not One: The Eight Rival Religions That Run the World* (New York: HarperOne, 2010), 25.

11. James Traub, "Is Modi's India Safe for Muslims? Hindu Nationalism Is on the Rise in the Country with the World's Second-Largest Muslim Population," *FP: The Magazine*, June 26, 2015, http://foreignpolicy.com/2015/06/26/narendra-modi-india-safe-for-muslims-hindu-nationalism-bjp-rss/.

12. Beverly Milton-Edwards, *Islamic Fundamentalism since 1945* (New York: Routledge, 2005), 5.

13. Hugh Kennedy, *The Great Arab Conquests: How the Spread of Islam Changed the World We Live In* (Philadelphia: Da Capro Press, 2008), 3.

14. Ibid.

15. For a substantial account of the social and economic dimensions of the early spread of Islam, especially about the paradigm shift from a circulatory to a centralized economic system, see Mohammed A. Bamye, *The Social Origins of Islam: Mind, Economy, Discourse* (Minneapolis: University of Minnesota Press, 1999).

16. Kennedy, *The Great Arab Conquests*, 375.

17. Ibid.

18. Ira M. Lapidu, *A History of Islamic Societies*, 3rd ed. (New York: Cambridge University Press, 2014), 32.
19. Ibid.
20. Karen Armstrong, *Muhammad: A Prophet for Our Times* (San Francisco: HarperOne, 2006), 28.
21. Before Islam, the Kaaba (Kaʿba) was "a polytheist sanctuary and was a site of pilgrimage for people throughout the Arabian Peninsula." http://www.britannica.com/topic /Kabah-shrine-Mecca-Saudi-Arabia.
22. Reza Aslan, *No God but God: The Origin, Evolution, and Future of Islam* (New York: Random House, 2006), 4; in this breaking of all the idols in the Kaaba, it is reported that Muhammad did not break the idol of Jesus and his mother, Mary, as reported by Aslan: "One by one he [The Prophet] carried the idols out before the assembled crowd and, raising them over his head, smashed them to the ground, . . . all, that is, except for the one of Jesus with his mother, Mary" (106).
23. Ibid., 10.
24. Tom Holland, *In the Shadow of the Sword: The Battle for Global Empire and the End of the Ancient World* (New York: Doubleday, 2012).
25. Armstrong, *Muhammad*, 29.
26. Ibid., 30.
27. Ibid.
28. Seyyed Hossein Nasr, *Islam: Religion, History, and Civilization* (New York: HarperSanFrancisco, 2003), 31.
29. "The Future of the Global Muslim Population: Sunni and Shia Muslims," *Pew Research Center: Religion and Public Life*, January 27, 2011, http://www.pewforum.org/2011/01/27 /future-of-the-global-muslim-population-sunni-and-shia/.
30. The percentages of Sunnis and Shias in the top four Muslim-majority countries are taken from Pew Forum, in ibid. For the estimate of Sunni and Shia Muslims in the world, I take my cues from John Esposito and Seyyed Hossien Nasr; the higher percentage for Sunnis is from Nasr's *Islam*, 10; and the lower percentage for the same is from Esposito's *The Future of Islam*, 52.
31. See, for example, Nasr, *Islam*, 80–87.
32. I will use IS (Islamic State), in conformity with the Council on Foreign Relations, to signify ISIL and ISIS. See Zachary Laub, "The Islamic State," CFR Backgrounders, August 10, 2016, http://www.cfr.org/iraq/islamic-state/p14811.
33. "About 90% of the Country Practices Islam; of the Remaining 10%, 9% Practices Coptic Christianity" in "Population of Egypt 2014," *World Population Statistics*, October 8, 2014, http://www.worldpopulationstatistics.com/egypt-population/.
34. Thomas Pakenham, *The Scramble for Africa: The White Man's Conquest of the Dark Continent from 1876 to 1912* (New York: Avon Books, 1992), 75.
35. Ibid.
36. Ahmad N. Amir, Abdi O. Shuriye, and Ahmad F. Ismail, "Muhammad Abduh's Contribution to Modernity," *Asian Journal in Management Sciences and Education* 1, no. 1 (April 2012): 68, http://www.ajmse.leena-luna.co.jp/AJMSEPDFs/Vol.1(1)/AJMSE2012(1.1 -07).pdf.
37. "Rashid Rida, Muhammad," *The Oxford Dictionary of Islam* (Oxford: Oxford University Press, 2003), via *Oxford Islamic Studies Online*, 2007 and updated regularly, http://www .oxfordislamicstudies.com/article/opr/t125/e1979.

38. "The term Salafism refers to an interpretation of Islam that seeks to restore Islamic faith and practice to the way they existed at the time of Muhammad and the early generations of his followers (known as the Salaf, or the Forefathers—hence the adjective Salafi). Since this early period represented the golden age of Islam in its pure form, Salafis believe it should be the example followed by all Muslims today." Jonathan Brown, *Salafis and Sufis in Egypt* (Washington, DC: Carnegie Endowment for International Peace, 2011), 3.

39. Hibbard, *Religious Politics and Secular States*, 60.

40. Ibid.

41. Karen Armstrong, *Fields of Blood: Religion and the History of Violence* (New York: Alfred A. Knopf, 2014), 320.

42. Nabeel Jabbour, *The Rumbling Volcano: Islamic Fundamentalism in Egypt* (Pasadena, CA: Mandate Press, 1993), 71.

43. Milton-Edwards, *Islamic Fundamentalism since 1945*, 27.

44. Jabbour, *The Rumbling Volcano*, 109.

45. John Calvert, *Sayyid Qutb and the Origins of Radical Islamism* (New York: Columbia University Press, 2010), 14.

46. John Calvert, "The Afterlife of Sayyid Qutb," *Foreign Policy*, December 15, 2010, http://foreignpolicy.com/2010/12/15/the-afterlife-of-sayyid-qutb/.

47. Amr Elshobaki, "The Muslim Brotherhood—Between Evangelizing and Politics: The Challenge of Incorporating the Brotherhood into the Political Process," in *Islamist Politics in the Middle East: Movements and Change*, ed. Amer Said Shehata (New York: Routledge, 2012), 113.

48. See Tarek Masoud, *Counting Islam: Religion, Class, and Elections in Egypt* (New York: Cambridge University Press, 2014), 207–25.

49. Carrie Rosefsky Wickham has a section titled "The Brotherhood under the Dome of the Parliament" in her book *The Muslim Brotherhood: Evolution of an Islamist Movement* (Princeton, NJ: Princeton University Press, 2013), 52.

50. Peter Beaumont, "Mohamed Morsi Signs Egypt's New Constitution into Law," *The Guardian*, December 26, 2012, http://www.theguardian.com/world/2012/dec/26/mohamed-morsi-egypt-constitution-law.

51. Bruce Livesey, "The Salafist Movement," *Frontline*, January 25, 2005, http://www.pbs.org/wgbh/pages/frontline/shows/front/special/sala.html.

52. Valentine M. Moghadam, *Globalization and Social Movements: Islamism, Feminism, and the Global Justice Movement*, 2nd ed. (Lanham, MD: Rowman & Littlefield Publishers, 2013), 99.

53. For a well-researched essay on the influence of the Brotherhood beyond Egypt, see Hazem Kandil, *Inside the Brotherhood* (Cambridge, UK: Polity Press, 2015), 146–74.

54. Manfred B. Steger, *Globalization: A Very Short Introduction* (New York: Oxford University Press, 2009), 8.

55. Ibid., 10.

56. To cut through all the complicated and tangled theorizing on globalization, Manfred categorizes this twenty-first-century transformation in the world into three distinct components: "globality" refers to the social *condition*, "globalization" points to the set of social *processes*, and "global imaginary" lifts up the social *consciousness* of belonging to a global community. See ibid., 8–16.

57. Mark Juergensmeyer, *Global Rebellion: Religious Challenges to the Secular State, from*

Christian Militia to Al Qaeda (Berkeley, CA: University of California Press, 2008), 205–6. Apart from suggesting some version of these two factors for the rise of global jihad after 2001, Juergensmeyer also identifies battle-hungry U.S. foreign policy and the failure of the secular state as two other contributors to this "bitterly violent" phenomenon that arose as a "new religious incarnation of ideological confrontation" (211).

58. Reza Aslan, *Beyond Fundamentalism: Confronting Religious Extremism in the Age of Globalization* (New York: Random House, 2009), 32.

59. As quoted in ibid., 31.

60. In his first recorded speech as self-acclaimed caliph, Baghdadi reveals his political theology: "O Muslims everywhere, glad tidings to you and expect good. Raise your head high, for today—by Allah's grace—you have a state and khilāfah [caliphate], which will return your dignity, might, rights, and leadership. It is a state where the Arab and non-Arab, the white man and black man, the easterner and westerner are all brothers. . . . Their blood mixed and became one, under a single flag and goal, in one pavilion, enjoying this blessing, the blessing of faithful brotherhood. If kings were to taste this blessing, they would abandon their kingdoms and fight over this grace. So all praise and thanks are due to Allah." As translated by Abu Bakr al-Janabi, "What Did Abu Bakr al-Baghdadi Say [re the Islamic State]?," *Middle East Eye*, July 5, 2014, http://www.middleeasteye.net/news/what-did-baghdadi-say-320749010.

61. Graeme Wood, "What ISIS Really Wants," March 2015, http://www.theatlantic.com/magazine/archive/2015/03/what-isis-really-wants/384980/.

62. Ibid.

63. Bernard Haykel, "ISIS: A Primer," *Princeton Alumni Weekly*, June 3, 2015, https://paw.princeton.edu/issues/2015/06/03/pages/0027/index.xml.

64. Ibid.

65. Karima Bennoune, *Your Fatwa Does Not Apply Here: Untold Stories from the Fight against Muslim Fundamentalism* (New York: W. W. Norton, 2013), 336.

66. Let me give a brief synopsis of the other four pillars of Islam. The second pillar of Islam sets out the rhythmic pattern of daily submission to God. *Salat*, meaning to bow or to worship, is obligatory to Muslims all over the world. The third pillar of Islam is almsgiving, or *zakat*. Similar to the tithe offering expected of Jews and Christians, Muslims are required to give 2.5 percent of both one's income and possessions, including wealth such as gold, silver, and commercial assets. The fourth pillar of Islam is fasting, or *sawm*. Muslims are required to fast during the ninth month of the Islamic calendar, Ramadan. During the 29 or 30 days of Ramadan, all adult Muslims must give up any kind of food and drink, smoking, and sexual activity during the daylight hours. The fifth pillar of Islam is hajj. This is the pilgrimage to Mecca in Saudi Arabia that every Muslim, those physically capable and financially able, must undertake at least once in their lifetime. Hajj takes place in the twelfth month of the Islamic calendar. Hajj has a physical, spiritual, and social aspect to it. For more on the five pillars of Islam, see Musharraf Hussain, *The Five Pillars of Islam: Laying the Foundations of Divine Love and Service to Humanity* (Markfield, UK: Kube Publishing Ltd, 2012); Aslan, *No God but God*, 144–51; and Nasr, *Islam*, 7–15.

67. For more than ten years (1980–84 and 1996–2005) I was awakened by a piercing call to prayer that originated from the local mosque in Bangalore, India. Well before sunrise, "Allahu Akbar" (God is great) is cried out, almost as a form of auspicious greeting cum religious witness.

68. The second part of this affirmation states the decisive role of Muhammad as the "messenger" of God. These are the two parts of the Sunni creed. Often Shia Muslims add some version of a faith statement that lifts up Ali as the *"wali* [friend, custodian, or helper] of God" as a third part of this credo. Caliph Ali, the fourth successor of Prophet Muhammad, was his cousin and son-in-law, who ruled from 656 to 661. Ali is regarded as the first imam by the Shiites.

69. See Terry McDermott, *Perfect Soldiers: The Hijackers: Who They Were, Why They Did It* (New York: HarperCollins, 2005). Let me cite one passage that summarizes McDermott on this issue: "Most of the men of September 11 came from apolitical and unexceptional backgrounds. They evolved into devout, pious young men who, over time, drew deeper and deeper into Islam. As they did, they debated endlessly how best to serve their God, how to fulfill what they came to regard as sacred obligation. They saw themselves as soldiers of God" (xvi). Also see Bruce Lincoln, *Holy Terrors: Thinking about Religion after September 11*, 2nd ed. (Chicago: University of Chicago Press, 2006); Lawrence Wright, *The Looming Tower: Al-Qaeda and the Road to 9/11* (New York: Vintage Books, 2006); and Jessica Stern, *Terror in the Name of God.*

70. Helen Pidd and Ewen MacAskill, "Fort Hood Gunman Shouted 'Allahu Akbar' as He Opened Fire," *The Guardian*, November 6, 2009, http://www.theguardian.com /world/2009/nov/06/fort-hood-shooter-alive.

71. Mary Abdelmassih, "Egyptian Policeman Shouted 'Allahu Akbar' Before Shooting Six Christians," *Assyrian International News Agency*, January 12, 2011, http://www.aina.org /news/20110112115752.htm.

72. "Charlie Hebdo: Gun Attack on French Magazine Kills 12," *BBC News*, http://www .bbc.com/news/world-europe-30710883.

73. Andrew C. McCarthy, "The 'Secular' Muslim Brotherhood," *National Review*, February 12, 2011, http://www.nationalreview.com/article/259614/secular-muslim-brotherhood -andrew-c-mccarthy.

74. Quoted in Stein, *For Love of the Father*, 25, emphasis added by Stein.

75. Nasr, *Islam*, 77.

76. Seyyed Hossein Nasr, *The Heart of Islam: Enduring Values for Humanity* (New York: HarperSanFrancisco, 2002), 119.

77. Jabbour, *The Rumbling Volcano*, 89.

78. Richard P. Mitchell, *The Society of the Muslim Brothers* (1969; New York: Oxford University Press, 1993), 8, as quoted by Armstrong, *Fields of Blood*, 320.

79. Ray Takeyh and Nikolas K. Gvosdev, *The Receding Shadow of the Prophet: The Rise and Fall of Radical Political Islam* (Westport, CT: Praeger Publishers, 2004), 6.

80. Kandil, *Inside the Brotherhood*, 175.

81. Michael Cook, *The Koran: A Very Short Introduction* (New York: Oxford University Press, 2000), 144.

82. Hans Küng, *Islam: Past, Present and Future* (Oxford, UK: Oneworld Publications, 2007), 66–67.

83. Kandil, *Inside the Brotherhood*, 19

84. "The term 'Boko Haram' comes from the Hausa word *boko*, figuratively meaning 'western education' (often said to be literally 'alphabet,' from English 'book,' but the Hausa expert Paul Newman says it derives from a Hausa word with meanings such as 'fraud' as 'inauthenticity')." From Dan Murphy, "'Boko Haram' Doesn't Really Mean 'Western Education Is a Sin,'" *Christian Science Monitor*, May 6, 2014,

http://www.csmonitor.com/World/Security-Watch/Backchannels/2014/0506/Boko-Haram-doesn-t-really-mean-Western-education-is-a-sin.

85. Wickham, *The Muslim Brotherhood*, 23.
86. Seyyed Hossein Nasr, "Reflections on Islam and the West: Yesterday, Today and Tomorrow," in *Islam in Transition: Muslim Perspectives*, ed. John Donohue and John Esposito (New York: Oxford University Press, 2007), 372.
87. Kandil, *Inside the Brotherhood*, 1–2.
88. Ibid., 2.
89. Ibid.
90. Ibid.
91. Calvert, *Sayyid Qutb*, 14.
92. Mansoor Moaddel, *Islamic Modernism, Nationalism, and Fundamentalism: Episode and Discourse* (Chicago: University of Chicago Press, 2005), 198.
93. Efraim Karsh, *Islamic Imperialism: A History* (New Haven, CT: Yale University Press, 2007), 238.
94. Milton-Edwards, *Islamic Fundamentalism since 1945*, 10.
95. Khaled Abou El Fadl, "Peaceful Jihad," in *Taking Back Islam: American Muslims Reclaim Their Faith*, ed. Michael Wolfe and the producers of Beliefnet (Emmaus, PA: Rodale, 2004), 37.
96. Ibid.
97. Ayesha Jalal, *Partisans of Allah: Jihad in South Asia* (Cambridge, MA: Harvard University Press, 2010), 7.
98. Ibid.
99. Ahmed S. Hashim, "The Islamic States: From al-Qaeda Affiliate to Caliphate," *Middle East Policy Council* 21, no. 4 (Winter 2014), http://www.mepc.org/journal/middle-east-policy-archives/islamic-state-al-qaeda-affiliate-caliphate.
100. David A. Graham, "The Mysterious Life and Death of Abdelhamid Abaaoud," *The Atlantic*, November 19, 2015, http://www.theatlantic.com/international/archive/2015/11/who-was-abdelhamid-abaaoud-isis-paris/416739/. In his conviction that he was chosen by Allah to crusade against the Western crusaders against Muslims, Abaaoud recruited his 13-year-old brother (Younes Abaaoud) in 2014 to join him in this jihad. Younes was killed as he carried out the Paris attack on November 13, 2015. See David Jones, "Even His Own Family Wanted the Paris Mastermind Dead," *Daily Mail.com*, November 18, 2015, http://www.dailymail.co.uk/news/article-3324589/Even-family-wanted-dead-Privately-educated-Spoilt-parents-nightclub-loving-playboy-spurned-spread-hatred-slaughter.html.
101. Graham, "Life and Death of Abdelhamid Abaaoud."
102. Juergensmeyer, *Terror in the Mind of God*, 61.
103. Bernard Lewis, *What Went Wrong? The Clash Between Islam and Modernity in the Middle East* (New York: Oxford University Press, 2004), 151.
104. Aslan, *No God but God*, 248.
105. Ibid.
106. "The Islamic State (IS) and Saudi Arabia prescribe near-identical punishments for a host of crimes, according to documents circulated by the militant group," report Rori Donaghy and Mary Atkinson, "Crime and Punishment: Islamic State vs. Saudi Arabia," *Middle East Eye*, January 20, 2015, http://www.middleeasteye.net/news/crime-and-punishment-islamic-state-vs-saudi-arabia-1588245666#sthash.STzM8YHE.dpuf.

107. "Saudi Arabia becomes world's top arms importer," *RT News*, 9 (March 2015), https://www.rt.com/news/238881-saudi-arabia-arms-import/.

108. See, for example, Tariq Ramadan, *The Messenger: The Meanings of the Life of Muhammad* (New York, Oxford University Press, 2007); Ziauddin Sarda, *Muhammad: All That Matters* (London: Hodder Education, 2012); and Armstrong, *Muhammad*.

109. Armstrong, *Fields of Blood*, 180–81.

110. Aslan, *No God but God*, 59–61.

111. Armstrong, *Muhammad*, 116.

112. Esposito, *The Future of Islam*, 49.

113. Nasr, *The Heart of Islam*, 217.

Chapter Four: Hindu Fundamentalism

1. Prothero, *God Is Not One*, 135.

2. The Ottoman (Turkish Sunni Empire, 1299–1922), Safavid (Iranian Shiite Empire, 1502–1736), and Mughal (Turkic-Mongol Empire, 1526–1757) dynasties, who established control over Turkey, Iran, and India by using advanced firearms between the 15th and 16th centuries, are referred to as "Gunpowder Empires."

3. Catherine Blanshard Asher, *Architecture of Mughal India*, vol. 1.4 of *The New Cambridge History of India* (Cambridge, UK: Cambridge University Press, 1992), 25.

4. Ibid., 29.

5. John F. Richards, *The Mughal Empire* (Cambridge: Cambridge University Press, 1996), 171.

6. Ibid., 175.

7. Ibid., 177.

8. Faruqui, *The Princes of the Mughal Empire, 1504–1719* (Cambridge: Cambridge University Press, 2012), 9.

9. William Dalrymple, *The Last Mughal: The Fall of a Dynasty, Delhi, 1857* (New York: Vintage, 2008), 5.

10. William Dalrymple, "The East India Company: The Original Corporate Raiders," *The Guardian*, March 4, 2015, http://www.theguardian.com/world/2015/mar/04/east-india-company-original-corporate-raiders.

11. "The East India Company: The Company That Ruled the Waves," *The Economist*, December 17, 2011, http://www.economist.com/node/21541753.

12. Ibid.

13. Edna Fernandes, *Holy Warriors: A Journey into the Heart of Indian Fundamentalism* (New Delhi: Viking, 2006), xvi.

14. Here I am indebted to the work of Chetan Bhatt, who talks of "primordialism" as "an overarching framework that serves to provide ideological coherence to the idea of a primordial nationalism, primarily defined through an invention of archaic Vedic Hinduism." See his work *Hindu Nationalism: Origins, Ideologies and Modern Myths* (Oxford, UK: Berg, 2001), 10.

15. Angana P. Chatterji, *Violent Gods: Hindu Nationalism in India's Present* (Gurgaon, India: Three Essays Collective, 2009), 41.

16. For a convincing essay on how the "militant chauvinism" and "authoritarian fundamentalism" of Savarkar's Hindutva is the antithesis of Gandhi's Hinduism, see Rudolf C. Heredia, "Gandhi's Hinduism and Savarkar's Hindutva," *Economic and Political Weekly* 44, no. 29 (July 18, 2009): 62–67.

17. "Savarkar, Modi's Mentor: The Man Who Thought Gandhi a Sissy," *The Economist*, December 17, 2014, http://www.economist.com/news/christmas-specials/21636599 -controversial-mentor-hindu-right-man-who-thought-gandhi-sissy.

18. Ibid.

19. Bhatt, *Hindu Nationalism*, 79.

20. Vinayak Damodar Savarkar, *Hindutva: Who Is a Hindu?*, 2nd ed. (Bombay: Veer Savarkar Prakashan, 1969), 82.

21. Ibid., 86.

22. Ibid., 84–85.

23. Ibid., 91–92.

24. The most celebrated society of Brahmanism in India compares Savarkar's invention of the idea of Hindutva to the revelation given to the Vedic Seers. The Web site committed to documenting and propagating the philosophy of Veer Savarker (1883–1966), which was inaugurated by Prime Minster Modi while chief minister of Gujarat, states: "Veer Savarkar was and continues to be one of the tallest exponents of Hindutva and Hindu nationalism. His definition of the term 'Hindu' caused the Arya Samaj leader Swami Shraddhanand to exclaim, 'It must have been one of those Vedic dawns indeed which inspired our seers with new truths that revealed to the author of Hindutva this *mantra*, this definition of Hindutva.'" "Hindutva," *Veer Savarkar*, http://www.savarkar.org/en/hindutva.

25. Satish Deshpande, *Contemporary India: A Sociological View* (New Delhi: Viking, 2003), 80.

26. Savarkar, *Hindutva*, 101

27. Ibid., 113.

28. Christophe Jaffrelot, introduction in *The Sangh Parivar: A Reader*, ed. Christophe Jaffrelot (New Delhi: Oxford University Press, 2006), 1.

29. For an excellent study on Azariah as an evangelist, ecumenical leader, and national figure (including his conversations with Gandhi on the legitimacy of mass movements through the first few decades of the twentieth century), see Susan Billington Harper, *In the Shadow of the Mahatma: Bishop V. S. Azariah and the Travails of Christianity in British India* (Grand Rapids: Wm. B. Eerdmans Publishing, 2000).

30. J. Waskom Pickett, *Christian Mass Movements in India* (Nashville: Abingdon Press, 1933).

31. Ibid., 2.

32. Walter K. Anderson and Shridhar D. Damle, "RSS: Ideology, Organization, and Training," in Jaffrelot, *The Sangh Parivar*, 28.

33. Martha C. Nussbaum, *The Clash Within: Democracy, Religious Violence, and India's Future* (Cambridge, MA: Belknap Press, 2007), 154.

34. Christophe Jaffrelot, "The RSS: A Hindu Nationalists Sect," in Jaffrelot, *The Sangh Parivar*, 59.

35. Bhatt, *Hindu Nationalism*, 110.

36. Jawaharlal Nehru (1889–1964), "Speech on the Granting of Indian Independence, August 14, 1947," *Internet Modern History Sourcebook*, http://legacy.fordham.edu/halsall /mod/1947nehru1.html.

37. As cited in Hibbard, *Religious Politics and Secular States*, 127.

38. Jaffrelot, introduction in Jaffrelot, *The Sangh Parivar*, 4.

39. M. S. Golwalkar's words via Bhatt, *Hindu Nationalism*, 128.

40. M. S. Golwalkar, as cited in ibid., 135.

41. Ram Puniyani asserts that rising on the wings of RSS, "Hindu fundamentalism is

becoming more assertive from 1980s," in his work *Contours of Hindu Rashtra: Hindutva, Sangh Parivar and Contemporary Politics* (New Delhi: Kalpaz Publications, 2006), 262.

42. Christopher J. Fuller, *The Camphor Flame: Popular Hinduism and Society in India*, rev., expanded ed. (Princeton, NJ: Princeton University Press, 2004), 258.

43. For an excellent critique of secularism that was first published in 1987, see T. N. Madan, "Secularism in Its Place," in *Secularism and Its Critics*, ed. Rajeev Bhargava (Delhi: Oxford University Press, 1998), 297–320.

44. The phrase "archaic religious emotions" is adopted by Walzer from V. S. Naipaul. See Michael Walzer, *The Paradox of Liberation: Secular Revolutions and Religious Counterrevolutions* (New Haven, CT: Yale University Press, 2015).

45. Deshpande, *Contemporary India*, 82–83.

46. "As per the Institute for Scientific Research on Vedas (I-SERVE), planetarium software has ascertained the birth of Lord Rama as 10th January 5114 BCE in Ayodhya. As per the Indian calendar the time of the birth is in-between 12 noon and 1pm." Reported under a news article titled "Lord Rama's Date of Birth Scientifically Calculated," in *Zeenews Bureau*, August 27, 2012, http://zeenews.india.com/news/nation/lord-ramas-date-of-birth-scientifically-calculated_796118.html.

47. This has reference to Hanuman's (the monkey-faced God) army, which helped liberate Rama from the demon king Ravana.

48. Faruqui, *The Princes of the Mughal Empire*, 1.

49. For a succinct and precise history of events stemming from this sacred site, see Krishna Pokharel and Paul Beckett, "Ayodhya, the Battle for India's Soul: The Complete Story," *Wall Street Journal*, December 10, 2012, http://blogs.wsj.com/indiarealtime/2012/12/10/ayodhya-the-battle-for-indias-soul-the-complete-story/.

50. Hibbard, *Religious Politics and Secular States*, 150.

51. Hassan Gardezi and Hari Sharma, "Introduction," *Bulletin of Concerned Asian Scholars* 31, no. 2 (1999): 3.

52. Ibid., 4.

53. See the following essays: Gail Omvedt, "The Hindutava Bomb," *The Hindu*, June 20, 1998; Kalpana Sharma, "The Hindu Bomb," *The Bulletin of Atomic Scientists* 54, no. 4 (July–August 1988): 30–33.

54. The objective to build nuclear capacities, including for purposes of weapons, goes back to Congress era. Thus the label Hindutva or Hindu bomb fails to account for the complexity of the process that led to Pokhran. For a good assessment of this complexity, see Rajesh M. Basrur "On Indian Perspectives on the Global Elimination of Nuclear Weapons," in *Unblocking the Road to Zero: China and India*, ed. Barry Blechman, Stimson Nuclear Security Series (Washington, DC: Harry L. Stimson Center, March 2009), 2, https://www.stimson.org/sites/default/files/file-attachments/UnblockingRoadZeroChinaIndia_1.pdf.

55. Carey Sublette, "1998: The Year of Testing," *Pakistan's Nuclear Weapons Program*, http://nuclearweaponarchive.org/Pakistan/PakTests.html.

56. Meera Nanda, *Prophets Facing Backward: Postmodern Critiques of Science and Hindu Nationalism in India* (New Brunswick, NJ: Rutgers University Press, 2003), 37.

57. Ibid.

58. "Indian Astrology vs. Indian Science," *BBC World Service*, May 31, 2001, http://www.bbc.co.uk/worldservice/sci_tech/highlights/010531_vedic.shtml.

59. Meera Nanda, "Vedic Science and Hindu Nationalism: Arguments against a Premature

Synthesis of Religion and Science," in *Science and Religion in a Post-Colonial World: Interfaith Perspectives*, ed. Zainal Abidin Bagir (Hindmarsh, AUS: ATU Press, 2005), 28.

60. Karen Gabriel and P. K. Vijayan, "Fighting for Our Soul: Education under the Modi Regime," in *365 Days: Democracy and Secularism under the Modi Regime*, ed. John Dayal and Shabnam Hashmi (New Delhi: Anhad Publishers, 2015), 77, http://www .sanjosepeace.org/fmd/files/One%20year%20under%20Modi%20regime%20-%20 ANHAD%20-%202015%20for%20web.pdf..

61. "Statistics: Formal Education," *Vidya Bharati = Akhil Bhartiya Shiksha Sansthan*, http:// vidyabharati.net/statistics.php.

62. "Philosophy, Aims, and Objectives," *Vidya Bharti*, vidyabharti.net/philosphy_aim.php.

63. I am conscious of the unsuitability of using a Sanskrit term to describe this non-Sanskritic category consisting of informal, vernacular, local, oral traditions. I am employing the Sanskrit to keep this in sync with the other two canonical forms of scripture with the anticipation that this term will be incorporated into the catalogs of classifying Hindu scripture. Dr. David C. Scott, Hindu scholar and friend, made me aware that I have a choice between using *kujati* with the primary sense of murmur as a lament or complaint and *jalpita* that renders murmur as a soft spoken utterance. In consultation with him I have chosen the latter term.

64. Meera Nanda, "Response to My Critics," *Social Epistemology* 19, no. 1 (January–March, 2005): 155, http://www.physics.nyu.edu/sokal/Nanda_SocEpist.pdf.

65. Romila Thapar, "Syndicated Hinduism," in *Hinduism Reconsidered*, ed. Günther-Dietz Sontheimer and Hermann Kulke (New Delhi: Manohar Publications, 2001), 55; originally published as "Syndicated Moksha," *Seminar*, no. 313 (September 1985); also separately as *Syndicated Hinduism* (New Delhi: Critical Quest, 2010).

66. Badri Narayan, *Fascinating Hindutva: Saffron Politics and Dalit Mobilisation* (New Delhi: Sage Publications, 2009), 12.

67. Ibid., 13.

68. Among the literary sources the Manusmriti, or Manu Smriti (Manu Dharma Shastra), compiled around 500 BCE, most explicitly and systematically enumerates the degrading ways in which the Sudras and outcastes ought to be treated by the dominant caste community.

69. Anderson and Damle, "RSS: Ideology, Organization, and Training," 28.

70. Deendayal Upadhyaya, *Integral Humanism*, four lectures of April 22–25, 1965, http:// antibjp.tripod.com/archives/chapter3.html.

71. Dipankar Gupta, *Mistaken Modernity: India between Worlds* (New Delhi: Harper Collins, 2000), 35.

72. Ibid.

73. S. P. Udayakumar, "Nukes as a Way of Life? Contextualizing the Nuclear Madness in South Asia," *Bulletin of Concerned Asian Scholars* 31, no. 2 (1999): 80.

74. Chatterji, *Violent Gods*, 52.

75. Similar to this is Martha Nussbaum's description of this event as a "genocide." See her chapter "Genocide in Gujarat," in *The Clash Within*, 17–51.

76. Paul Brass, "Contemporary Conflicts: The Gujarat Pogrom of 2002," *Social Science Research Council*, March 26, 2004, http://conconflicts.ssrc.org/archives/gujarat/brass/.

77. Ibid.

78. Parvathi Menon and T. S. Subramanian, "Communalism: A Hate Campaign," *Frontline* 17, no. 15 (July 22–August 4, 2000), http://www.frontline.in/static/html/fl1715 /17150340.htm.

79. From the Ahmadnagar journal *Gyanodaya*, "The Recent Attacks on Christians in Kandhamal and Its Impacts," in *The Recent Attacks on Christians in Orissa: A Theological Response*, ed. Patna Regional Theological Centre (Patna: Prabhat Prakashan, 2009), 6.

80. Ibid., 7.

81. Kalyani D. Menon, "Converted Innocents and Their Trickster Heroes: The Politics of Proselytizing in India," in *The Anthropology of Religious Conversion*, ed. Andrew Buckser and Stephen D. Glazier (Lanham, MD: Rowman & Littlefield Publishers, 2003), 44.

82. Ibid.

83. J. M., *Hindu Nationalism in the United States: A Report on Nonprofit Groups*, July 2014, released via *South Asia Citizens Wire*, http://www.sacw.net/IMG/pdf/US_HinduNationalism_Nonprofits.pdf.

84. Ingrid Therwath, "'Far and Wide': The Sangh Parivar's Global Network," in Jaffrelot, *The Sangh Parivar*, 425, emphasis added.

85. Chatterji, *Violent Gods*, 41.

86. Ibid., 42.

87. "Executive Summary," in Dayal and Hashmi, *365 Days*, 8.

88. Let me furnish the whole quotation: "Hindutva feeds on Islamophobia, and to a lesser extent on Christianophobia. Its long-term goal is the hinduization of the whole of India. Its short-term goal is the intimidation of the minorities, especially Muslims and Christians—their persons, properties and institutions—and places of worship are under constant threat from Hindu fundamentalists" (Parel, introduction in Saha, *Religious Fundamentalism in the Contemporary World*, 1).

Chapter Five: Countering Violence and Nurturing Peace amid Competing Religious Fundamentalisms

1. George W. Dollar, *A History of Fundamentalism in America* (Greenville, SC: Bob Jones University Press, 1973), vi, via Humphrey and Wise, *Fundamentalism*, 25.

2. Charles Kimball, *When Religion Becomes Lethal: The Explosive Mix of Religion and Politics in Judaism, Christianity, and Islam* (San Francisco: Jossey-Bass, 2011), 98.

3. Ibid., 99.

4. Seyyed Hossein Nasr, *Islam in the Modern World: Challenged by the West, Threatened by Fundamentalism, Keeping Faith with Tradition* (New York: HarperOne, 2010), 9.

5. Ibid., 61.

6. Antoun, *Understanding Fundamentalism*, 141.

7. Bennoune, *Your Fatwa Does Not Apply Here*, 31.

8. Ibid., 53.

9. Jeff Haynes's early but influential comparative global study provides a clear distinction between religions in which "singular scriptural revelations are central to each fundamentalist dogma" (Islam, Judaism, and Christianity) and religions that are driven by "their desire to recapture a national identity" (Hinduism and Buddhism). See his work *Religion, Fundamentalism and Ethnicity: A Global Perspective*, Discussion Paper 65 (Geneva: United Nations Research Institute for Social Development, May 1995), 21, http://www.unrisd.org/80256B3C005BCCF9/(httpPublications)/265FAA83B0EA35EB80256B67005B67F6.

10. Amartya Sen, *The Argumentative Indian: Writings on Indian History, Culture, and Identity* (New York: Picador, 2005), 72.

11. "While scripturalism reaches back to the ancient roots and professes the will of God

according to a literal and a-historical use of texts in order to highlight the core fundamentals of religion, traditioning is an attempt to provide further authority to these fundamentals by indicating their stand and value in the tradition of the particular religion. Consequently, fundamentalism has a strong inclination to the history of its tradition" (Vorster, "Core Characteristics of Religious Fundamentalism," 49).

12. Richard T. Antoun, *Understanding Fundamentalism*, 37.
13. As quoted by Julie Jones, *Being the Chosen*, 112.
14. "But I want you to understand that Christ is the head of every man, and the husband is the head of his wife, and God is the head of Christ" (1 Corinthians 11:3).
15. As quoted by Julie Jones, *Being the Chosen*, 122.
16. "At least 11 people have been killed in attacks on abortion clinics in the United States since 1993," reports Liam Stack, "A Brief History of Deadly Attacks on Abortion Providers," *The New York Times*, November 29, 2015, http://www.nytimes.com/interactive /2015/11/29/us/30abortion-clinic-violence.html?_r=0.
17. Mona Chalabi, "Deadly Shootings Are Rare at US Abortion Clinics—but 'Disruptions' Are Common," *The Guardian*, November 30, 2015, http://www.theguardian .com/us-news/datablog/2015/nov/30/planned-parenthood-colorado-springs-shooting -abortion-clinics-violence.
18. Jabbour, *The Rumbling Volcano*, 89.
19. Mitchell, *The Society of the Muslim Brothers*, 8, as quoted by Armstrong, *Fields of Blood*, 320.
20. "The Arabic word *madrasa* (plural: *madaris*) generally has two meanings: (1) in its more common literal and colloquial usage, it simply means 'school'; (2) in its secondary meaning, a madrasa is an educational institution offering instruction in Islamic subjects including, but not limited to, the Quran, the sayings (*hadith*) of the Prophet Muhammad, jurisprudence (*fiqh*), and law." So stated by Christopher M. Blanchard, "Islamic Religious Schools, Madrasas: Background," *CRS [Congressional Research Service] Report for Congress*, January 23, 2008, https://www.fas.org/sgp/crs/misc/RS21654.pdf.
21. As quoted in Bennoune, *Your Fatwa Does Not Apply Here*, 14.
22. Nina Shen Rastogi, "Decapitation and the Muslim World: Is There Any Special Significance to Beheading in Islam?," *Slate*, February 20, 2009, http://www.slate.com /articles/news_and_politics/explainer/2009/02/decapitation_and_the_muslim_world.html. Although vaguely connected with a couple of instances where Allah calls for beheading (Qur'an, sura 47.4, "Therefore, when ye meet the Unbelievers (in fight), smite at their necks"; and sura 8.12, "I am with you: give firmness to the Believers: I will instill terror into the hearts of the Unbelievers: smite ye above their necks and smite all their fingertips off them"), this form of Islamic punishment has more legitimization from vested interpretations of the Hadith.
23. Janine Di Giovanni, "When It Comes to Beheading, ISIS Has Nothing over Saudi Arabia," *Newsweek*, October 14, 2014, http://www.newsweek.com/2014/10/24/when -it-comes-beheadings-isis-has-nothing-over-saudi-arabia-277385.html.
24. Moghadam, *Globalization and Social Movements*, 150.
25. Bennoune, *Your Fatwa Does Not Apply Here*, 81.
26. Ibid., 15.
27. Alongside the scores of interviews with women activists and feminist collectives in Bennoune's book *Your Fatwa Does Not Apply Here*, also see Theodore Friend, *Woman, Man, and God in Modern Islam* (Grand Rapids: Wm. B, Eerdmans Publishing, 2012);

and Priscilla Offenhauer, *Women in Islamic Societies: A Selected Study of Social Scientific Research* (Washington, DC: Federal Research Division, Library of Congress, 2005).

28. Article 48 in The Constitution of India 1949 (as of November 9, 2015), p. 23, declares: "The State shall, in particular, take steps for preserving and improving the breeds, and prohibiting the slaughter, of cows and calves and other milch and draught cattle"; http://lawmin.nic.in/olwing/coi/coi-english/coi-4March2016.pdf.

29. Sami Khan, "Beef Ban: States Where Cow Slaughter Is Legal and Illegal," *International Business Times*, October 5, 2015, http://www.ibtimes.co.in/beef-ban-states-where -cow-slaughter-legal-illegal-649249.

30. Ibid.

31. Meryl Sebastian, "'Maharashtra's Beef Ban Is Not Merely Communal, It Is Theocratic': Kancha Ilaiah," interview, *Daily News and Analysis*, March 4, 2015, http://www.dnaindia .com/india/interview-maharashtra-s-beef-ban-is-not-merely-communal-it-is-theocratic -kancha-ilaiah-2066223.

32. Aditi Vatsa, "Dadri: Mob Kills Man, Injures Son over 'Rumours' That They Ate Beef," *The India Express*, December 25, 2015, http://indianexpress.com/article/india/india -others/next-door-to-delhi-mob-kills-50-year-old-injures-son-over-rumours-they-ate-beef/.

33. Vishal Sharma, "Cow Activist, 4 Others Held after 2 Muslim Cowherds Hanged to Death," *Hindustan Times*, March 20, 2016, http://www.hindustantimes.com/india /five-arrested-after-two-muslim-cowherds-hanged-to-death-in-jharkhand/story-KcHi7 nNS22Y6CXAych5eBJ.html.

34. Article 25.1 of The Constitution of India, 1949 (as of November 9, 2015), p. 13, http:// lawmin.nic.in/olwing/coi/coi-english/coi-4March2016.pdf.

35. Anita Joshua, "Rajnath Pitches for Anti-conversion Law," *The Hindu*, April 28, 2015, http://www.thehindu.com/news/national/states-should-act-against-communal-incidents -rajnath/article7150757.ece.

36. Ruth Gledhill, *Christianity Today* contributing editor, "India: 600 Violent Attacks on Christians and Muslims since May," *World*, March 23, 2015, http://www.christiantoday .com/article/india.600.violent.attacks.on.christians.and.muslims.since.may/50574 .htm.

37. John Dayal, "Their Cross to Bear: The Christian Situation under Mr. Narendra Modi," in Dayal and Hashmi, *365 Days*, 118.

38. Shamik Ghosh, ed., "Rapes Occur in India, Not Bharat, Says RSS Chief Mohan Bhagwat," *NDTV Convergence* [*New Delhi Television*], January 4, 2013, http://www.ndtv.com /india-news/rapes-occur-in-india-not-bharat-says-rss-chief-mohan-bhagwat-509401.

39. Sikata Banerjee, "Gender and Nationalism: The Masculinization of Hinduism and Female Political Participation in India," *Women's Studies International Forum* 26, no. 2 (2003): 177.

40. Santosh C. Saha, "Hindu Revivalist Cultural Policies," in *Religious Fundamentalism in the Contemporary World*, 150.

41. Ibid., 155.

42. Bennoune, *Your Fatwa Does Not Apply Here*, 81.

43. Monica Duffy Toft, Daniel Philpott, and Timothy Samuel Shah, *God's Century: Resurgent Religion and Global Politics* (New York: W. W. Norton, 2011), 22.

44. Charles B. Strozier, "Opening the Seven Seals of Fundamentalism" in Strozier et al., *The Fundamentalist Mindset*, 119.

45. George H. W. Bush (U.S. president in 1989–93), "Address before a Joint Session of the

Congress on the Cessation of the Persian Gulf Conflict," March 6, 1991, *The American Presidency Project*, http://www.presidency.ucsb.edu/ws/?pid=19364.

46. Ibid.

47. Joseph Nye first distinguished "soft power" from "hard power" in the field of international relations, in his *Soft Power: The Means to Success in World Politics* (New York: Public Affairs, 2005); then he introduced the notion of "smart power" as an effective balance between the two as he suggested a third way for American foreign policy, in his *The Powers to Lead* (New York: Oxford University Press, 2008).

48. It is beyond the scope of this work to get into interpretations of this millennium (thousand-year rule of Christ; cf. Revelation 20) apart from noting that there are three major views: premillennialism holds that Christ will come *before* the millennium; postmillennialism maintains that Christ will come *after* the millennium; and amillennialism, or nonmillennialism, rejects any belief in the literal thousand-year rule of Christ on the earth. For a brief and pointed study, see Catherine Wessinger, ed., *The Oxford Handbook of Millennialism* (Oxford: Oxford University Press, 2011).

49. Kimball, *When Religion Becomes Lethal*, 167.

50. Ibid.

51. Even though conservative Christians are split on their support of Donald Trump, the Republican presidential nominee, in his first foreign policy speech on April 27, 2016, talked about "making America strong again" so that it can "save . . . humanity itself." Via Ryan Teague Beckwith, "Read Donald Trump's 'America First' Foreign Policy Speech," *Time*, April 27, 2016, http://time.com/4309786/read-donald-trumps-america-first-foreign-policy-speech/.

52. Qur'an, sura 9.31–33, translated by Dr. Rashad Khalifa, http://www.quran-islam.org/main_topics/quran/quran_in_english/sura_5_to_9_(P1323).html.

53. Sayyid Qutb, *Milestones*, first published in Arabic as *Ma'ālim fī al-ṭarīq* (Cairo: Maktabat Wahbah, 1964), quoted from p. 47 of *Studies in Islam and the Middle East* journal's online PDF, http://majalla.org/books/2005/qutb-nilestone.pdf.

54. As noted earlier, I am aware of Karsh's indefatigable scholarly zeal for lionizing the resistance of Zionism and pardoning the excesses of Israel against the backdrop of the imperialistic history of Islam. For a devastatingly critical perspective of Karsh, see the scathing essay written by one of his Jewish academic challengers, Benny Morris, who accuses his scholarship as being "completely politically motivated, often unscholarly, and, in large part, propagandistic": "My Response to Efraim Karsh," *American Thinker*, July 17, 2011, http://www.americanthinker.com/articles/2011/07/my_response_to_efraim_karsh.html#ixzz48qkuSdm4.

55. Efraim Karsh, *Islamic Imperialism*, 212.

56. Graeme Wood, "What ISIS really Wants," *The Atlantic* (March 2015), http://www.theatlantic.com/magazine/archive/2015/03/what-isis-really-wants/384980/.

57. Ibid.

58. Barak Mendelsohn, "The Jihadi Threat to International Order," *Islam and International Order* (New York: The Project on Middle East Political Science, July 22, 2015), 10, http://pomeps.org/wp-content/uploads/2015/07/POMEPS_Studies_15_Islam_Web.pdf.

59. Ashok Singhal died shortly after this statement, on November 17, 2015.

60. "By 2020, India Will Be Hindu nation, World by 2030: Ashok Singhal," *The Times of India*, July 18, 2015, http://timesofindia.indiatimes.com/india/By-2020-India-will-be-Hindu-nation-world-by-2030-Ashok-Singhal/articleshow/48125440.cms.

61. Amit Shah, at Vrindavan, "Modi Govt Promoting Sanatan Dharma: Amit Shah," *Press Trust of India*, via *Struggle for Human Existence*, February 8, 2016, https://hinduexistence.org/2016/02/10/modi-govt-is-promoting-sanatan-dharma-amit-shah/.

62. Aslan, *How to Win a Cosmic War*, 136.

63. James W. Jones, "Conclusion: A Fundamentalist Mindset?," in Strozier et al., *The Fundamentalist Mindset*, 216.

64. John Micklethwait and Adrian Wooldridge, *God Is Back: How the Global Rise of Faith Is Changing the World* (London: Penguin, 2010), 303–4.

65. Prothero, *God Is Not One*, 3.

66. Ibid., 3.

67. Walzer, *The Paradox of Liberation*, 103.

68. Eleazer S. Fernandez, *Burning Center, Porous Borders: The Church in a Globalized World* (Eugene, OR: Wipf & Stock, 2011), 180.

69. Moghadam, *Globalization and Social Movements*, 6–29.

70. Steger, *Globalization*, 98–128.

71. Grace Davie, *The Sociology of Religion: A Critical Agenda* (London: Sage Publications, 2007), 183.

72. Office of the Director of National Intelligence, National Counterterrorism Center, "2011 Report on Terrorism," NCTC, Washington, DC, as of March 12, 2012, http://fas.org/irp/threat/nctc2011.pdf.

73. I am playing with the phrase from Bronislaw Malinowski, "An Anthropological Analysis of War," in *Magic, Science, and Religion* (Glencoe, IL: Free Press, 1948), 285: "Aggression like charity begins at home," quoted in Marty, *When Faiths Collide*, 30–31.

74. McTernan, *Violence in God's Name*, 158.

75. Thomas L. Friedman, *The World Is Flat: A Brief History of the Twenty-first* Century (New York: Farrar, Straus & Giroux, 2005).

76. From prologue of Thomas L. Friedman, *Longitudes and Attitudes: Exploring the World after September 11* (New York: Farrar, Straus & Giroux, 2002), 6, https://books.google.com/books?id=qounE_g_j2EC&q=angry+men#v=snippet&q=angry%20men&f=false.

77. Bernard Lewis, *Islam and the West* (New York: Oxford University Press, 1994), 7.

78. Huntington, *Who Are We?*, 356.

79. Tisaranee Gunasekara, "National Security, in Peace Time," *The Island*, August 1, 2015, http://www.island.lk/index.php?page_cat=article-details&page=article-details&code_title=129277.

80. Robert Wuthnow and Matthew P. Lawson, "Sources of Christian Fundamentalism in the United States," in *Accounting for Fundamentalism: The Dynamic Character of the Movement*, ed. Martin E. Marty and R. Scott Appleby (Chicago: University of Chicago Press, 1994), 26.

81. Peter Herriot, *Religious Fundamentalism: Global, Local, Personal* (London: Routledge, 2009), 3.

82. G. Almond, E. Sivan, and R. S. Appleby, "Fundamentalism: Genus and Species," in *Fundamentalisms Comprehended*, ed. Martin Marty and Scott Appleby (Chicago: University of Chicago Press, 1995), 403.

83. Toft, Philpott, and Shah, *God's Century*, 13.

84. Grace Davie, *The Sociology of Religion: A Critical Agenda*, 2nd ed. (London: Sage Publications, 2013), 199.

85. Toft, Philpott, and Shah, *God's Century*, 14.

Chapter Six: Countering Violence and Nurturing Peace amid Competing Religious Fundamentalisms

1. World Council of Churches, Pontifical Council for Interreligious Dialogue, and World Evangelical Alliance, *Christian Witness in a Multi-Religious World: Recommendations for Conduct*, June 28, 2011, principle 6, via download, https://www.oikoumene.org /en/resources/documents/wcc-programmes/interreligious-dialogue-and-cooperation /christian-identity-in-pluralistic-societies/christian-witness-in-a-multi-religious-world.

2. John Kerry, "We Ignore the Global Impact of Religion at Our Peril," September 14, 2015, http://www.americamagazine.org/issue/religion-and-diplomacy.

3. Steffen, *The Demonic Turn*, 267.

4. Walter Wink, *Engaging the Powers: Discernment and Resistance in a World of Domination* (Minneapolis: Augsburg Fortress, 1992), 13.

5. The following two books have had a huge influence on nonviolent movements in the United States through the last quarter century: John Howard Yoder, *The Politics of Jesus* (1972), 2nd ed. (Grand Rapids: Wm. B. Eerdmans Publishing, 1994); and *The War of the Lamb: The Ethics of Nonviolence and Peacemaking* (Grand Rapids: Brazos Press, 2009).

6. Walter Wink, *Jesus and Nonviolence: A Third Way* (Minneapolis: Augsburg Fortress, 2003).

7. Baselios Cleemis Cardinal Thottunkal, "Majority of Hindus in India Are Secular, says Cardinal," *Deccan Herald*, March 2, 2016, http://www.deccanherald.com/content /532115/majority-hindus-india-secular-says.html.

8. Sunanda Y. Shastri and Yagneshwar S. Shastri, "Ahimsa and the Unity of All Things: A Hindu View of Non-violence," in *Subverting Hate: The Challenge of Nonviolence in Religious Traditions*, ed. Daniel L. Smith-Christopher (Maryknoll, NY: Orbis Books, 2007), 58.

9. Bennoune, *Your Fatwa Does Not Apply Here*, 330–31.

10. Ibid., 330.

11. Jack Nelson-Pallmeyer, *Is Religion Killing Us? Violence in the Bible and Quran* (New York: Continuum, 2005), xiv.

12. Ibid., xiv–xv.

13. Daniel L. Migliore, *Faith Seeking Understanding: An Introduction to Christian Theology*, 3rd ed. (Grand Rapids: Wm. B. Eerdmans Publishing, 2014), 52.

14. Ibid.

15. In these comments on Marcion, I am drawing from the well-established scholarship of Joseph B. Tyson, *Marcion and Luke-Acts: A Defining Struggle* (Columbia: University of South Carolina Press, 2006).

16. Eric A. Seibert, *The Violence of Scripture: Overcoming the Old Testament's Troubling Legacy* (Minneapolis: Fortress Press, 2012), 4.

17. Hector Avalos, *Fighting Words: The Origins of Religious Violence* (Amherst, NY: Prometheus Books, 2007), 360; after arguing that religion incites and sustains violence by creating scarce resources though its scriptures and theology, Hector Avalos advocates that our twenty-first-century efforts be united to eliminate violent scriptures in their entirety.

18. Hector Avalos, *The End of Biblical Studies* (Amherst, NY: Prometheus Books, 2007), 29.

19. Hector Avalos, "The Letter Killeth," *Journal of Religion, Conflict, and Peace* 1, no. 1 (Fall 2007), http://www.religionconflictpeace.org/volume-1-issue-1-fall-2007/letter-killeth.

20. Avalos (ibid.) comments on why certain texts need to be cut off from the refashioned biblical canon: Genesis 6–7, 22; Exodus 12:29; 22:18; Leviticus 20:13; Numbers 31:17; Deuteronomy 7:1–5; 22:13–30; 1 Samuel 15:1–3; 2 Samuel 12:21; 1 Kings 18:40; 2 Kings 23; Matthew 10:34–37; chap. 27; Luke 14:26; Hebrews 9:22; and Revelation.

21. Ibid.

22. John Dominic Crossan, *How to Read the Bible and Still Be a Christian: Struggling with Divine Violence from Genesis through Revelation* (New York: HarperOne, 2015), 28.

23. Jerome F. D. Creach, *Violence in Scripture: Interpretation Resources for the Use of Scripture in the Church* (Louisville, KY: Westminster John Knox Press, 2013), 3.

24. Ibid., 5.

25. Quoted by Donald G. Bloesch in Alister E. McGrath, *The Christian Theology Reader*, 4th ed. (Chichester, UK: Wiley-Blackwell, 2011), 136.

26. Ibid.

27. In a careful study of the historical Jesus, Crossan argues for an overall portrait of his nonviolent teachings and practice: "Only in John is there any mention of a 'whip of chords'—not for the money changers but for the herd of animals. That was an act of religiopolitical demonstration or of nonviolent resistance, not an act of violence with a whip used against people" (Crossan, *How to Read the Bible*, 8).

28. Walter Brueggemann, *The Prophetic Imagination*, 2nd ed. (Minneapolis: Augsburg Fortress, 2001). In a more recent book Brueggemann makes a similar distinction between "*official truth*" on the one hand, which is carried forward by "urban elites of dynasty and temple" in continuity with "the scribal community allied with other establishment parties,"—and "*counter truth*" on the other hand, which is carried out by "Jesus and his followers" with a view to "subvert" and "bewilder" the establishment; see his *Truth Speaks to Power: The Countercultural Nature of Scripture* (Louisville, KY: Westminster John Knox Press, 2013), 3, emphasis added.

29. Crossan, *How to Read the Bible*, 28.

30. In this vein of opening up the historical Jesus to the resurrected Christ, one might also point to the continued expansiveness of the Divine to the Christian Trinity. This includes the question of how Christians might find the working of the threefold modality/person/movement of the triune God in the Christian Bible, if one only confines divine presence and activity to Jesus Christ.

31. L. Juliana Claassens and Bruce C. Birch, eds., *Restorative Readings: The Old Testament, Ethics, and Human Dignity* (Eugene, OR: Pickwick Publications, 2015).

32. Derek Flood, *Disarming Scripture: Cherry-Picking Liberals, Violence-Loving Conservatives, and Why We All Need to Learn to Read the Bible Like Jesus Did* (San Francisco: Metanoia Books, 2014).

33. Nelson-Pallmeyer, *Saving Christianity from the Empire*, 109; he identifies three kinds of Divine violence that can be found through the Bible: God's liberating violence, God's punishing violence, and God's vindicating violence (109–10).

34. Nelson-Pallmeyer, *Is Religion Killing Us?*, 32.

35. Ibid., 59.

36. Charles B. Strozier, "Opening the Seven Seals of Fundamentalism," in Strozier et al., *The Fundamentalist Mindset*, 110.

37. In discussing Luke 9:51–10:12 in this chapter, I draw from an earlier article: see Sathianathan Clarke, "Global Cultural Traffic, Christian Mission, and Biblical Interpretation:

Rereading Luke 10:1–12 through the Eyes of an Indian Mission Recipient," *Ex Auditu* 23 (2007): 162–78.

38. Scott Cunningham, *"Through Many Tribulations": The Theology of Persecution in Luke-Acts* (Sheffield, UK: Sheffield Academic Press, 1997), 95–96.
39. Charles H. Talbert, *Reading Luke: A Literary and Theological Commentary on the Third Gospel*, rev. ed. (Macon, GA: Smyth & Helwys Publishing, 2002), 123.
40. Robert C. Tannehill, *Luke* (Nashville: Abingdon Press, 1996), 176.
41. See 1 Corinthians 4:1: "Think of us in this way, as servants of Christ and stewards of God's mysteries."
42. See Ephesians 6:15: "As shoes for your feet put on whatever will make you ready to proclaim the gospel of peace."
43. Desmond Tutu, *God Is Not Christian: And Other Provocations* (New York: HarperOne, 2011), 14.
44. Leonardo Boff, "Trinity," in *Mysterium Liberationis: Fundamental Concepts of Liberation Theology*, ed. Ignacio Ellacuría and Jon Sobrino (Maryknoll, NY: Orbis Books, 1993), 389.
45. Stephen B. Bevans and Roger P. Schroeder, *Prophetic Dialogue: Reflections on Christian Mission Today* (Maryknoll, NY: Orbis Books, 2011), 9.
46. To guide the reader to some basic texts on the Trinity that have influenced this reflection, I suggest the following: Leonardo Boff, *Trinity and Society* (Maryknoll, NY: Orbis Books, 1988); Stanley J. Grenz, *Rediscovering the Triune God: The Trinity in Contemporary Theology* (Minneapolis: Fortress Press, 2004); Mark Heim, *The Depth of the Riches: A Trinitarian Theology of Religious Ends* (Grand Rapids: Wm. B. Eerdmans Publishing, 2001); Elizabeth A. Johnson, *Quest for the Living God: Mapping Frontiers in the Theology of God* (New York: Continuum, 2007); Jürgen Moltmann, *The Trinity and the Kingdom: The Doctrine of God* (Minneapolis: Fortress Press,1993); Panikkar, *The Rhythm of Being*; and R. Kendall Soulen, *The Divine Name(s) and the Holy Trinity: Distinguishing the Voices* (Louisville, KY: Westminster John Knox Press, 2011).
47. Rowan Williams, *On Christian Theology* (Oxford, UK: Blackwell, 2000), 180.
48. Rowan Williams, "Dialogue Is a Means of 'God-Given Discovery,'" *Current Dialogue* 54 (July 2013): 7.
49. Theodore Friend, *Man, Woman, and God in Modern Islam*, 330–31.
50. I am drawing from the argument in Moltmann, *The Trinity and the Kingdom*, 98–102.
51. Jürgen Moltmann, *The Crucified God: The Cross of Christ as the Foundation and Criticism of Christian Theology* (Minneapolis: Fortress Press, 1993), 241.
52. Panikkar, *The Rhythm of Being*, 225.
53. Narrated by Dr. Jeremiah Guen Seok Yang of Sungkonghoe University.
54. I am aware that there are many versions of this quote that stem from the one that says, "The longest journey you will ever take is the 18 inches from your head to your heart." It has been attributed to a Christian leader, Archbishop Donald Coggan; a Buddhist teacher, Thich Nhat Hanh; and a British politician, Andrew Bennett, among others.
55. I am aware that this verse from Ephesians could well be influenced by Isaiah 52:7: "How beautiful upon the mountains are the feet of the messenger who announces peace, who brings good news, who announces salvation, who says to Zion, 'Your God reigns.'" One cannot miss how feet, messenger, peace, good news, and salvation are tied together in this passage.

56. Terrence J. Rynne, *Jesus Christ, Peacemaker: A New Theology of Peace* (Maryknoll, NY: Orbis Books, 2014).

57. Ibid., 98.

58. Martin Marty, *When Faiths Collide*, 178.

59. Raimundo Panikkar, preface in *Nucleus: Reconnecting Science and Religion in the Nuclear Age*, by Scott Eastham (Santa Fe, NM: Bear, 1987), xxv.

60. Raimon Panikkar, "Nine Sutras on Peace," *Religion East & West* 5 (October 2005): 122.

61. Aslan, *How to Win a Cosmic War*, 136.

62. Elisabeth Schüssler Fiorenza's classic book comes to mind: *Bread Not Stone: The Challenge of Feminist Biblical Interpretation* (Boston: Beacon Press, 1984).

Bibliography

Aftab, Safiya. "Poverty and Militancy." *Conflict and Peace Studies* 1, no. 1 (October–December 2008): 1–18.

Ahmed, Akbar, and Brian Forst. "Toward a More Civil Twenty-First Century." In *After Terrorism: Promoting Dialogue among Civilizations*, edited by Akbar Ahmed and Brian Forst, 3–12. Cambridge, UK: Polity Press, 2005.

Alexander, Jeffrey C. "Analytic Debates: Understanding the Relative Autonomy of Culture." In *Culture and Society: Contemporary Debates*, edited by Jeffrey C. Alexander and Steven Seidman, 1–30. Cambridge: Cambridge University Press, 1990.

Ali, Tariq. *The Clash of Fundamentalisms: Crusades, Jihads and Modernity*. London: Verso, 2003.

Almond, G., E. Sivan, and R. S. Appleby. "Fundamentalism: Genus and Species." In *Fundamentalisms Comprehended*, edited by Martin E. Marty and Scott Appleby, 402–9. Chicago: University of Chicago Press, 1995.

Amir, Ahmad N., Abdi O. Shuriye, and Ahmad F. Ismail. "Muhammad Abduh's Contribution to Modernity." *Asian Journal in Management Sciences and Education* 1, no. 1 (April 2012): 63–75.

Antoun, Richard T. *Understanding Fundamentalism: Christian, Islamic, and Jewish Movements*. 2nd ed. Lanham, MD: Rowman & Littlefield Publishers, 2008.

Appleby, R. Scott, Gabriel Almond, and Emmanuel Sivan. *Strong Religion: The Rise of Fundamentalisms around the World*. Chicago: University of Chicago Press, 2003.

Armstrong, Karen. *The Battle for God*. New York: Ballantine Books, 2001.

———. *Fields of Blood: Religion and the History of Violence*. New York: Alfred A. Knopf, 2014.

———. *Muhammad: A Prophet for Our Times*. San Francisco: HarperOne, 2006.

Asher, Catherine Blanshard. *Architecture of Mughal India*. Vol. 1.4 of *The New Cambridge History of India*. Cambridge: Cambridge University Press, 1992.

Aslan, Reza. *Beyond Fundamentalism: Confronting Religious Extremism in the Age of Globalization*. New York: Random House, 2010.

———. *How to Win a Cosmic War: God, Globalization, and the End of the War on Terror*. New York: Random House, 2009.

———. *No God but God: The Origin, Evolution, and Future of Islam*. New York: Random House, 2006.

Asthana, N. C., and Anjali Nirmal. *Urban Terrorism: Myths and Realities*. Jaipur: Pointer Publishers, 2009.

Avalos, Hector. *The End of Biblical Studies*. Amherst, NY: Prometheus Books, 2007.

———. *Fighting Words: The Origins of Religious Violence*. Amherst, NY: Prometheus Books, 2007.

Bamye, Mohammed A. *The Social Origins of Islam: Mind, Economy, Discourse*. Minneapolis: University of Minnesota Press, 1999.

Banerjee, Sikata. "Gender and Nationalism: The Masculinization of Hinduism and Female Political Participation in India." *Women's Studies International Forum* 26, no. 2 (2003): 167–79.

Barber, Benjamin R. *Fear's Empire: War, Terrorism, and Democracy*, New York: W. W. Norton, 2004.

———. *Jihad vs. McWorld: Terrorism's Challenge to Democracy*. New York: Random House, 2001.

Bennoune, Karima. *Your Fatwa Does Not Apply Here: Untold Stories from the Fight against Muslim Fundamentalism*. New York: W. W. Norton, 2013.

Bevans, Stephen B., and Roger P. Schroeder. *Prophetic Dialogue: Reflections on Christian Mission Today*. Maryknoll, NY: Orbis Books, 2011.

Bhargava, Rajeev, ed. *Secularism and Its Critics*. Delhi: Oxford University Press, 1998.

Bhatt, Chetan. *Hindu Nationalism: Origins, Ideologies and Modern Myths*. Oxford, UK: Berg, 2001.

Boyd, Gregory A. *The Myth of a Christian Nation: How the Quest for Political Power Is Destroying the Church*. Grand Rapids: Zondervan, 2005.

Bruce, Steve. *Fundamentalism*. 2nd ed., rev., updated. Cambridge, UK: Polity Press, 2008.

Brueggemann, Walter. *The Prophetic Imagination*. 2nd ed. Minneapolis: Augsburg Fortress, 2001.

———. *Truth Speaks to Power: The Countercultural Nature of Scripture*. Louisville, KY: Westminster John Knox Press, 2013.

Calvert, John. *Sayyid Qutb and the Origins of Radical Islamism*. New York: Columbia University Press, 2010.

Chatterji, Angana P. *Violent Gods: Hindu Nationalism in India's Present*. Gurgaon, India: Three Essays Collective, 2009.

Ciment, James, ed. *World Terrorism: An Encyclopedia of Political Violence from Ancient Times to the Post-9/11 Era*. New York: Routledge, 2015.

Claassens, L. Juliana, and Bruce C. Birch, eds. *Restorative Readings: The Old Testament, Ethics, and Human Dignity*. Eugene, OR: Pickwick Publications, 2015.

Clarke, Sathianathan. "Dalits Overcoming Violation and Violence: A Contest between Overpowering and Empowering Identities in Changing India." *Ecumenical Review* 54, no. 3 (July 2002): 278–95.

———. "Global Cultural Traffic, Christian Mission, and Biblical Interpretation: Rereading Luke 10:1–12 through the Eyes of an Indian Mission Recipient." *Ex Auditu* 23 (2007): 162–78.

———. "Hindutva, Religious and Ethnocultural Minorities, and Indian-Christian Theology." *Harvard Theological Review* 95, no. 2 (2002): 197–226.

———. "The Promise of Religious Conversion: Exploring Approaches, Exposing Myths,

Expounding Modalities." In *Religiöse Grenzüberschreitungen: Studien zu Bekehrung, Konfessions- und Religionswechsel = Crossing Religious Borders: Studies on Conversion and Religious Belonging,* edited by Christine Lienemann-Perrin and Wolfgang Lienemann, 590–610. Wiesbaden: Harrassowitz, 2012.

———. "Viewing the Bible through the Eyes and Ears of Subalterns in India." *Biblical Interpretation* 10, no. 3 (2002): 245–66. http://www.religion-online.org/showarticle.asp?title=2444.

Clarke, Sathianathan, and Philip Peacock. "Dalits and Religious Conversion: Slippery Identities and Shrewd Identifications." In *Dalit Theology in the Twenty-first Century: Discordant Voices, Discerning Pathways,* edited by Sathianathan Clarke, Deenabandhu Manchala, and Philip Peacock, 178–98. New Delhi: Oxford University Press, 2010.

Collier, Paul. *The Bottom Billion: Why the Poorest Countries Are Failing and What Can Be Done about It.* New York: Oxford University Press, 2007.

Cook, Michael. *The Koran: A Very Short Introduction.* New York: Oxford University Press, 2000.

Cox, Harvey. *The Future of Faith.* New York: HarperOne, 2009.

Creach, Jerome F. D. *Violence in Scripture: Interpretation Resources for the Use of Scripture in the Church.* Louisville, KY: Westminster John Knox Press, 2013.

Crossan, John Dominic. *How to Read the Bible and Still Be a Christian: Struggling with Divine Violence from Genesis through Revelation.* New York: HarperOne, 2015.

Cunningham, Scott. *"Through Many Tribulations": The Theology of Persecution in Luke-Acts.* Sheffield, UK: Sheffield Academic Press, 1997.

Dalhouse, Mark Taylor. *An Island in the Lake of Fire: Bob Jones University, Fundamentalism, and the Separatist Movement.* Athens, GA: University of Georgia Press, 1996.

Dalrymple, William. *The Last Mughal: The Fall of a Dynasty, Delhi, 1857.* New York: Vintage, 2008.

Davie, Grace. *The Sociology of Religion: A Critical Agenda.* London: Sage Publications, 2007. 2nd ed. London: Sage Publications, 2013.

Dayal, John, and Shabnam Hashmi, eds. *365 Days: Democracy and Secularism under the Modi Regime.* New Delhi: Anhad Publishers, 2015. http://www.sanjosepeace.org/fmd/files/One%20year%20under%20Modi%20regime%20-%20ANHAD%20-%202015%20for%20web.pdf.

Deshpande, Satish. *Contemporary India: A Sociological View.* New Delhi: Viking, 2003.

Domke, David, and Kevin Coe. *The God Strategy: How Religion Became a Political Weapon in America.* New York: Oxford University Press, 2010.

Donohue, John, and John Esposito, eds. *Islam in Transition: Muslim Perspectives.* New York: Oxford University Press, 2007.

Elshobaki, Amr. "The Muslim Brotherhood—Between Evangelizing and Politics: The Challenge of Incorporating the Brotherhood into the Political Process." In *Islamist Politics in the Middle East: Movements and Change,* edited by Samer Said Shehata, 107–19. New York: Routledge, 2012.

Esposito, John. *The Future of Islam.* New York: Oxford University Press, 2010.

Faruqui, Munis D. *The Princes of the Mughal Empire, 1504–1719.* Cambridge: Cambridge University Press, 2012.

Fernandes, Edna. *Holy Warriors: A Journey into the Heart of Indian Fundamentalism.* New Delhi: Viking, 2006.

Fernandez, Eleazer S. *Burning Center, Porous Borders: The Church in a Globalized World.* Eugene, OR: Wipf & Stock, 2011.

Foucault, Michel. *The Archaeology of Knowledge*. New York: Pantheon Books, 1972.
———. *The Order of Things: An Archaeology of the Human Sciences*. New York: Vintage Books, 1994.
———.*Power/Knowledge: Selected Interviews and Other Writings, 1972–1977*. New York: Pantheon Books, 1980.
Freeman, Donald C. "Old American Myths; New World Realities." In *Civilizations—Conflict or Dialogue?*, edited by Hans Köchler and Gudren Grabher, 83–91. Vienna: International Progress Organization, 1999.
Friedman, Thomas L. *Longitudes and Attitudes: Exploring the World after September 11*. New York: Farrar, Straus & Giroux, 2002.
———. *The World Is Flat: A Brief History of the Twenty-First Century*. New York: Farrar, Straus & Giroux, 2005.
Friend, Theodore. *Woman, Man, and God in Modern Islam*. Grand Rapids: Wm. B. Eerdmans Publishing, 2012.
Fuller, Christopher J. *The Camphor Flame: Popular Hinduism and Society in India*. Rev., expanded ed. Princeton, NJ: Princeton University Press, 2004.
Gottschalk, Peter, and Gabriel Greenberg. *Islamophobia: Making Muslims the Enemy*. Lanham, MD: Rowman & Littlefield Publishers, 2008.
Gupta, Dipankar. *Mistaken Modernity: India between Worlds*. New Delhi: Harper Collins, 2000.
Harding, Susan Friend. *The Book of Jerry Falwell: Fundamentalist Language and Politics*. Princeton, NJ: Princeton University Press, 2000.
Hardt, Michael, and Antonio Negri. *Empire*. Cambridge, MA: Harvard University Press, 2001.
Harris, Harriet A. *Fundamentalism and Evangelicals*. Oxford: Oxford University Press, 2008.
Haynes, Jeff. *Religion, Fundamentalism and Ethnicity: A Global Perspective*. Discussion Paper 65. Geneva: United Nations Research Institute for Social Development, May 1995. http://www.unrisd.org/80256B3C005BCCF9/(httpPublications)/265FAA83B0EA35 EB80256B67005B67F6.
Heredia, Rudolf C. "Gandhi's Hinduism and Savarkar's Hindutva." *Economic and Political Weekly* 44, no. 29 (July 18, 2009): 62–67.
Herriot, Peter. *Religious Fundamentalism: Global, Local, Personal*. London: Routledge, 2009.
Hibbard, Scott W. *Religious Politics and Secular States: Egypt, India, and the United States*. Baltimore: Johns Hopkins University Press, 2010.
Holland, Tom. *In the Shadow of the Sword: The Battle for Global Empire and the End of the Ancient World*. New York: Doubleday, 2012.
Hughes, Richard T. *Christian America and the Kingdom of God*. Urbana: University of Illinois Press, 2009.
Humphrey, Fisher, and Philip Wise. *Fundamentalism*. Macon, GA: Smyth & Helwys, 2004.
Huntington, Samuel P. "The Clash of Civilizations?" *Foreign Affairs* 72, no. 3 (Summer 1993): 22–49.
———. *The Clash of Civilizations and the Remaking of World Order*. New York: Simon & Schuster, 1996.
———. *Who Are We? The Challenges to America's National Identity*. New York: Simon & Schuster, 2004.
Hussain, Musharraf. *The Five Pillars of Islam: Laying the Foundations of Divine Love and Service to Humanity*. Markfield, UK: Kube Publishing Ltd., 2012.

Iannaccone, Laurence R., and Eli Berma. "Religious Extremism: The Good, the Bad, and the Deadly." *Public Choice* 1, no. 1 (2006): 109–29.

Ignatieff, Michael. *The Lesser Evil: Political Ethics in an Age of Terror*. Princeton, NJ: Princeton University Press, 2004.

Jabbour, Nabeel. *The Rumbling Volcano: Islamic Fundamentalism in Egypt*. Pasadena, CA: Mandate Press, 1993.

Jaffrelot, Christophe, ed. *The Sangh Parivar: A Reader*. New Delhi: Oxford University Press, 2006.

Jalal, Ayesha. *Partisans of Allah: Jihad in South Asia*. Cambridge, MA: Harvard University Press, 2010.

Jenkins, Philip. *Laying Down the Sword: Why We Ignore the Bible's Violent Verses*. New York: HarperOne, 2011.

Jewett, Robert, and John Shelton Lawrence. *Captain America and the Crusade against Evil: The Dilemma of Zealous Nationalism*. Grand Rapids: Wm. B. Eerdmans Publishing, 2003.

Jones, James W. *Blood That Cries Out from the Earth*. Oxford: Oxford University Press, 2008.

Jones, Julie Scott. *Being the Chosen: Exploring a Christian Fundamentalist Worldview*. Farnham, UK: Ashgate Publishing, 2010.

Jones, Robert P. *Progressive and Religious: How Christian, Jewish, Muslim, and Buddhist Leaders Are Moving beyond Wars and Transforming American Public Life*. Lanham, MD: Rowman & Littlefield Publishers, 2008.

Juergensmeyer, Mark. *Global Rebellion: Religious Challenges to the Secular State, from Christian Militia to Al Qaeda*. Berkeley: University of California Press, 2008.

———. *The New Cold War: Religious Nationalism Confronts the Secular States*. Berkeley: University of California Press, 1993.

———. *Terror in the Mind of God: The Global Rise of Religious Violence*. Berkeley: University of California Press, 2003.

Kakar, Sudhir. *The Colours of Violence: Cultural Identities, Religion, and Conflict*. Chicago: University of Chicago Press, 1996.

Kandil, Hazem. *Inside the Brotherhood*. Cambridge, UK: Polity Press, 2015.

Karsh, Efraim. *Islamic Imperialism: A History*. New Haven, CT: Yale University Press, 2007.

Kennedy, Hugh. *The Great Arab Conquests: How the Spread of Islam Changed the World We Live In*. Philadelphia: Da Capro Press, 2008.

Khanna, Parag. *The Second World: Empires and Influence in the New Global Order*. New York: Random House, 2008.

Khosrokhavar, Farhad. "The Psychology of the Global Jihadists." In *The Fundamentalist Mindset*, edited by Charles B. Strozier, David M. Terman, and James W. Jones, with Katherine A. Boyd, 139–55. New York: Oxford University Press, 2010.

Kimball, Charles. *When Religion Becomes Evil: Five Warning Signs*. Rev., updated ed. New York: HarperOne, 2008.

———. *When Religion Becomes Lethal: The Explosive Mix of Religion and Politics in Judaism, Christianity, and Islam*. San Francisco: Jossey-Bass, 2011.

Kippenberg, Hans G. *Violence as Worship: Religious Wars in the Age of Globalization*. Stanford, CA: Stanford University Press, 2011.

Küng, Hans. *Islam: Past, Present and Future*. Oxford: Oneworld Publications, 2007.

Lapidu, Ira M. *A History of Islamic Societies*. 3rd ed. New York: Cambridge University Press, 2014.

Lewis, Bernard. *Islam and the West*. New York: Oxford University Press, 1994.

———. *What Went Wrong? The Clash Between Islam and Modernity in the Middle East.* New York: Oxford University Press, 2004.

Lincoln, Bruce. *Holy Terrors: Thinking about Religion after September 11.* 2nd ed. Chicago: University of Chicago Press, 2006.

Marsden, George M. *Militant Christianity: The Rise of Fundamentalism in American Culture.* Online: Now and Then Reader, 2012. http://www.nowandthenreader.com /militant-christians-the-rise-of-fundamentalism-in-american-culture/preview/.

———. *Understanding Fundamentalism and Evangelicalism.* Grand Rapids: Wm. B. Eerdmans Publishing, 1991.

Marty, Martin E. *When Faiths Collide.* Malden, MA: Blackwell, 2005.

Masoud, Tarek. *Counting Islam: Religion, Class, and Elections in Egypt.* New York: Cambridge University Press, 2014.

McDermott, Terry. *Perfect Soldiers: The Hijackers: Who They Were, Why They Did It.* New York: HarperCollins, 2005.

McGrath, Alister E. *The Christian Theology Reader.* 4th ed. Chichester, UK: Wiley-Blackwell, 2011.

McTernan, Oliver. *Violence in God's Name: Religion in an Age of Conflict.* Maryknoll, NY: Orbis Books, 2003.

Menon, Kalyani D. "Converted Innocents and Their Trickster Heroes: The Politics of Proselytizing in India." In *The Anthropology of Religious Conversion,* edited by Andrew Buckser and Stephen D. Glazier, 43–53. Lanham, MD: Rowman & Littlefield Publishers, 2003.

Migliore, Daniel L. *Faith Seeking Understanding: An Introduction to Christian Theology.* 3rd ed. Grand Rapids: Wm. B. Eerdmans Publishing, 2014.

Milton-Edwards, Beverly. *Islamic Fundamentalism since 1945.* New York: Routledge, 2005.

Moaddel, Mansoor. *Islamic Modernism, Nationalism, and Fundamentalism: Episode and Discourse.* Chicago: University of Chicago Press, 2005.

Moghadam, Valentine M. *Globalization and Social Movements: Islamism, Feminism, and the Global Justice Movement.* 2nd ed. Lanham, MD: Rowman & Littlefield Publishers, 2013.

Moltmann, Jürgen. *The Coming of God: Christian Eschatology.* Minneapolis: Fortress Press, 1996.

———. *The Crucified God: The Cross of Christ as the Foundation and Criticism of Christian Theology.* Minneapolis: Fortress Press, 1993.

———. *Sun of Righteousness, Arise! God's Future for Humanity and the Earth.* Minneapolis: Fortress Press, 2010.

———. *The Trinity and the Kingdom: The Doctrine of God.* Minneapolis: Fortress Press, 1993.

Müller-Fahrenholz, Geiko. *America's Battle for God: A European Christian Looks at Civil Religion.* Grand Rapids: Wm. B. Eerdmans Publishing, 2007.

Nanda, Meera. *Prophets Facing Backward: Postmodern Critiques of Science and Hindu Nationalism in India.* New Brunswick, NJ: Rutgers University Press, 2003.

———. "Response to My Critics. *Social Epistemology* 19, no. 1 (January–March 2005): 147–91. http://www.physics.nyu.edu/sokal/Nanda_SocEpist.pdf.

———. "Vedic Science and Hindu Nationalism: Arguments against a Premature Synthesis of Religion and Science." In *Science and Religion in a Post-Colonial World: Interfaith Perspectives,* ed. Zainal Abidin Bagir, 27–36. Hindmarsh, AUS: ATU Press, 2005.

Nandy, Ashis. "Cultural Frames for Social Transformation: A Credo." *Alternatives* 12, no. 1 (January 1987): 113–23.

————. *Time Warps: Silent and Evasive Pasts in Indian Politics and Religion*. New Brunswick, NJ: Rutgers University Press, 2002.

Narayan, Badri. *Fascinating Hindutva: Saffron Politics and Dalit Mobilisation*. New Delhi: Sage Publications, 2009.

Nasr, Seyyed Hossein. *The Heart of Islam: Enduring Values for Humanity*. New York: HarperSanFrancisco, 2002.

————. *Islam: Religion, History, and Civilization*. New York: HarperSanFrancisco, 2003.

Nelson-Pallmeyer, Jack. *Is Religion Killing Us? Violence in the Bible and Quran*. New York: Continuum, 2005.

————. *Saving Christianity from the Empire*. New York: Continuum, 2007.

Nussbaum, Martha C. *The Clash Within: Democracy, Religious Violence, and India's Future*. Cambridge, MA: Belknap Press, 2007.

Nye, Joseph. *The Powers to Lead*. New York: Oxford University Press, 2008.

————. *Soft Power: The Means to Success in World Politics*. New York: Public Affairs, 2004. New ed., 2005.

Offenhauer, Priscilla. *Women in Islamic Societies: A Selected Study of Social Scientific Research*. Washington, DC: Federal Research Division, Library of Congress, 2005.

Omer, Atalia, and Jason A. Spring. *Religious Nationalism: A Reference Handbook*. Santa Barbara, CA: ABD-CLIO, 2013.

Pakenham, Thomas. *The Scramble for Africa: The White Man's Conquest of the Dark Continent from 1876 to 1912*. New York: Avon Books, 1992.

Panikkar, K. N., ed. *The Concerned Indian's Guide to Communalism*. New Delhi: Viking Press, 1999.

Panikkar, Raimon. *The Experience of God: Icons of the Mystery*. Minneapolis: Fortress Press, 2006.

————. *The Rhythm of Being: The Gifford Lectures*. Maryknoll, NY: Orbis Books, 2010.

Pratt, Douglas. "Terrorism and Religious Fundamentalism: Prospects for a Predictive Paradigm." *Marburg Journal of Religion* 11, no. 1 (June 2006): 1–15.

Prothero, Stephen. *God Is Not One: The Eight Rival Religions That Run the World*. New York: HarperOne, 2010.

Puniyani, Ram. *Contours of Hindu Rashtra: Hindutva, Sangh Parivar and Contemporary Politics*. New Delhi: Kalpaz Publications, 2006.

Ramadan, Tariq. *The Messenger: The Meanings of the Life of Muhammad*. New York: Oxford University Press, 2007.

Richards, John F. *The Mughal Empire*. Cambridge: Cambridge University Press, 1996.

Robertson, Pat. *The New World Order*. Dallas: Word Publishing, 1991.

Rynne, Terrence J. *Jesus Christ, Peacemaker: A New Theology of Peace*. Maryknoll, NY: Orbis Books, 2014.

Saha, Santosh C., ed. *Religious Fundamentalism in the Contemporary World: Critical Social and Political Issues*. Lanham, MD: Lexington Books, 2004.

Said, Edward W. *Orientalism*. New York: Pantheon, 1978.

————. *Covering Islam: How the Media and the Experts Determine How We See the Rest of the World*. New York: Pantheon, 1981.

————. *Culture and Imperialism*. New York: Random House, 1993.

Sarda, Ziauddin. *Muhammad: All That Matters*. London: Hodder Education, 2012.

Savarkar, Vinayak Damodar. *Hindutva: Who Is a Hindu?* 2nd ed. Bombay: Veer Savarkar Prakashan, 1969.

Seibert, Eric A. *The Violence of Scripture: Overcoming the Old Testament's Troubling Legacy.* Minneapolis: Fortress Press, 2012.

Sen, Amartya. *The Argumentative Indian: Writings on Indian History, Culture, and Identity.* New York: Picador, 2005.

Sharma, Arvind, ed. *The Study of Hinduism.* Columbia: University of South Carolina Press, 2003.

Sharma, Kalpana. "The Hindu Bomb." *Bulletin of Atomic Scientists* 54, no. 4 (July–August 1988): 30–33.

Shastri, Sunanda Y., and Yagneshwar S. Shastri. "Ahimsa and the Unity of All Things: A Hindu View of Non-violence." In *Subverting Hate: The Challenge of Nonviolence in Religious Traditions*, edited by Daniel L. Smith-Christopher, 57–75. Maryknoll, NY: Orbis Books, 2007.

Sontheimer, Günther-Dietz, and Hermann Kulke, eds. *Hinduism Reconsidered.* Rev. ed. New Delhi: Manohar Publishers, 2001.

Steffen, Lloyd. *The Demonic Turn: The Power of Religion to Inspire and Restrain Violence.* Cleveland: Pilgrim Press, 2003.

Steger, Manfred B. *Globalization: A Very Short Introduction.* New York: Oxford University Press, 2009.

Stein, Ruth. *For Love of the Father: A Psychoanalytical Study of Religious Terrorism.* Stanford, CA: Stanford University Press, 2010.

Stern, Jessica. *Terror in the Name of God: Why Religious Militants Kill.* New York: HarperCollins, 2003.

Strozier, Charles B., David M. Terman, and James W. Jones, with Katherine A. Boyd, eds. *The Fundamentalist Mindset: Psychological Perspectives on Religion, Violence, and History.* New York: Oxford University Press, 2010.

Takeyh, Ray, and Nikolas K. Gvosdev. *The Receding Shadow of the Prophet: The Rise and Fall of Radical Political Islam.* Westport, CT: Praeger Publishers, 2004.

Talbert, Charles H. *Reading Luke: A Literary and Theological Commentary on the Third Gospel.* Rev. ed. Macon, GA: Smyth & Helwys Publishing, 2002.

Tannehill, Robert C. *Luke.* Nashville: Abingdon Press, 1996.

Toft, Monica Duffy, Daniel Philpott. and Timothy Samuel Shah. *God's Century: Resurgent Religion and Global Politics.* New York: W. W. Norton, 2011.

Tutu, Desmond. *God Is Not Christian: And Other Provocations.* New York: HarperOne, 2011.

Tuveson, Ernest. *Redeemer Nation: The Idea of America's Millennial Role.* Chicago: University of Chicago Press, 1968.

Tyson, Joseph B. *Marcion and Luke-Acts: A Defining Struggle.* Columbia: University of South Carolina Press, 2006.

Udayakumar, S. P. "Nukes as a Way of Life? Contextualizing the Nuclear Madness in South Asia." *Bulletin of Concerned Asian Scholars* 31, no. 2 (1999): 79–84.

Vidino, Lorenzo. *Countering Radicalisation in America: Lessons from Europe.* Special Report 262. Washington, DC: United States Institute of Peace, November 22, 2010. http://www.usip.org/sites/default/files/resources/SR262%20-%20Countering_Radicalization_in_America.pdf.

Vorster, Jakobus M. "Perspectives on the Core Characteristics of Religious Fundamentalism Today." *Journal for the Study of Religions and Ideologies* 7, no. 21 (Winter 2008): 44–66.

Walzer, Michael. *The Paradox of Liberation: Secular Revolutions and Religious Counterrevolutions.* New Haven, CT: Yale University Press, 2015.

Wickham, Carrie Rosefsky. *The Muslim Brotherhood: Evolution of an Islamist Movement.* Princeton, NJ: Princeton University Press, 2013.

Williams, Rowan. "Dialogue Is a Means of 'God-Given Discovery.'" *Current Dialogue* 54 (July 2013): 5–8.

———. *On Christian Theology.* Oxford: Blackwell, 2000.

Wink, Walter. *The Powers That Be: Theology for a New Millennium.* New York: Doubleday, 1999.

———. *Engaging the Powers: Discernment and Resistance in a World of Domination.* Minneapolis: Augsburg Fortress, 1992.

———. *Jesus and Nonviolence: A Third Way.* Minneapolis: Augsburg Fortress, 2003.

Witham, Larry. *Marketplace of the Gods: How Economics Explains Religion.* New York: Oxford University Press, 2010.

———. "Was Adam Smith an 'Economist of Religion'?" Paper presented at the Association for the Study of Religion, Economics and Culture, Arlington, VA, April 8, 2011, 1–11. http://www.thearda.com/asrec/archive/papers/witham_adam_smith.pdf.

Wolfe, Michael, and the producers of Beliefnet, eds. *Taking Back Islam: American Muslims Reclaim Their Faith.* Emmaus, PA: Rodale, 2004.

Wuthnow, Robert, and Matthew P. Lawson. "Sources of Christian Fundamentalism in the United States." In *Accounting for Fundamentalism: The Dynamic Character of the Movement*, edited by Martin E. Marty and R. Scott Appleby, 18–56. Chicago: University of Chicago Press, 1994.

Index

terrorism (*continued*)
    catastrophic events of, 33
    Christian, 60, 196n89
    Jewish, 33
    religious, 2, 24, 190n40
    and sexual roles, 191n56
    "War on Terror," 45
    See also specific events, e.g., September
        11, 2001
texts, sacred/religious
    absolute character of, 193n41
    disarming exclusive and explosive,
        173–77
    literalist use of, 193n41
    "terror texts," 6, 173–75
    "toxic," 6, 173–75
    See also Scripture/scriptures
Thapar, Romila, 116
theology
    absoluteness of God in, 55
    counterfundamentalist, 178
    historical-critical theories, 37
    liberation, 171
    See also political theology
Thottunkal, Cleemis Cardinal, 166
Tiller, Dr. George, 60, 196n90
tithe offering, 93, 200n66
Toft, Monica Duffy, Daniel Philpott, and
        Timothy Samuel Shah, 161
tolerance, 98, 157, 177. *See also*
    intolerance
totalitarianism, 136
"toxic texts," 6, 173–75
tradition, absolute character of, 193n41
traditioning, 133, 148, 193n41, 208n11
Traub, James, 66
Trinity/triune God, 178–82, 185, 213n30,
        214n46
tripolar geopolitical framework, 19
Trump, Donald J., 191nn2–3, 210n51
truth, 172
    absolute, claims of, 193n41
    belt of, 182
    the Bible's, 130
    "counter," 213n28
    embodied expressions of, 177
    for Muslims, 85
    "official," 213n28
    "religion of truth" claims, 148

    Spirit of, 172
    universal, 115, 152
Tunisia, 77–78
Turkey, 203n2
Turkmenistan, 67
Tutu, Desmond, 178
Tuveson, Ernest, 62
twentieth century. *See under specific*
        fundamentalisms, e.g., Hindu
        fundamentalism: twentieth-century
twenty-first century
    religious fundamentalism in, 7–33
    transformation in the world, 199n56
    See also under specific fundamentalisms,
        e.g., Hindu fundamentalism:
        twentieth-century
Tyson, Joseph B., 212n15

Udayakumar, S. P., 120
ummah (community of Muslims), 4, 65, 71,
        77, 79, 87, 89–90, 92–93, 143, 150
unipolar geopolitical framework, 19
United Kingdom, 63
United Nations, 13, 19, 92
United States, 19–20, 35–62
    African Americans in, 66
    "America First," 36, 210n51
    the American Creed, 12
    anti-Americanism, 89
    "chosen nation," 57–58, 61, 130,
        145–46
    Christian fundamentalism in, 5, 35–62,
        130
    Constitution of, 130
    foreign policy of, 58–59, 62, 200n57,
        210n47, 210n51
    fundamentalist agenda in, 192n35
    as global superpower, 45
    manifest destiny, 57, 100, 195n76
    nonviolent movements in, 212n5
    See also Christian fundamentalism;
        culture: American; *specific topics and*
        events, e.g., empire; nationalism;
        September 11, 2001
unity, 8
    of the Bible, 168, 170
    Divine, 179
    of religions, 127, 155
    with the universe, 120

CPSIA information can be obtained
at www.ICGtesting.com
Printed in the USA
FSOW01n1949090717
36109FS